EXPLORING THE AFTERLIFE
SERIES

VOL. I

Voyages into the Unknown

Bruce Moen

HAMPTON ROADS
PUBLISHING COMPANY, INC.

for the evolving human spirit

Cover design by
Marjoram Productions
Cover painting by Francine Barbet

For information write:

Hampton Roads Publishing Company, Inc.
134 Burgess Lane
Charlottesville, VA 22902

Or call: (804)296-2772
FAX: (804)296-5096
e-mail: hrpc@hrpub.com
Web site: http://www.hrpub.com

If you are unable to order this book from your local
bookseller, you may order directly from the publisher.
Quantity discounts for organizations are available.
Call 1-800-766-8009, toll-free.

ISBN 1-57174-068-6

10 9 8 7 6 5 4 3 2 1

Printed on acid-free paper in the United States of America

Dedicated to

The Mysterious Teacher (here called Rebecca), without whose Love, Understanding, and Support none of this would have been possible;

Robert A. Monroe, whose courage and technology provided the path and the tools;

The Staff of The Monroe Institute, whose Guidance and Teaching taught me to explore the Afterlife;

My Family, whose Love and Patience has been with me from the beginning;

My wife Pharon, whose Love and Courage helped bring this into being;

My friends, physical and nonphysical, who have helped me learn to explore.

CONTENTS

Prologue

I'm just an ordinary human being whose curiosity about human existence beyond death led me to extraordinary experiences. I have never had a near-death experience. No supernatural happening changed me. I wasn't born with some special psychic gift or talent. If there is any difference between you and me, it is *only* that my curiosity has already led me to explore and know what lies beyond death in the Afterlife.

For centuries we have been told that Afterlife knowledge is unattainable. My experience, however, has convinced me that any ordinary human being with curiosity can learn to explore human existence beyond death.

Not so many years ago, almost everyone believed the Earth was flat. None holding that belief ventured too far out to sea for fear of sailing off the edge and falling into the great abyss of death. Earth's true nature was unknown. Some suggested a reality in which the Earth was not flat but round and shaped like a ball. But most, lacking knowledge of what existed beyond the horizon, lived lives limited by their acceptance of beliefs held by most in the culture of their time.

A few desired to know the truth. Curiosity drove them beyond the horizon, far beyond safe boundaries set by their beliefs. The Vikings, Columbus, and unnamed others sailed beyond, bringing back word of a strange New World and strange new people. Their word and maps encouraged others to explore and gather knowledge. Others followed, who explored and mapped, blazing trails for settlers.

From today's perspective we can laugh at the ignorance of those poor souls whose lives were limited to sailing near the shore. We know now that the edge beyond which they feared to sail existed only in their beliefs; we can sail beyond the horizon without fear of what lies beyond. Knowledge of Earth's true nature gave us that freedom.

In our culture, most still fear sailing beyond the edge of life, from this physical world into death. Yet none of us can stay Here forever. We are all inescapably sailing, most with uncertainty and fear, toward the edge of this life we call death. Lacking knowledge of the truth, those holding to "modern" beliefs still live in fear of death.

But some claim to have sailed out past the edge of this life and returned. Psychics, mediums, and those who have had near-death experiences say they have crossed over by intent or accident. They return with word of a strange new world and strange new people. People tend to think of them as crackpots, mostly.

I'm certain future cultures will look back at us and laugh at the ignorance that forced us to live our lives in fear of death. I hope this book will help demystify the subject of human experience beyond death in the *Afterlife*. Led by curiosity, I have sailed out and back many times. Each time, I have returned with more knowledge through my own direct experience. I have discovered that death is nothing to be feared.

Hopefully, reading this book will help you realize that you need not limit yourself to the beliefs and descriptions of others. You can learn to safely sail out past the edge of this life, explore There and return. You can bring back your own first-hand knowledge of the New World that lies across this ocean we call life. Out of curiosity that's what I did, and so can anyone, including you.

This book is not specifically intended to teach anyone *how* to explore the Afterlife, although Appendix C contains some guidelines for those with interest. Schools such as The Monroe Institute in Faber, Virginia, can teach you to sail. Rather, this is the log book of my journeys, and the maps I have drawn. It may provide compass headings, map coordinates, and landfalls you may recognize on your own journey. Some of you may recognize that you've been on this journey in your own way without knowing it. For others, it may only be an old salt's tale. For all, I hope, it will go some measure toward replacing the fear of death so many of us harbor.

This story is, to the best of my ability, a true account of my experience, with some changes of name and place to protect the privacy of those who desire it. You don't have to accept this as the truth. You can learn to explore, and discover the truth for yourself. I hope that you who embark on this journey find at least bits and pieces here that ring true to your own experience, and I hope that finding those bits and pieces will encourage you to continue.

The specific path of my journey is, of course, unique to me. It has been colored by all the beliefs and preconceptions about the Afterlife I've taken from my culture, my religion, and many other sources. This *Exploring the Afterlife* series chronicles my own experiences and discoveries. I urge you not to take my word for any of this. Sail your own ship and explore on your own. When you come back, share what you have found with anyone who is interested. It's so very important that many more of us acquire Afterlife knowledge and pass along to others what we discover about who and what we really are. It is important too for many more of us to know how our experience in the Afterlife is affected by our beliefs and how we live our lives here in the physical world. I believe that as more of us know the truth, both this world and the Afterlife will be better places in which to live.

I began writing the *Exploring the Afterlife* series long before I knew that I'd become an author or that it would become a book. I started a month after a friend and teacher named Robert Monroe died. Bob wrote three books that had an impact on my life—*Journeys Out of the Body, Far Journeys,* and *Ultimate Journey*—and founded The Monroe Institute, where I learned to explore the Afterlife.

It was in April of 1995, right after the Oklahoma City bombing, that I began writing. I had gone, nonphysically, to the site of the bombing the day it happened to do what I could to assist those who had been killed in the explosion and its aftermath. Later I had to find a way to express and release emotional energies I had picked up. The method of emotional release I chose was writing about the experience. About halfway through this process, Bob Monroe contacted me from the Afterlife to talk about what I was writing.

"Well, Bruce," I felt Bob say, "I see you're writing about Oklahoma City."

"Yeah, it seems to be working as a way to release something I picked up there," I thought back at him.

"I'm glad you're writing, Bruce. I'd like to see you continue writing. If you put enough down on paper I'll do what I can from my side to get it published as a book."

I didn't make any promises. I was working full-time as a mechanical engineer and the only time I had for writing was from when I got home from work at 5:30 until I went to sleep. But as I could make the time I kept on writing, and this book and those that will follow are the result.

Starting with my experience with the Oklahoma City bombing is jumping way ahead of what you'll need to know to understand it all, but then we'll backtrack, and the story will become clear.

As I said at the beginning, I'm just an ordinary human being. If there is any difference between you and me it is *only* that my curiosity has *already* led me to know what lies beyond death in the Afterlife. Follow your curiosity and it can lead you to your own Afterlife knowledge. Then you'll know, too.

I. Oklahoma City: April 19, 1995

For several years I'd been sailing back and forth between this world and the Afterlife. Ashore on many uncharted islands, I'd searched for hidden treasures, as I call the knowledge my exploring brings. On some, my discoveries showed there was a lot more to learn. The terrorist bombing in Oklahoma City on April 19, 1995, proved to be just such an island.

I was working as a contract engineer in Colorado. Word of the bombing started floating through the office in the late morning. Early reports said that many people had been killed but none of us knew the extent of the carnage.

Learning to assist people who have just recently died was how I first learned to explore the Afterlife, so I had brief thoughts that there might be some way I could help those who had been killed. I decided to try to do something when I got home from work.

As I drove the freeway home that night, National Public Radio filled in more details of the bombing. It was pretty clear by the time I switched on the television in my apartment that many, many people had died. As darkness approached I began to feel a restless, raspy, fidgety energy that seemed to fill the air around me. A strong desire to be with other people pulled me out to a nearby Bennigan's restaurant for dinner. At least there the loud music and noisy, crowded atmosphere matched the energy I felt surrounding me when I was alone at home.

Sitting at a small table by myself, I'd just finished placing my order for a seafood platter when I remembered earlier thoughts about trying to assist victims of the bombing. Still thinking it was something I'd actually do later, I sat on a stool in Bennigan's, quietly expressing my willingness to provide assistance. That's how it always starts. I just express the intent to proceed. I thought I'd have plenty of time to finish my meal, go home, lie down, and then begin to carry out my intent to assist. I have done such things before and it has always worked out just fine. But hidden treasure is a tricky thing. You're never sure what you're going to find. Moments after expressing my willingness to assist, I felt the voice of Coach, a nonphysical friend you'll come to know later. Amidst the overly loud music and many people's voices, I focused on Coach's voice.

"Okay Bruce," I felt him saying, "they can use the help."

In the next instant, sitting on a tall stool in Bennigan's and remaining aware of those surroundings, suddenly I was also rushing through blackness toward three infants who had died in the blast.

As I approached I could see them sitting close together, seemingly unharmed and perhaps a little dazed. I'd never retrieved more than one person at a time before, but this didn't seem much different. Besides, these were babies and I could easily hold all three of them together in my arms. I scooped the babies up into my arms and spun around, feeling for the direction of the Reception Center.

The Reception Center is a port of entry for the newly deceased in the Afterlife. Whatever needs they have will be provided for in this calm setting with a familiar Earth-like appearance. For some who arrive here, those needs include soothing the trauma of dying. The Helpers at the Reception Center are good at that. They get lots of practice.

The Reception Center in the Focus 27 area of the Afterlife looks very much like the physical world. The Park there has grass, trees, sidewalks, benches, and flower gardens. As on every previous trip I have made there, I knew people would be waiting when I arrived. They would take these babies in and then begin the process of helping them adjust to their new lives in their New World.

As the Reception Center came into view I could see the people standing on the grass in the Park, waiting. Out of my habit of always trying to get verifying information, I tried to get identities of some of those people waiting on the ground. I felt aunts, uncles and non-related volunteer Helpers take the babies from my arms. I paused a moment, again out of habit, to imprint in memory the impressions I'd received about those who had been waiting. Then I turned around, focused in on the location of the blast site, and accelerated into the blackness again. In the few seconds before my arrival I checked and noted I was feeling little emotion as a result of what I had just done. There were some feelings of sadness for the babies' early loss of life but not much more.

Several more quick-paced trips followed as I went back and forth between the blast site and the Reception Center. The first few trips were with children, ages maybe two to eight. Out of habit I continued to gather and store in memory impressions that might be useful later to verify what I thought I was doing. Early in my training, gathering verifiable information was important to me: I needed proof I wasn't making it all up. I'd gotten that proof so many times by now that there was no real need to continue gathering data, but some old habits just become so ingrained you continue to do them without thinking.

Next a woman named Charlotte materialized in the blackness in front of me. She seemed dazed and in shock. She became aware of my presence almost immediately and looked at me through a shell-shocked face and glazed-over eyes. I explained that I'd been sent to bring her back home. I sensed that somewhere inside her it registered from her religious upbringing that when she died someone was supposed to come for her. In her dazed state of shock she was willing to go wherever I would take her. I reached out and took her by the hand. Then we lifted off and flew away in the direction of the Park. When we arrived, again out of habit, I tried to get an impression of the name of the person who met her there. Then I turned back toward the blast site.

There were several more adults in rapid succession. A man named Ralph or Rob or something like that was the last one I felt I had time to identify. I was beginning to feel a bit overwhelmed by the sheer number of people I was encountering. I usually do this sort of thing with one person at a time and there might be several days or weeks between such trips. As I moved back and forth from the blast site to the Park, people's names and faces all began to run together in my memory.

At times I would come back more fully to awareness of my loud, noisy surroundings sitting on the stool at Bennigan's. Awareness of my activities at Oklahoma City would fade a little and I'd just be eating my dinner or sipping my beer. Then the sights and sounds would begin to fade and I'd be moving through the blackness again.

A year and a half before Oklahoma City, I had met a special group of Helpers—people who have lived in the Afterlife long enough to understand how to assist with the special needs of the new arrivals—while they were assisting after an earthquake in India in which some 68,000 people had died. I was then a participant in a research group at The Monroe Institute, exploring how to assist the deceased after a large-scale natural disaster; the earthquake, which had happened just a few days before our regularly scheduled exploration session, presented an opportunity to gather information. I learned much about the inner workings of assisting with large groups of newly deceased people there.

As I stood now at the Oklahoma City blast site peering into the blackness trying to find another victim, I felt one of those Helpers approach me from behind, and recognized his "voice." (I have never seen this man.) He suggested that I stop making trips back and forth to the Reception Center by myself. "Bruce, just get their attention. Get them to walk toward you," I felt him say. "As they move closer to you, Helpers will step out from behind you to greet them. Let the Helpers transport them to the Reception Center. No sense using up your valuable time making all those trips back and forth. You're better at getting their attention than we are anyway. Remember how you used that ability to assist us in India? Just bring them in close and let us take care of the rest."

"Okay," I said.

Two more Helpers from that previous experience appeared, looking like very, very bright lights, so bright as to be almost blinding to the eye. They took up positions one on either side of me, and together they illuminated the blackness like two huge searchlights, making it easier to find victims of the blast. We began moving forward together, penetrating more deeply into the site.

I quickly lost track of the numbers or names or anything else about the people we found who had been killed in the blast. I was so overwhelmed by their numbers that I gave up my old habit of gathering verifiable information. They came into view, I got their attention, and they moved toward us. As each approached, I could feel a Helper, standing close behind, step out into view. Taking the person by the hand, talking softly, moving gently, the Helper would turn toward the direction of the Reception Center. Then they would move off together slowly, disappearing into the blackness.

As I continued scanning for more people, Rebecca, one of the most loving people I know in this or any other world and my most loved and revered friend in the physical world, came into view. Rebecca had also participated in the India earthquake exercise. Now, in Oklahoma City, she was doing the same thing. Standing, smiling, her arms spread out in Love, she was providing a portal that was draining off the emotional blackness of fear. By extending her Love into the blast site she was relieving the pressure, casting light into darkness. We acknowledged each other with smiles, then I moved on with the two bright-light Helpers still at my sides.

As we continued searching I became aware of something very strong—just the hint of a feeling at first. I realized it had been there all along but I'd been able to ignore it until then. It must be something like what a firefighter experiences going into a burning building to rescue a buddy. At first he is so busy trying to locate and rescue his friend he is barely aware of the surrounding maelstrom. If he stops to think about his surroundings all of a sudden he can see the flames and feel the heat. Firefighters probably know better than to stop and do such a thing. I'm not a firefighter; I didn't know.

I stopped for a moment, naively opening up my awareness to the now strong feeling I had been only dimly aware of in the background. I realized immediately that it was emotional energy of incredible power. Then all of a sudden, man . . . could . . . I . . . feel . . . the . . . heat! The burning, searing power and intensity of these emotional energies was incredible. Grief and confusion were so strong that when they first hit me I felt my awareness begin to quiver, wavering toward unconsciousness. Unbelievably horrendous levels of grief, fear, anger, frustration, and rage surged through me.

This part of the hidden treasure I was not prepared for in the least. Instants passed like years as I struggled to push the door of my awareness closed against the tremendous pressure of these emotions! Finally, after I was able to move my attention away from the emotional energies of the blast site, I could stop and catch my breath.

It took me several moments to regain my composure. As I hovered in the blackness, resting for a while, I thought about what had just happened, and realized that those powerful emotional energies to which I had opened up were coming not from the people I was assisting, but from physically alive people at the site and throughout the country. The bombing had focused the emotional energies of millions onto the blast site. Rescue workers, victims' family members, and people around the world were all feeling frustration, anger, grief, and more as they worked, waited, and watched. Those emotions were being projected into the blast site area because people's attention was focused there while they were feeling them.

After resting for another minute I cooled down and felt a little better. Then the bright-light Helpers and I moved back into the blackness again.

My awareness was jarred by the feeling of someone off to my right and downward, somewhere in the twisted pile of steel and broken concrete that had been the Federal

Building. Those we had found so far had been sort of out in the open, easy to find and easy to move. Sensing where she was, we turned and approached the debris pile. I moved right up against it until I could feel its mass resisting further progress. I exerted slight forward pressure and overcame the resistance, and we pushed into the debris. Moving through it slowly, I scanned back and forth in front of me trying to locate whomever it was I could feel. It didn't take long. A few seconds after we entered the debris pile we found her, stretched out face-down, surrounded and covered by broken chunks of the building. I stopped perhaps fifteen feet away and called out to get her attention. She could move her head and she lifted it, looking in my direction. She looked at me and screamed. "Help me! Get me out of here! Something's fallen on my legs. I'm pinned down and my legs are stuck and I can't get free."

She was very frightened, nearly hysterical. In the logical, tactless approach I was using at the time, I tried to explain to her a bomb had gone off and she had died in the blast. I could tell she thought I was nuts. As far as she was concerned, something heavy had fallen down on her and she was stuck. Nothing I could say was going to convince her otherwise. I was at a complete loss as to what to do to help her until someone suggested using a technique I'd learned on previous trips called *seeing it not there*.

"Seeing it not there"—I do so like the sound of that. It is a subtle difference, but *seeing it not there* is not the same as *making something disappear*. Rebecca had taught the technique to me.

I focused my attention on the debris pile surrounding the woman and began to see it—not there. A spherical shape perhaps two of her body lengths in diameter began to take form around her. This ball shape replaced the debris with a dim whitish-gray light. In a few moments she was floating freely inside the ball. From her floating position it was a simple matter for her to move toward me. She was greeted by a Helper who stepped out from behind where I was standing. With a somewhat puzzled look on her face, she left with the Helper, heading for the Reception Center.

With the bright-light people still at my sides illuminating the darkness, I began moving quickly through the debris pile scanning for other trapped victims of the blast. The same *seeing it not there* technique worked repeatedly for every person we found. I don't remember how many people we recovered this way. By then I had lost all interest in counting or identifying.

While still searching with the bright-light Helpers, I finished my seafood platter in what I'm sure must have looked like a dazed state to those around me. Throughout this experience I'd been aware of my surroundings in Bennigan's simultaneously with my activities in Oklahoma City. At times one area or the other would fade, though never completely. I paid my bill and, leaving a half-finished beer on the table, headed straight for my Jeep and drove home to my apartment.

Shortly after arriving home I began to feel the way I do when I've spent too much time out in the sun. It felt like radiation burns from exposure to the emotional energies at the blast site. These burns didn't show on the outside; these were emotional burns, on the inside. Like sunburn, they burned more and more as time went by. Grief, rage, and anger engulfed me. Anxiety, sadness, and frustration rolled over me like twenty-foot breakers crashing on the beach during a storm. I phoned Rebecca to tell her what had happened and to compare notes. My old habit of verification had returned. I also wanted her advice about the emotional energy burns I'd sustained and specifically how to avoid them in the future. Sometimes, by talking about hidden treasures with someone who has found them previously, you can learn a lot more quickly.

Her first words were, "Oh, Bruce, the babies." I felt a crest of grief rise up and then crash down through me. As we talked, my experience of the emotional waves changed. They were no longer waves of giant surf pounding the beach. Instead, they became more like gigantic swells out at sea with rising crests and dropping troughs of intensity. I'd feel anger, rage, or frustration below me and rising upward with great power. A wave of emotion would pass upward through my body until I was completely submerged and overwhelmed by the feeling. This was not a pleasant experience! At the peak of intensity, with the crest of a wave high above my head, I'd lose almost all emotional control. Grief and rage, the most prominent, were the most powerful and difficult to deal with. Through my confusion and disorientation, Rebecca and I continued to talk about our experiences. After ten minutes or so I calmed down some and began to feel physically exhausted. After hanging up the phone I spent fifteen minutes doing Tai Chi, successfully restoring a little energy, and then I collapsed into bed to rest.

Lying there, I felt the continual rise and fall of the strong emotions I'd felt at the blast site in Oklahoma City. Those energies had stuck to my nonphysical body like hot black tar and I had carried them into my physical world awareness. Too strong a dose of this stuff, left in place too long, can make a person physically ill. Luckily I had previous experience with this hot black tar and knew how to remove it.

I relaxed into Focus 10, a specific state of consciousness I'd learned to reach during my early training at The Monroe Institute. Then I envisioned many small, hollow balls in the air above my body. Mentally, I directed anything within my energy field that was not mine into an appropriate ball. When it felt as though everything had been transferred from my field into the balls, I mentally sent each one back to its rightful owner. I felt great relief from the pressure of all that emotional energy as the envisioned balls carried it away. Waves of emotion that moved through me after that were still strong but manageable. I was no longer in any danger of totally losing emotional control. Within ten minutes I was feeling a little better, so I contacted Coach to offer further assistance in Oklahoma City.

"I think you've had enough for now," was his reply. With that I drifted off to sleep.

Most of Thursday and Friday and portions of Saturday were emotionally rough seas. Waves of grief would bring tears to my eyes. During waves of anger I'd stomp around my apartment, wanting to strike out and hurt the bastards who had set off the bomb. Over those three days the waves gradually came fewer and further between, until on Sunday their intensity began to diminish. My exposure in Oklahoma City had stirred up every bit of my own unresolved emotional baggage. That was all that was left to deal with after I had sent the energies I'd picked up back to their rightful owners. To release what they had stirred up in me I had to welcome in my feelings and give them expression. As I cried and raged and talked and fretted, the strength of the waves gradually subsided.

I awoke Monday morning to a suggestion from Coach to form a *reball* before getting out of bed. It is an energy-charging technique I also learned during training at The Monroe Institute. Think of it as visualizing a large balloon of energy surrounding your entire body. Within this balloon, visualize currents and flows of energy passing through your body, cleaning and recharging the energy field that surrounds and permeates you. This particular reball turned out to have a rather intricate appearance. It had a pair of counter-rotating helixes. One carried energy from below my feet, inside my body, to above my head. The other helix shape rotated in the opposite direction outside my body. It carried energy from above my head to back down below my feet. Each helix fed the other, circulating fresh, clean, clear energy throughout my body. Lying in bed with my eyes closed, I watched the reball do its work. Within three or four minutes the last of the emotional goo I'd stirred up in me in Oklahoma City was cleared away. After thirty-five minutes of Tai Chi I felt fully energized and back to what is normal for me. On Monday I finally felt really good again.

My mother always used a line on me as a kid about experience being both the best teacher and a hard master. Oklahoma City made her point again. There was much to learn from the experience of this voyage into the Afterlife.

From my friend Rebecca, I learned how to prepare for such emotionally charged encounters in the future. Her technique is taken from *The Course In Miracles*, which says that any defense serves only to invite attack. Pushing the door of my awareness closed against the pressure of those emotions had been a mistake. My preparation for trips to places like Oklahoma City now begins with her affirmation. "All my energy channels are clean, clear, open and functioning perfectly. Any energies I encounter pass through me easily with no effect." I try to remember to use this one all the time.

Starting my assistance while sitting in a busy, noisy public place like a Bennigan's restaurant had not been a wise choice either. It may have been the raucous atmosphere that drew me there. The whole experience would have been better done in the quiet and privacy of my apartment. A better choice yet would have been to work in the company of someone else with experience. I'd approached it entirely too lightly without respect for the potential power of the experience.

This was my first experience in which I realized that previous contact with an organized group of Helpers could lead to my getting their assistance should the need arise. The team of Helpers I'd met a year and a half before at the earthquake in India came to help me without my having remembered or asked them. They had provided logistical support and guidance to me, a novice who had jumped into something way over his head. I am grateful for the assistance that they and others like them have given me. This experience taught me that in the New World of the Afterlife you can make friends that you can depend on.

People have asked if I would ever attempt such a thing again. Of course I will. I learned a lot about how to do it by the mistakes I made. I'll know better how to approach such an experience in the future. Besides, each time I voyage out into the Afterlife in this way I learn more about the thing I'm most curious about. I learn more about what it means to be a human being.

II. Initial Forays

A Childhood Daydream

I've always had a great curiosity about my *Three Great Questions*. They are: Where did I come from before I was born? What am I supposed to do while I'm living here? Where do I go when I die? Finding answers to those questions is a journey I know I started somewhere in the past. It has always been difficult for me to pinpoint the exact place or time. All the events of my life seem so woven together and interconnected that the best I have ever been able to do is to remember landmarks along the way.

One such landmark is a daydream that recurred once or twice a week over many months when I was five or six years old, in 1953 while I was living in Alaska.

It always started with the same opening scene. In the middle of whatever I was doing suddenly it would be dark. I would be standing at the back corner of a house, looking up at the stars on a clear, cloudless night. I was in a small city or village without street lights to obscure all those bright stars. The house, extending off to my right toward the street that ran in front of it, was white with a stucco texture. At my back was another house, same style and construction, not six feet away. To my left a dark unpaved alley had served as a path for me to move, unseen, to the back of the house. In front of me a wooden staircase led up the back of the house to a landing with a door providing entry to the second floor. I reached out for the railing as I started quietly climbing those creaky, wooden stairs on my way to the landing and the second-floor door. At the landing I turned to my right, facing the door. I reached for the latch, opened the door, and entered the second-floor room. It was a dimly lit room. I could see that the ceiling was the underside of the roof, its peak running the length of the house from back to front. On the left side of the room there might have been a dresser with a candle burning, providing dim illumination of the rest of the room. On the far wall I could see a white cotton curtain moving slowly, fluttering in a very light breeze. The window behind the curtain must have been open or there was no glass. On the right side of the room, halfway down the wall, was a large brass rail bed. On the side of the bed nearest me, a woman beckoned, motioning with her hand for me to come and join her. I fully entered the room and closed the door behind me. Walking around to the far side of the bed, I looked at the woman, who raised the covers as I eagerly climbed into the bed with her. As a five- or six-year-old boy, I never understood what we did in that bed. I only felt the frolicking atmosphere, pleasure, and a lot of bouncing and moving. I enjoyed whatever it was until I heard those footsteps, heavy footsteps coming up the same stairs I had climbed just a little while before—heavy footsteps that struck such terror in me that something in my chest leaped up into my throat. I felt frightened beyond belief. I rolled off the woman onto the side of the bed closest the window. My eyes were riveted on the door. For a moment, lying there on my back, my body weight propped on my elbows, I was frozen in fear. I kept looking at that door. When the door flew open I could see a man, huge, standing in the doorway silhouetted against the night sky. He was wearing a broad-brimmed, flat-topped hat that was nearly touching the door jam over his head. His bulk filled the doorway. I knew in that instant if he got his hands on me I would be dead or worse. As a five- or six-year-old I never understood why the man would want to kill me. In that daydream there was time only to act, not to question. In one motion, I lifted the light thick blanket with my left hand, rolled out of the bed, and ran naked toward the window. I put my hands out in front of me like a diver as I leapt toward that white cotton curtain. I was terrified beyond belief as I jumped. Just before my fingers touched the curtain, the day dream would always end. And there I'd be, back in the daylight, playing with my dump trucks in the dirt, my heart still pounding with fear.

As a five- or six-year-old, I never gave much thought to what this meant or why it happened. To me it was just another dream. All kids have dreams they remember all the time. It didn't seem unusual to me that it happened when I was wide awake during the daytime playing outside. It was just another dream, one that I had at least once a week for months on end.

Later in life I began to wonder, *so where had this daydream come from? How could I as a young boy have any knowledge of brass rail beds, sex, or another man's jealousy that was strong enough that he wanted to kill me?* And the feelings that accompanied the experience—*where had they come from? The pleasure, joy and frolic I'd felt with the woman. The throat-gripping terror I'd felt with the knowledge I'd be killed or worse if the man in the doorway caught me. Where did those feelings come from?*

By my early twenties, it was clear to me that I had no reasonable, logical explanation for how a five- or six-year-old boy could have such a daydream. Parents didn't take their kids to see such movies back then, and that kind of story would not have been broadcast on television in 1953.

After many years I came to accept the only possible answer, reincarnation. I had lived in another time, in another place, in a different body under different circumstances. Somehow as a child I had remembered the details of my final minutes alive in that lifetime. The memory was so vividly portrayed in that childhood daydream, the feelings were so real, that I still remember every detail today, forty-two years later.

As someone told me a long time ago, if you eliminate all other possibilities, whatever is left, no matter how incongruous it might seem, must be the answer. For me reincarnation is that answer.

(One further note. Often, as I have told other people about my recurring childhood dream, their response has been to relate a reoccurring childhood dream of their own. These kinds of dreams seem to stick in people's memories forever. The details they tend to remember thirty or forty years later are really quite remarkable considering the passage of time.)

Carl Jung, one of the fathers of modern psychology, said that the earliest dream a person can remember often sets the tone and purpose for his entire life. In my case that daydream is the *only* dream I can remember from that period of my life. And for me Carl Jung was right: Its content, and my wondering at its source and meaning, made it a landmark on my journey. It has set the tone and given definition to my life.

Who Are You?

By my mid-twenties my curiosity had led me to read everything I could find relating to my Three Great Questions. I read the Bible and books on automatic writing, reincarnation, astrology, numerology, hypnosis, dreams, and many more subjects relating to the paranormal. I played with Ouija boards. I listened to audio tapes claiming to be information channeled through mediums from the beyond. Finally, I felt that I had a pretty good basic idea about where I came from before I was born. My curiosity then began to focus on where I would go after I died.

I devoured every source of information I could find. I read books about Edgar Cayce and others by authors such as Ruth Montgomery, Judy Boss, and many more. I read *The Search for Bridey Murphy*, a story about past-life regression using hypnosis, and hypnosis became another hobby.

Much of what I read indicated that where we go after we die may be connected to the world in which we dream. I decided to try to find a way to consciously enter the world of dreams. When I came across the writings of Carlos Castaneda, I got my first real clues about how to do so consciously.

Castaneda, a student of anthropology, wrote a series of books about his study of the role of sorcerers or shamans in the Yaqui Indian culture of Mexico. In one book he described how his teacher, a man he called don Juan Matus, had instructed him to find his hands while he was dreaming. His hands would serve as a reference point to help him become "lucid," and thus able to consciously explore the dream world.

Finally I had come across a method I could use to become conscious in the world of dreams. I felt certain that, once there, I could explore the places we go to when we die. In my usual obsessive manner, I immediately began to put major effort into practicing don Juan's instructions to Castaneda to think about finding his hands many times during his waking hours as a way of inducing that act during his dreams. As many times a day as I could remember to do so, I would look down at my hands and tell myself, *I'm going to look down while dreaming tonight and see my hands in my dreams.* Every night I would go to sleep thinking about finding my hands. For over a month, every morning I awakened disappointed at not having accomplished what I'd set out to do.

Then, one night it happened! Asleep, I suddenly realized I was looking down at my hands! I had found them and I knew I was asleep and dreaming. I looked at them carefully. *Yup, those are my hands all right. So . . . now what am I suppose to do?* I had been so obsessed with the idea of finding my hands I had spent no time thinking ahead to plan what I might do next! I remembered one of don Juan's instructions. *Hmmm, well maybe I'll just look around.*

Okay . . . so I looked up from my hands to see that I was standing in a second floor hallway of an old house. I could see a few doors along the hallway on my left and a blank wall on my right. The hallway extended out in front of me perhaps twenty feet to a blank wall at its end. *Big deal*, I thought to myself, *I'm standing in the hallway of a house, so what. There must be something more interesting to do than stand here looking at a hallway in an old house!*

Handsprings! In all my life I've never been strong enough or coordinated enough to do handsprings—that's what I'll do. It will be easy here, I don't have a heavy body to move around.

This will be great! These thoughts were so loud I am sure anyone else in or near the house must have been laughing. I jumped forward, landing on my hands, and sprang over to my feet. Two or three more times I joyfully did handsprings down the second-floor hallway. Abruptly, I stopped. For no apparent reason, I turned to look at the blank wall of the hallway on my right. As I did, a window began to form in the wall in front of me. An old-fashioned doublehung, wooden framed window materialized in the wall right in front of me. The lower half of the window opened and I was looking out into the distance at a man.

This guy was big! I knew he had to be big because we were looking straight and level into each other's eyes. I was standing on the floor of the second story of a house; he was standing on the ground. I couldn't be positive he was actually standing on the ground as his feet were obscured by the plain, grayish, white robe he was wearing. It hung loosely from his shoulders two stories down to the ground. His feet might not actually be touching the ground but that didn't matter at this point. I was looking at a very big guy.

As I stared at his face I was trying to place his nationality. For some reason I thought it was very peculiar. His skin looked dark, more Asian than Negro, but his features were small and more characteristic of northern Europeans. There was something very odd and squinty about his eyes, not slanted as an Asian's, but still something about them caught my attention. As I continued to look at him I decided he must be a Norwegian Oriental. Sounds pretty silly now but that was the only combination that took into account all the peculiarities of his appearance.

"Who are you?" I called out to him in a casual, conversational tone.

He never moved a muscle, but he began slowly moving toward me. The expression on his face never changed the whole time I looked at him. He kept one of those completely non-threatening, I-know-something-you-don't-know smiles on his face the entire time. I became alarmed at his moving toward me.

"Who Are You?" I asked with a little more force in my voice this time.

Nothing in his face or movements acknowledged my question. He just continued moving slowly, ever closer to where I stood in the hall. By the time he got really close, terror had taken over my being and I was screaming *"Who are you?"* at the top of my lungs.

Just as I felt I was a goner, the window closed and then disappeared back into the smoothness of the blank wall. I was doing handsprings again down the hall like nothing had happened. The fear was gone and I was happy again. *Wheeeee, look at me, I'm doing handsprings down the hall.* I became bored with the handsprings in a fairly short time. Didn't seem much of a challenge any more. *What should I do next?*

I'd like to spring through the wall and land somewhere besides this boring hallway, I could hear myself thinking. Sure enough, the next time my hands hit the floor I leaped forward, leading with my feet, and felt myself fly out through the wall. I entered a strange blackness like none I had ever seen before. I could feel I was moving downward, feet first, after exiting the second-floor hallway through the wall. I could see I was moving, too. I was in some sort of coarse-grained, uniform field of blackness that had a three-dimensional quality to it. It was a blackness that had depth. As I looked into it I could see it going by at tremendous speed and that gave me a sense of motion. I couldn't feel this blackness, as you might feel air, but I could see its course-grained structure. It was more fluid than solid as I dropped through it on my way to wherever I was going.

Okay, I remarked to myself, *where shall I land?* The image of a beautiful sunlit field came into my mind. In a moment or two I landed, feet first, on a well-worn dirt path that wound its way through the grass off toward a horizon. The terrain was hilly, the grass greener than I remember seeing anywhere here on Earth. There were trees, short and tall, sparsely scattered around the countryside. The path I had landed on wound its way across an open grassy meadow then curved to the left up a low hill in the distance. With my eyes I followed the path from where I was standing to where it disappeared over the hill. In the distance, at the crest of the hill, I could see people, maybe five or six, walking down the path toward me. They were still quite a distance away, posing no threat, and yet the most reasonable thing that occurred to me was to attack them. Running toward them as fast as I could, I waded into them swinging. As I had approached them they seemed happy to see me, almost as if they knew me. It felt as though they had been waiting for me to come and meet them. I attacked them anyway with all the fury I could muster. I stood in their midst flailing away at them, intending to inflict as much harm as possible. These innocent folks treated me well considering my belligerent actions. They encircled me and, placing their hands and arms above me, gently pushed me down against the ground. I could tell they meant me no harm as they held me down. It was more like they thought they had encountered a crazy man and were merely restraining him. I was still struggling to get free and continue my attack when I gradually began to feel myself lose consciousness. The next thing I was aware of was waking up in bed in Minnesota, in a house I was building by a lake.

I remembered! I had succeeded in finding my hands in my dreams! I had become lucid and I remembered everything that had happened after that too. I wondered who that was, the big guy I had become so frightened of as I looked out the window. I wondered about the strange blackness I had fallen through after leaving the house through the wall. *Where was that place with the path, sunlit and so beautiful?* I felt a little sheepish for having attacked those nice people who were walking toward me on the path. *Who were those nice people anyway?* They had seemed to have known I was coming and were waiting for me. It felt as though they were coming down that path to meet me. Probably wanted to tell me some great secret I would be just dying to hear and instead of listening I went in and tried to beat the holy hell out them. I felt so stupid and ashamed. I wondered what all the things had meant that I had seen and done during my first lucid dream. I went to sleep that night with lots of questions on my mind.

A Shocking, Noisy Awakening

The next morning I awoke in my bedroom, or at least thought I did. It looked just like my bedroom, but it was filled with a strange golden-yellow light. The light that filled my room was so strange at first that I just kept trying to figure out how such a thing could be possible. I finally rationalized away the odd room lighting as just the glow of a hazy sunrise coming in through the window. (Amazing how easily we reject things we can't explain and then fail to probe them any further. Hours later I realized that the strange golden-yellow glow could not have been sunlight— the only window in that bedroom faces west.)

Then a slight buzzing, vibrating noise in my head grabbed my attention and quickly spread throughout my body. It built up to a very unpleasant level, feeling like a very strong, coarse, low-frequency current passing through my entire body. This current, giving a sensation of being electrocuted, reminded me of scenes from old movies when the bad guy *gets the chair*. The buzzing, jolting shock of it was completely overpowering. The sound accompanying this sensation was like I had my head stuck inside a jet aircraft engine at full afterburner. The deafening roar that filled my head excluded all possibility of thought except the sheer terror that filled my entire being. I could not move a muscle. I felt certain I was in the grip of some overpowering electrocuting force that was in the process of ending my life.

I struggled furiously, trying to move my body against the grip of this force holding me immobile. Nothing worked. My eyes still seemed to be open, as I could clearly see the bedroom around me, but I could not move even a finger. My body felt dead except for the strong terrifying electric, roaring, buzzing feeling passing through me. I concentrated on trying to move my legs thinking, *They're the biggest, strongest muscles in my body. If I could move anything at all it would probably be my legs.* I was panicked, frantically struggling to move something, anything. Then I felt a tiny muscle behind my left knee twitch just slightly. The power of the buzzing, roaring, electrocuting current weakened, wavered, and then faded away.

The room went black for just a moment and then I opened my eyes. I was still in my bedroom but the eerie yellowish light was gone. My body moved easily to a sitting position and then up out of bed. That awful buzzing was gone, and everything seemed back to normal. I had no idea what it was, where it came from, or what made it happen. I thought I had either had a close brush with death or I was going nuts. I knew I didn't what a repeat of it, whatever it was.

Over a period of the next two weeks the buzzing, roaring, vibrating, electrocuting experience repeated itself several times. Sometimes I would go through an experience similar to the first one as I woke up in the morning. Sometimes just as I was falling asleep I would feel it starting, softly at first, then very quickly building to a terrifying teeth-chattering level. The shock always frightened me; I would recoil back awake to avoid the sensation.

Over those two weeks I gradually decided that whatever it was wouldn't kill me, at least not right away. I also found that if I really concentrated I could make some part of my body move. Moving any part, no matter how small the movement, broke me free of the roaring, buzzing grip of terror. It became an annoyance that would catch me off guard as I went into or out of sleep, but I feared it only when it was going on. Otherwise I thought it was something strange that would go away on its own, so I kept it to myself.

Nearly two weeks to the day after the *Who Are You* dream, I went to the public library to check out a book on hypnosis. Hypnosis was still a hobby of mine at the time and I hadn't read a new book on the subject in quite a while. So at least that is why I thought I was going there. I went to the card catalogue, and jotted down a couple of call numbers, and headed back for the book shelves. It wasn't long before I spotted the first book on my list up on the top shelf, a little above eye level. I casually looked up at the book as I reached for it, got my finger on top of the binding and pulled it out and off the shelf. As I pulled the book toward me I absentmindedly opened it and began reading halfway down the left-hand page. It said:

A tall, rather dark-skinned woman in a long, straight dress or robe stood almost beside me. My first impression was that she was Negro, with small and even features, dark straight hair, and evenly cut bangs across the forehead. (In retrospect, I realized from the description, she could have been Middle Eastern or Egyptian, but not oriental, as I would have noticed the eye structure).

Something about those lines seemed oddly familiar and I could feel that something rushing toward my awareness. It was coming very fast, building up pressure, and then it exploded into thoughts I could recognize. *Wait a minute! That description matches the person I was screaming at in the Who Are You dream I had just a couple of weeks ago!* I thought to myself. I closed the book and read the cover. *Journeys Out of the Body*, by Robert A. Monroe. *This isn't the book I reached for!* I wasn't at all sure how I had accidentally picked out this book, but it seemed like one of those coincidences you don't mess around with. After all, I had been screaming *Who are you?* at someone in my first lucid dream two weeks ago and the book in my hand seemed to be whoever it was answering back.

I began thinking about the coincidence involved. To get to the library I had driven about fourteen miles. There were at least three other libraries closer to my home where I could have stopped instead. There were several other hypnosis books on my list. I could have reached for any of those other books first. I couldn't help wondering, what were the odds I would *accidentally* grab this *wrong* book? Furthermore, what were the odds I would open this *wrong* book "at random" and read the answer to a question I shouted in a dream two weeks before? I decided odds had nothing to do with it. I left the hypnosis book on the shelf and went home with *Journeys Out of the Body*.

Once home, I began to read Monroe's book. Monroe claimed he had spontaneously begun consciously traveling nonphysically several years before he wrote it. The passage I had stumbled upon in the library referred to beings he called Helpers. In his out-of-body travels these Helpers often lent assistance. I also found an explanation for the buzzing, roaring electrocution I had experienced the day after my *Who Are You* dream. Monroe talked in his first chapter about a strong vibration that held him, in his words, "like a vise." He called it the "vibration state," saying it was a precursor to moving to an out-of-body state. He outlined techniques that could be used to facilitate inducing this vibration state and using it to go consciously out of one's body. This sounded much better than mere lucid dreaming! He wrote about being able to go anywhere in the physical or nonphysical world in this out-of-body state, consciously!

After reading his book cover to cover, I enthusiastically began to practice the techniques he gave. His instructions seemed a little obscure, referring to many things I didn't understand. But I did my best to use his techniques to initiate his vibration state and then increase the frequency of the vibrations to a high, smooth feel and then go out-of-body. I put all my energy into accomplishing that goal. I practiced every chance I had. It wasn't long before I began to get results, but I still had the problem of fear. As I would drift off to sleep I would start the technique and many times suddenly find myself locked in the grip of that buzzing, roaring state. My first reaction was always to recoil away in fear, followed by disgust that I had gotten the vibration started and then pulled out of what I wanted so desperately to achieve. I can't say I ever got good control of Monroe's vibration state technique. I was never able to induce it at will.

It was, however, during this time that I had my first verifiable out-of-body experience. It was probably a result of having pushed so hard to make it happen and then backing off on the effort. I had lain down for an afternoon nap. I was tired and drifted quickly off to sleep. Some time later I woke up, or—more honestly—became aware of what I was rather absentmindedly doing. I sat up in bed, swung my legs over the side, and stood up facing the open doorway. I walked to the doorway, turned right, and continued down the hall in the direction of my living room. Everything I saw was just as in my physical-world house. Stopping at a short staircase that led up to a loft, I turned left facing the stairs and began moving toward them. Instead of going up the stairs I reached out with my right hand and pushed it through them. Passing the rest of my body through the stairs, I moved into that same three-dimensional blackness I had seen in the *Who Are You* dream. When I came out of the blackness I was up near the ceiling of a room, in a corner, looking down at a large dark round table. Everything was in black, white, and shades of gray. There were two people sitting at the table with small jars in front of them. They were picking up the jars, rubbing their fingers on something in them and then rubbing their faces. They would alternate between doing this and, looking at each other, erupting in uproarious laughter. I watched this scene for several minutes, not knowing what was going on, and then at some point I lost awareness of it. Later I woke up again, this time physically, and got out of bed.

"Becky, I had the strangest dream while I was napping," I said when I reached the living room where she had been sitting when I lay down for the nap.

Becky and I shared the house and she was familiar with my efforts to learn this out-of-body stuff. When I told her all the details she got one of those *Oh My God* looks on her face. She told me that after I had gone down for my nap she went across the street to visit her friend Debby, whose mother was a cosmetics salesman. Debby's mom had dropped of a bag full of sample jars of creams and makeup. Becky and Debby had been sitting at Debby's large, dark dining room table with those jars doing exactly what I had seen the two people doing in the *dream*.

Along with my out-of-body practice, my episodes of lucid

dreaming continued for quite some time. They were great fun and I enjoyed them immensely as I kept working to gain controlled access to the out-of-body state. Most of the time I would wake up in a dream where I was in a sports car, cruising down a newly paved road at high speed on a bright sunny day.

Then one summer day I was driving to work along Excelsior Boulevard, a four-lane city street in Minneapolis. I was in my 1960 Austin Healey with the top down. It was back in the days before Dutch Elm disease claimed all those beautiful trees, and as I drove east the rising sun illuminated the green brilliance of the elms that canopied the street. I remember looking up at the leaves, back-lit by the sun, and thinking how beautiful they looked. I remember thinking, *If I'm dreaming, I can fly up and get a better look.* My attention was sharply focused on those leaves perhaps forty feet above the ground. They seemed within arm's reach as I gazed at them wondering if I was dreaming or not. I continued looking straight up at the leaves, trying to decide if I was dreaming. Shock suddenly overtook me as I realized that I wasn't dreaming. I was driving at about thirty-five miles an hour down a crowded, morning rush hour street. I wasn't watching traffic! I was looking straight up at the colorful leaves of the trees. My head snapped back down so I could see the road and traffic ahead of me. *God looks after fools*, I thought, as I realized where I was and the danger of what I had been doing.

That event scared the living feces out of me as I thought about it later. I realized I could no longer tell for certain at any given moment whether I was lucid dreaming, with my body safely asleep in my bed, or driving in traffic or anywhere else for that matter. I decided to stop attempting to lucid dream and stop experimenting with the vibration state that led to out-of-body experience. It seemed too dangerous to continue. Somewhere inside me I think I made the decision to stop all this kind of activity, and after several months I lost all interest in inducing the vibration state Monroe had described. Gradually the ability to do so at all faded away; my life pulled me to other, more pressing things, and I moved on. But I have never forgotten the experience and can't stress too much its importance as I continued to quest after answers to my Three Great Questions.

Waking Vision of a Disk

One day in March 1975, my friend Ron called to ask if I would help him haul some scrap steel from a salvage site. Ron had located three old, burned-out box cars and the property owner was willing to let Ron cut them up for scrap and haul them away just to get rid of them. It was a sunny morning, a rarity in Minnesota springtime, when I met Ron to lend a hand. What happened that day was the next major landmark on my journey.

Ron had built a makeshift toboggan out of scrap lumber. We loaded his cutting torch, oxygen, and acetylene tanks on the toboggan and hauled them over hard-packed snow about forty yards from the road to where the old box cars were. After unloading the toboggan, Ron fired up his torch and began cutting the first box car into chunks small enough for us to handle. We both loaded the toboggan and then I pulled it, loaded with steel, to the trailer parked just off the road. It was physically demanding work but I could get to the trailer, unload, and be back before Ron had enough steel cut to reload and haul out.

After about three trips I decided to lie down for a few minutes, to shake off my exhaustion. With my heavy winter coat and stocking hat, I was comfortable lying there in the warm springtime sun. I closed my eyes and relaxed into the warm feeling of the sun on my face.

After a short time with my eyes closed, my attention was drawn to a vivid, full-color, 3-D scene seemingly floating in the empty space in front of me. It looked so real, like a lucid dream, and yet I could still hear Ron's cutting torch burning through steel not thirty feet away. As I began to look more closely at the scene, the sound of Ron's torch faded away. Then I was alone, silently and curiously looking at every detail of the scene before me.

Throughout the experience I was not aware of doing any analyzing, just watching, moving, and feeling. I was so amazed by what I saw that later I wrote down a description in as fine a detail as I could remember. But its meaning didn't get much clearer until September 1991. The following is taken from the journal I was keeping at the time. If you find yourself wondering what it means, you'll know how I felt about it for the next seventeen years.

Here it is:

I'm looking at a figure, humanoid in shape, standing in the air about ten feet in front of me. At first it looks like a male but as I look closer it's really more asexual then either male or female. The figure, seen only in profile, is dressed in a sort of close-fitting body stocking that is only one color. It could be beige but the lighting makes it difficult to see what color, if any, it really is. The body stocking gives the figure an overall smoothness to its shapes and lines, taking away any distinctive features that would help identify its gender.

This figure is standing between a very bright yellow-white light and the place I am looking from. The background color is the deepest, most vivid sky blue you can imagine. If the sky were putting on a special display of its shades of blue this would be a rare display of its deepest, deepest blue. The air around the figure is hazy and the haze gives it a surrounding glow. It looks very much like when, on a hot, hazy summer day, you hold your hand out to shield your eyes from the sun and then look at your hand.

As I feel myself becoming curious about the figure's face I realize I'm moving closer and looking at its face. The expression is interesting, one of awe and total amazement with everything it's seeing as it peers into the world around itself. Like the expression on the face of a baby, there's a feeling of fascination in the eyes that expresses awe.

Backing away a short distance, I notice something behind the figure. I know he's not aware of what I am looking at. Perhaps he's so taken with the view in front he's never looked behind himself. It looks like a crystal-clear glass rod about an inch or so in diameter. It seems to be glowing from within with a greenish-yellow light. I move closer to get a better look at the rod. It's connected to the humanoid figure directly between the shoulder blades and seems to be flexible rather than rigid. I am very close to the rod now and turn my head to the right to see how long it is. It extends off into the distance further than I can see. Backing away from the eerily lit rod to get a better view, I follow it to see how far away it extends. I still can't see the end of it so I begin to move along its path, my eyes transfixed on it as I do.

As I follow the rod off into the distance, I notice the background color is changing now. The deep vivid blue is softening into progressively paler pastel blues. It is like I am approaching dusk without the usual pinks and yellows of the approaching nighttime sky. The soft, pastel blues then begin fading into black as I cross the boundary between day and night. The rod is changing form now too. Its diameter is the same but now it's made of three smaller rods closely packed together. As the background color dims, fading to twilight, the rod divides and divides again. Its diameter is still the same but after several divisions it's now made of perhaps twenty or thirty thinner strands, like a crystal-clear, multi-stranded cable. I keep moving along following the cable. The background now is past twilight and into night. What started out as faintly twinkling stars are now shining brightly in a deep black, nighttime sky.

It feels like the humanoid figure I left just moments ago is now light years away and I am continuing to move through some distant night sky following what started out as a single solid bar. It has divided into smaller strands so many times it's just a bundle of fine filaments too numerous to count. Something is changing. The filaments are spreading out. I stop to get a closer look at what I am seeing. The filaments are fanning out in graceful parabolic curves toward a place where I can just make out the elliptical shape of a disk. I can't really see a disk but I know it's there because the stars behind it are blocked from view by its presence. I know it's round; it only looks elliptical because I am viewing it at an angle. The filaments are fanning out in smooth uniform patterns to connecting points on the disk.

I start to move again slowly, moving first closer to the filaments, then picking out one to follow. It leads toward its connection point on the disk. Approaching the disk, I can see connection points for many filaments. They're near small, round, yellow disks. The little disks at the connection points form rings of concentric circles on the large disk. There might be thousands of the smaller disks, one for every filament. I continue to follow the one I picked out earlier. Closer now, I see that each of the small yellow disks next to each filament connection point has a picture on it. They are pictures of faces. Each face depicts a set of human feelings or emotions. As I look at each one I can see from this distance, I get the feeling that each one represents a separate, distinct personality. I move my focus back to the filament I have been following for quite a while now and notice I am getting close to the place it is connected to the disk. The face on its yellow disk reminds me of a mustachioed villain named Snidely Whiplash, a cartoon character from a Saturday morning kids' series called Rocky and His Friends. Closer now, I see that Snidely's face is animated, his mustache jiggling back and forth, his eyebrows bouncing up and down. There's a little red button sticking out of the disk next to Snidely's picture and I know he wants me to push his button. That is what all his facial antics are for. He is trying to get me to push the little red button. I reach out with my hand. My hand?

This is the first time I have any awareness of having a body. To this point I have just been watching without awareness of my eyes. I reach out and push the little red button next to Snidely's image. I hold the button in. I watch as greenish-yellow light emerges from the disk into the previously empty filament. A few moments later I remove my finger from the button and the greenish-yellow light stops coming out. It has formed a pulse of light about four inches long that is continuing to move through the filament at the same speed it emerged from the disk.

As the pulse of light moves away to my left, toward the direction of the humanoid figure now standing many light years away, I follow it. As I do, other filaments begin to come back into view in the background. Some have light pulses in them, moving like the one I am following, some do not. The

*other pulses I can see are out of phase. They evidently emerged
from the disk at different times. As I follow the pulse, moving
back in the direction of the humanoid figure, the filaments
are beginning to gather back together on the way to forming
the cable again. As they narrow together I am seeing hundreds
of fibers. At least half of them have light pulses traveling to
my left. The cable is forming again, same diameter as before,
as I continue following the pulse emitted when I pressed the
little red button next to Snidely Whiplash's image. For a while
I can still see the pulse I have been following amongst the
others. Then, flying alongside the cable, I lose sight of it. There
are too many pulses moving together and the filaments are
rejoining into larger ones and fewer of them. The pulse is now
joined with so many others that they've all joined together into
a solid greenish-yellow glow within the clear glass-like rods.
Though I have lost sight of it I continue to fly alongside the
rods at the same speed as before, knowing I am keeping pace
with Snidely's pulse.*

*The background has gone from black starry night back to
twilight. I can just make out the fading stars against the
ever-lightening sky. As I move into the pale blues of dawn, the
rod has rejoined itself into three parallel rods as before. I
continue to keep pace with Snidely's pulse as the now-single
rod stands out against the deepening vivid blue sky background.
The humanoid figure is coming into view on my left and I
want to watch as Snidely's pulse, moving through the rod,
enters the figure from behind. I back away slightly as it does
and I can see through the expression on the face that whatever
it was viewing in the world at that instant was viewed through
the personality of Snidely Whiplash. Not just that this humanoid has experienced it through the personality of Snidely but
that Snidely was there to experience it. In a sense Snidely, still
residing on the disk, has come into this world briefly not only
to color how the universe looks to this humanoid but also to
be expressed in it.*

The image I was seeing faded away and I found myself
lying on the toboggan on a snow-covered little hill, warm
and cozy in the Minnesota springtime sun.

I opened my eyes and sat up on the toboggan. Then I stood up and stretched my body like a large upright cat. Looking over toward where Ron was working, I could see he had cut enough steel from the old box car to fill the toboggan again. I pulled it over, piled it high, and dragged another load across the snow to the trailer parked beside the road. All the while, my mind was filled with curiosity and wonder at what I had just seen. When I told Ron what I'd seen he said it sounded like a vision. That took me by surprise, as visions were not something I'd experienced before. As I worked the rest of the day I could see, clearly in my mind, all the scenes from the vision in great detail. Questions filled my mind: Why did I see it? What were all those things I saw—the figure, the light, the rod, the disk, the pulses, and all the faces? Most of all, I wondered, *What did it mean?* For the next seventeen years I continued to puzzle over this vision.

After the vision of the disk that spring day, life just continued on. I finished building the house on the lake, got divorced, and moved to Colorado. Several years passed by. I remarried, started a family, and was kept pretty busy by life in general. I frequented a metaphysical bookstore, took a few classes in things such as astrology and psychic development, and I continued to search for answers to my Three Great Questions, though my effort was muted by the distractions, responsibilities, and choices I had made for my life. When occasionally the memory of the disk vision wafted through my mind, it still brought a sense of wonder and curiosity. But gradually my questions about the meaning of that vision faded into the vague grayness of all past memories.

III. Gateway Voyage

While browsing through the Nic Nac Nook, my favorite metaphysical bookstore in Denver, I stumbled across Monroe's second book, *Far Journeys*. *Journeys Out of the Body* had had such an impact on me that I snapped up his newest one on sight. I read and reread *Far Journeys* several times over the next five years or so, trying to understand more about the experience and concepts it described. After each rereading I felt a desire to contact Monroe to tell him how his first book had found me and thank him for writing it. Can't say I ever made much of a real effort to find him though.

Then, in 1991, I caught a glimpse of Robert Monroe's picture on a magazine cover in a grocery store. I got all the way to my place in line at the checkout before it registered with me what I had seen. I went back to the magazine rack, grabbed a copy, and rushed back to my cart just in time to begin unloading it.

The article made reference to The Monroe Institute and included a phone number to call for information. The response to my phone call was a pamphlet describing available tapes and the activities of the Institute. I was impressed by the opening paragraph written by Robert Monroe:

The Monroe Institute is a nonprofit educational and research organization devoted to the following premise: Focused consciousness contains all the solutions to the questions of human existence. Greater understanding of such consciousness can be achieved only through coordinated research efforts using an interdisciplinary approach. The results of such research efforts are meaningful only if there are practical applications— something of value for our contemporary culture. The Monroe Institute proposes to introduce at all levels of human endeavor such abilities of mental functioning so as to change constructively man's direction and destiny.

I was once again on my quest after the Holy Grail of Out-of-Body-Experience. I became obsessed with learning how to consciously move out of my body again and explore the nonphysical world of human consciousness. I read both of Monroe's books again, looking for clues. I went back to practicing the vibration state techniques, trying to restart what I had stopped in 1975. I ordered the first set of home study audio tapes from the Institute, and got my first exposure to Hemi-Sync®, Monroe's technology of sound, and to Focus 10, a state of human consciousness evoked by certain Hemi-Sync sound patterns.

Several times a week I listened to the home study tapes and practiced moving into this strange, altered state of consciousness called Focus 10. It felt like a combination of extremely deep, physical relaxation coupled with a heightened state of mental alertness. The other name Monroe used to describe this state, "Mind Awake, Body Asleep," really seemed to fit. At times I lost all contact with my body and yet I remained wide awake, aware of my every thought.

Using the vague clues given in *Journeys Out of the Body*, coupled with Focus 10, I put concentrated effort into trying to have out-of-body experiences again. The buzzing, roaring vibration state began to occur at random times and I found myself again pulling back in fear. After several months of struggling to learn how to get out of my body, in frustration I contacted the Institute again. It seemed obvious to me that I could accelerate the learning process by attending a structured program there rather than continuing with the home study tapes. So I made my credit card deposit over the phone and reserved a September 1991 spot for myself in their entry-level program called Gateway Voyage. Not everyone in my family was happy with this decision. (Note: A more detailed description of The Monroe Institute, Hemi-Sync and all Gateway Voyage Focus levels is provided in Appendix A.)

September finally came and I found myself riding in a van from the Charlottesville airport toward The Monroe Institute in Faber, Virginia. As the van approached the building where the program takes place, some part of me began to feel anxious. Anxiety built up so fast and so high that I began to question just what in the world my obsession had brought me to. If I could have escaped without humiliation, I would have turned around and gone home. After the van stopped in front of the training center, I carried my suitcase into the building. All at once the anxiety and nervousness of just a few minutes before were gone. I can't explain how it happened, but as I walked into the building it felt like I'd left my home in Colorado and walked into my home in Virginia.

The Gateway Voyage program takes place in a facility where meals and lodging are provided during the participant's six-day stay. I emptied my suitcase into the closet and dresser provided in the small room I'd share with a roommate. Then I peeked into the CHEC unit (Controlled Holistic Environmental Chamber) in my room that would serve as both sleeping quarters and the place I'd listen to the Hemi-Sync tapes during the program.

The CHEC unit—which reminded me of a Pullman berth—is an enclosed space the size of the single bed mattress it contains. The small opening into the CHEC unit has a thick, black curtain that can be drawn for privacy as well as isolation from outside light and sound. Crawling inside, I found it comfortable and cozy, albeit small. I closed the curtain and played with different levels of red, yellow, and blue lighting available.

Feeling comfortable with my new surroundings, I strode downstairs to meet some of the other participants congregating in the dining room. There I met Darlene, one of the two program trainers, and we sat down to what's called the intake interview. During our little chat I explained I'd come to Gateway Voyage to learn how to have out-of-body experiences. She suggested that while a few participants might have had such experiences in the past it wasn't necessarily the main focus of the program. Furthermore, she suggested, it might be useful to consider approaching the program with few expectations. To me that meant if I pretended I wasn't hell-bent on getting out of my body and zooming around through the ether it would be easier to do so. Kind of like, "you get what you want when you least expect it, so try not to expect it too much." Throughout most of the program I struggled with trying to consciously go out-of-body while not expecting to. Lucky for me the confusion of that state of mind left room for something big to happen.

The program started with what for me was a reintroduction to Focus 10. Lying in my CHEC unit with Hemi-Sync sounds coming through my stereo headphones from the control room, I was surprised at the ease of seeing visual images. That hadn't happened using the home study tapes. These images were not in full color and sound, but rather, in a coarse-grained, black, white, and shades of gray. The image that stands out most from this reintroduction to Focus 10 is that of many faces. They were the faces of several adults looking down at me from above. I didn't recognize any of them as people I knew and as they peered down at me I felt as though I were lying on my back in a crib. It felt as if a number of strangers had happened by and they were peeking into the crib at the baby.

(During one Focus 10 tape exercise, I became very annoyed at the sound of snoring. I was convinced that my roommate was snoring so loudly it was disturbing my experience. Then I decided that someone had sneaked into my CHEC unit and that person was intentionally snoring loudly to disturb me. Then it hit me. It was me! I was lying there wide awake and conscious and at the same time my body was asleep snoring! Oh well, they did call Focus 10, "Mind Awake, Body Asleep"!)

We began to use Focus 10 to explore for answers to questions or to find information important to us personally.

In one tape I intended to contact the person I met in the "Who Are You?" lucid dream I had years ago. During that tape I sensed the presence of someone as he approached, but the only visual image I saw was a spinning pattern of white light. I wasn't aware of any communication, just a spinning ball of light.

After several tape-guided excursions to Focus 10, carrying out various activities, the "feel" of it became familiar. Familiar enough, in fact, that I was able to shift my awareness to it without needing the Hemi-Sync sounds of the tapes. With that accomplished, the program moved on to Focus 12.

Focus 12 is an altered state of consciousness different from Focus 10. In our pre-tape briefing, trainers described it as a state of awareness expanded beyond the physical body, an awareness level in which, among other things, exploration of nonphysical realities was possible. Excited by the prospects, I lay down in my CHEC unit, slipped on the stereo headphones, and waited to embark on a Focus 12 voyage.

My first experience of Focus 12 felt very planar. Everything seemed to exist in a flat plane which extended forever in all directions. Then a beautiful, full-color visual display of deep green, tree-covered countryside came into view below me. A thin column of dense white smoke began to rise from amongst the trees a quarter of a mile away. It continued to rise into the sky and perhaps a thousand feet above the ground it began to expand outward. As the mushroom-shaped cloud continued to expand outward from the smoke column, I felt myself expanding outward also. The feeling of Focus 12 for me was that of ever-expanding access to greater and greater volumes of information at levels beyond my normal awareness. Again, the trainer's description of Focus 12 as a state of expanded awareness seemed to fit nicely.

In later Focus 12 tapes we began learning how to access information there for decision making, problem solving, and enhanced creative expression. When we started taking problems into Focus 12, looking for solutions, I copped out and asked to see a problem. I found myself walking down an extremely steep, switchback mountain trail. I could see all the way to the bottom of this long trail; it ended in the back yard of my home in Colorado.

In a later Focus 12 tape exercise I asked for the meaning of the steep mountain trail problem. The answer came back, *When you come down from the mountain and go back home, how will you explain your experience to your wife to relieve her anxiety about what you're doing?* Asking for an answer to this problem, I saw the image of a hug, a rose, and a knot in a wooden board. Repeating the question with these symbols I got: express your warm, close love for her and flowers would be nice. The knot turned out to mean, *tell her what it's not.*

In another tape exercise, called the "Five Questions Exercise," we were to enter Focus 12 with the following questions: Who am I? Where and who was I before I entered this physical body? What is my purpose for existence in physical matter reality? What action can I now take to best serve this purpose? and What is the content of the most important message that I can receive and understand at this point in my existence? I was delighted that the Gateway Voyage program included some facets of my own Three Great Questions.

The answers came back so fast that I thought they were my symbols for asking the questions. You see, part of Gateway Voyage training is learning to communicate in pictures, symbols, and feelings instead of words. This method is called Nonverbal Communication or NVC. The technique involves first thinking about your question in words and then translating it into whatever NVC images feel appropriate. I had followed this procedure, first asking the questions verbally in my thoughts. Immediately after I did so, a series of images formed in my mind which I took to be my own NVC images for the question. These images appeared so quickly that at first I didn't realize they were the answer to my question. Whoever was answering was not playing by the program trainer's rules. In my confusion about this I became very angry to have not received any answers.

Two symbols appeared after I had verbalized the "Who am I?" question. The first was a huge cylinder shape which I knew symbolized the limits and extent of the far reaches of my perception. The second was a narrow, tightly focused, beam of white light which was sweeping the inside surface of the cylinder. It looked like a lighthouse beacon striking a distant fog bank. I knew this represented illumination of the limits of my perception.

Since I mistakenly took these to be my own NVC question symbols instead of the answer, I asked the same question again. I saw the same images.

Getting frustrated and angrier, I asked again. This time the image of the cylinder formed and then it changed into a hollow sphere. The narrow beam of white light scanned the inside surface of the sphere. Still believing these were my own NVC questions, I continued to ask the same question and see the same images. By the end of the tape exercise I was fuming mad and gave up.

After every tape exercise, the trainers and all participants gather together in a large, comfortable room for a debriefing session to discuss experiences during the exercise. During the debriefing session held after the Five Questions Exercise, one of the trainers responded to my complaining by suggesting perhaps the answer was contained in the images I thought were my NVC question. As I thought about that the angry smoke rolling out of my ears dissipated and I calmed down. Later, as I remembered the images, they translated themselves into something I could feel and understand. The answers to all five questions condensed themselves down to the following statement:

I am an awareness that illumines the unknown to make it known and expose more unknown to repeat the process. The light beam illuminated the inside of a hollow sphere representing the boundary of my perception. I am to continue to explore the unknown in all directions. This will bring what is presently unknown into my awareness and in a continuing process. More unknowns will be transformed into knowns, thereby expanding the limits of my perception.

After an appetite-whetting number of tape explorations of Focus 12, we moved on to Focus 15, the level of No Time. My first experience of Focus 15 had a sense of absolute stillness, a quiet, peaceful realm. While exploring there I was reminded of a complete loss of time episode when I was in my early teens. I had started to play a 45 rpm record on an old phonograph. I heard the first few bars of guitar music and the next thing I knew the tone arm was cycling back and forth after the end of the music. I had the distinct feeling that three minutes or three hundred years could have elapsed during my loss of time and I had no way of knowing which was true. The difference between my experience as a teenager and exploring Focus 15 was that I remained fully alert and conscious during my Gateway Voyage experiences. Learning to explore Focus 15 opened access to information without time acting as an obstacle. Moving my awareness from the present to the past or the future became as easy as the thought of doing so. It was very difficult for me to form any rational concepts to explain my experience in the altered state labeled Focus 15. Yet my experience exploring there taught me that time is not a barrier to the shifting or movement conscious awareness.

The next altered state we learned to explore had fascinating implications for me. Called Focus 21, this state of consciousness was also labeled, by the trainers, as The Edge of Time and Space. They described Focus 21 as an opportunity to explore other energy systems and other realities beyond what we call time-space-physical-matter. As I approached these tape exercises I felt that this was what I had really come for.

During my early exploration of Focus 21, a person I call *The Cliff Diver* appeared. This was a very visual experience. I felt myself standing, watching this person with a sleek smooth elongated body. He looked like the award they hand out annually to actors called the Oscar. He was standing up high among towering rock spires. The rocks were very tall, narrow column shapes bathed in a warm steamy atmosphere. Thin fog-like clouds swirled gently around him. As I watched, he executed, beginning from a standing position, an absolutely perfect swan dive from one of the high rock spires. I jumped, starting from a vantage point right next to him, and continued to watch him as I followed him down. I knew we had to be accelerating, gaining speed, but I had no sensation of falling. I kept following until I lost sight of him in the blackness below. It would be a while before I made sense of this.

Then came the afternoon when our group listened to a tape called The Patrick Tape, which had been recorded during an explorer session several years before. (Explorers worked with Hemi-sync sounds early on, to find out what was possible. Explorer sessions were conducted with the volunteer in an isolation booth, monitored via two-way microphone communication, with the monitor outside the booth guiding the explorer, often using pre-selected questions to explore some aspect of the nonphysical world. These sessions were tape recorded for future reference.)

In The Patrick Tape, the explorer was functioning as a channel, that is, allowing a nonphysical person to use her vocal cords to speak. Monroe was the outside monitor for the session. After some preliminary information, the person using her vocal chords said he wanted to try something new. After getting assurances that the explorer would not suffer any ill effects Monroe gave the go-ahead to proceed. What followed was a conversation with a person named Patrick who, it turned out, had been dead for about 100 years. I listened in utter fascination as the story unfolded. I could feel the implications for getting answers to the third of my three great questions. I could feel I was being exposed to a method that would allow me to explore and possibly learn answers to the question *Where do I go after I die?*

Patrick had been a cook on a small steam-powered ship in the middle 1800s. His ship hauled lumber from Scotland and Ireland to the southern part of England. After dark one night, the ship's boiler exploded and Patrick was thrown into the sea. He swam around until he happened on a timber from his destroyed ship floating in the water. He held onto that timber in the icy cold water, hoping that when daylight came he would be spotted by a passing ship and rescued. The tone and emotion in Patrick's voice gave a very real, genuine feel to the words he spoke through the explorer. I remember in my skepticism thinking, *If this is a fake story it's a very good, realistic fake.*

As I listened to Monroe's voice on the tape and Patrick's responses, it became clear that Patrick didn't know he was dead. As far as Patrick knew it was still that first night of the explosion. He was still waiting, over a hundred years later, for the sun to rise that next morning with the hope of being found and rescued.

The shiver in Patrick's voice and his comments about being so cold gave a clue as to what had happened. I got the impression that Patrick had hung onto that timber until he gradually lost consciousness due to hypothermia. He had probably faded in and out a few times before he died. During one of those fade-outs he had slipped beneath the icy water and drowned. When he became conscious again it was after he had died. The hope of hanging onto that floating timber until daylight had brought him back. He was still clinging to that timber.

I have to give Monroe credit. Using the suggestions he was given beforehand, channeled through the explorer in the booth before Patrick came through, Monroe rescued him. The suggestions had been to get Patrick's attention, join him in his present reality, and then somehow inform him that he had died. Monroe accomplished this and in the process learned where Patrick had lived, about his family and other details. It was clear that information Patrick gave about his life and death might be usable to verify that he had once been alive on this earth as the experience proposed.

Other suggestions were to bring Patrick up to a place that felt safe and tell him to *look for the light.* Monroe succeeded in getting Patrick to float up and out of the water. When Patrick told Monroe his mom had died during an epidemic, it gave an opening to explain to Patrick that he was dead. After first carefully skirting around the issue,

Monroe told Patrick he was like his mom now, he had died. There were a few moments between Patrick's incredulous disbelief and his acceptance of the possibility.

Patrick looked for the light and eventually saw it. That started the most emotionally moving part of the experience. Moments after Patrick saw the light, his mother appeared to him and a very emotional reunion took place. Patrick's mother had been waiting there to take him home and shortly after she arrived they left together. This was a very emotionally moving experience for me and I found myself trying, as it ended, to hide the fact that tears were streaming down my cheeks.

The staff member who made the presentation explained that the Institute was in the process of assembling this new program, Lifeline, based in part on The Patrick Tape experience. It would be a program in which participants would learn to assist individuals who, like Patrick, are stuck in an isolated reality of their own making. In learning how to retrieve people like Patrick, we would have the opportunity to learn much more about a greater part of ourselves. I was hooked! I felt such a strong pull to learn to do this kind of work that I knew before I left the presentation room I would be back for Lifeline at my earliest opportunity.

Meeting I/There

The Institute brochure's description of Focus 21 as *Other Energy Systems* didn't provoke any images or ideas about what I might expect to find there. That is probably just as well. Without expectations, my curiosity was free to wander anywhere and find anything. My interaction with the Cliff Diver was an example of an early encounter with Other Energy Systems. In this example the scenes had been visually stunning. I had the feeling the Cliff Diver was trying to communicate something to me by his actions but it was unclear to me what they meant. Other labels for Focus 21 imply more about the Cliff Diver's identity or origin. *The Edge of Time and Space* refers to Focus 21 as the last level of physical world reality, the boundary between the physical and nonphysical worlds in Monroe's cosmology. It is the edge that lies between the physical world and the Afterlife. Human consciousness can exist at levels of consciousness up to and including Focus 21 while remaining physically alive. Since physical reality is often referred to as the reality of time and space, Focus 21 can be thought of as the edge of time and space. (Then how is it possible for physically alive humans to explore beyond Focus 21? Monroe said that exploration and return from those levels was possible but one could not *take up residence there* as a physically alive human.)

The Bridge is another label for Focus 21—it is a crossing point for movement between the two worlds. It can serve as a place for meetings between people from the physical world and those who exist in nonphysical worlds. This Bridge aspect of Focus 21 turned out to be important to me personally as the Gateway Voyage program continued.

After we became comfortable with Focus 21 during the first few tape exercises, our trainers suggested we begin trying to make contact with anyone we might find there. I approached the next Focus 21 tape exercise with an open mind and few expectations, but I had my first introduction to nonphysical friends.

The program tapes have a pink sound, a hissing sound added, which serves to mask the Hemi-Sync tones. This is evidently done to reduce the tendency to focus one's attention on those tones and miss what else is going on. The steady hiss of the pink sound makes it easy to ignore tape sounds altogether and let the Hemi-Sync do its work in the background. During this Focus 21 tape, I found myself at times focusing my attention on the hissing, pink sound. When I did, I began to hear the sound of many human voices all jumbled together. They sounded so real that I thought at first they were actually recorded on the tape and I was hearing them through my headphones. Several times during this tape exercise, as I would focus my attention on the jumble of voices in the hiss, one male voice would come through, standing out from the rest. Each time I heard that male voice it would call out the same word—*apprentice*. Each time I heard it, the experience was accompanied by a feeling that whoever these voices were, apprentice is what they called me. These voices sounded so real that I asked the trainers during the de-briefing session that followed if they were recorded on the tape. They assured me there are no such voices recorded on that tape, and other program participants I talked to didn't hear them. I decided they must be something else.

During a later Focus 21 tape exercise, the Cliff Diver I had seen earlier returned. I saw him again standing amongst those same cathedral-like rock spires, hands at his sides, looking straight ahead, preparing to dive. Same beautifully executed swan dive into the swirling mists and fog. I followed again, on his right side, watching him intently as we plummeted through the darkness below. His dive was different this time. After falling a short distance straight down, he turned his dive upward in a long, graceful, sweeping arc. I followed at his side as the dive became an ever-faster, upward-climbing flight. We were climbing at a steep angle when the Cliff Diver turned his head and looked at me. I didn't see his lips move but I clearly heard his voice when he said, "Apprentice." Then he picked up speed, swept further upward, and rocketed out of sight. The similarity of appearance between the Cliff Diver and the humanoid in my vision of the Disk years ago still hadn't entered my mind.

When I attended Gateway Voyage, Bob Monroe was still physically alive. As part of the Gateway Voyage program he customarily attended a gathering of participants on Wednesday evenings in David Francis Hall. He would talk with participants in lecture fashion about his experiences, often giving details behind what was printed in his books. After he finished covering whatever topic he chose for the evening, he would participate in the ensuing discussion and answer questions.

This Wednesday night he discussed something he called his "cluster," a group of Beings he identified as parts of himself. Each Being had completed a cycle of lifetimes on the earth or elsewhere and then had taken up residence as a member of the cluster. Each was a member of the same single being, the cluster. Monroe understood himself to be an individual member of this group and at the same time all of them together. He called this cluster his Total Self or his I/There. He described himself as a portion of I/There still living on the earth in the physical world.

He talked about seeing other such clusters, and watching as individual members of a cluster returned after living a lifetime on the earth. He saw how what they had experienced and learned became part of the Total Self the cluster now represented to him. He told of watching as the last member rejoined the cluster after finishing its last lifetime on earth. When this happened, Monroe explained, the entire cluster would wink out. It disappeared from sight. He speculated on what happened to the cluster after that. Perhaps, he pondered out loud, with all the combined experience of the thousands of individual lifetimes each member had completed, the Total Self moved on. With the knowledge of all the cluster members rejoined together, maybe they left to create their own world in some other reality. He admitted he really didn't know, but said that many times thoughts along these lines had occurred to him as he watched the last member rejoin a cluster just before it winked out.

As he talked I began to feel uneasy, not knowing why. It was as though, as he spoke, some part of me that had been unconscious was beginning to wake up. I had no idea what it was or what it meant; I just began to feel, well, uneasy.

He talked about his first contact with the other members of his cluster, his I/There. On one of his out-of-body journeys, he said, he had found himself standing in something that appeared to be a large bowl. It was very dark and round and appeared to contain a cluster of small, bright lights. When I heard his description that uneasy something in me gave me a jolt.

He said that he could see that one of these small bright lights near where he was standing had a narrow beam of light emanating from it. As he looked around he saw narrow beams of light emanating from all of the small, bright lights in the bowl. These light beams seemed to emanate from the surface of the bowl. As I listened to him my uneasiness changed. I began to feel a mild shaking coming from somewhere deep inside me.

Feeling curiosity mixed with his fear about what might happen, Monroe had cautiously reached out his hand toward one of the light beams. As his hand passed through it he heard many voices laughing and then a single voice stood out from the rest.

"Well, 'bout time you figured this out, Bob," the voice said.

My light shaking became a light, constant quivering, not physically visible on the outside but I could feel it throughout my body.

Monroe further described this combination of a bowl of small bright lights and narrow light beams as something analogous to a computer up-link. He talked about it being like a connecting cable that carried information from him, living in the physical world on earth, up to the other members of his cluster.

My constant light quivering quickly changed to internal slamming and banging. Pressure inside me built up suddenly. It peaked. Then memory of my vision of the Disk woke up and exploded into my awareness. The quivering I had felt inside now felt more like a violent shaking of every molecule in my body. My mind flashed to images in my vision and the corresponding images Bob was describing as his cluster. In the space between the words in his sentences I saw my humanoid figure gazing intently into the physical world. I saw the clear, light-filled cable exiting at its shoulder blades and moving off into space to my right. I saw the cable divide into smaller and smaller fibers. I saw the fibers fan out as I approached the Disk. I saw the small, round lights laid out in patterns of concentric circles on the round blackness that defined the size and shape of the Disk. I saw the face of Snidely Whiplash and the red button I had pushed. I saw the greenish-yellow light, filling the filament and moving through it in the direction of the humanoid figure. I saw myself following that pulse of greenish-yellow light until it entered the body of that person from behind. I saw the expression of Snidely Whiplash as his light pulse colored and changed whatever experience in the physical world that person was having as it entered its body. I felt the satisfaction of Snidely at having his personality expressed in this world by that human being at the end of the cable. I saw the Cliff Diver. And I knew. I knew somehow, all of them were ME. I sat there stunned to silence as the air around me shook and vibrated and Monroe continued to talk and answer questions from the group. I could feel my mind going back over everything Monroe had said before I had begun to feel uneasy. Comparisons and connections between the meaning of my Disk vision seventeen years earlier and Monroe's discussion tonight were being made at light speed. I sat there stunned, watching and feeling as the who and what I had come to believe I was in the past was disassembled and rearranged into something else. It was as though hundreds of old-time telephone switchboard operators were yanking wires out of where they had been plugged in for years and plugging them in somewhere else. Circuits I had relied on for most of my life to process and understand information were being changed. Information was being rerouted through entirely different, unfamiliar concepts to arrive at new conclusions about who and what I am. In the process, the *me* I had known for over forty years was dissolving and disappearing right before my mind's eye.

Then suddenly it all stopped. I had found an incongruity between my vision and Monroe's description. He had talked only about his bowl and narrow light beams as a computer up-link. His metaphor described information only flowing from him as a physically alive being to his bowl, this I/There as he called it. My vision clearly indicated information also traveled from the Disk back to me. Snidely had influenced the perception of the humanoid on the end of the cable. The old version of me jumped on this inconsistency as a way to make all this rerouting of circuits stop and go away. This could save the status quo! I could go back being to my old understanding of who and what I am if I could prove Monroe's vision was different from mine and I had the key. His description of his bowl of lights had not included any talk of a computer-like down-link from the bowl to him!

I pulled myself together and got enough of a grip to function through my old self to try to stop it from dissolving. I raised my hand to ask the question that would either save me or confirm my vision's I/There meaning.

He was still answering someone else's question but nodded to acknowledge that he would take my question next. I lowered my hand and waited. I could feel the air close to my skin buzzing, crackling, and snapping as I hung suspended between the old me and the new. When he finished answering someone else's question, Monroe looked in my direction, pointing to where I was sitting in the back of the room. "You had a question?"

"Bob, that computer-like up-link also serves as a down-link doesn't it? I mean information flows in both directions. It's carried both from you to the cluster and from individual cluster members to you, isn't it?"

With a quizzical look on his face he looked straight into my eyes as he answered. "Why, yes. Yes it does. Sometimes the various members of the cluster will interject something that affects the way I experience a particular event. Yes, you could say it's both an up-link and a down-link, I suppose."

My face felt ashen. I slumped back in my chair. The internal rerouting process I had been temporarily able to halt began again. I watched as new insights and realizations about who and what I am came and went in a continuously whirling fury.

I know the strain a steam boiler must feel as internal pressure builds up beyond its capacity to hold together. I was in a state of extreme, jumpy agitation. Something internal was shaking, banging, and gyrating until I felt that I had to get out of the building before I exploded in front of Bob all those other people. Fortunately his talk concluded shortly after I asked my question. Other people in the room stood up and moved toward Bob to shake his hand and talk to The Man. I jumped up out of my chair and bolted straight for the door.

I ran out into the cool evening air and headed for an open grassy field. Something inside me was being overwhelmed. The old me was dissolving into thin air and a new unfamiliar me was taking its place. I pulled off my shirt and began rolling around in the grass, trying to get a grip on myself. I wasn't sure why I felt the need to do so, but rolling on the ground seemed quite reasonable at the time. The feelings of agitation and internal chaos flying around inside me were overpowering. It felt like rushing waves of some new reality crashing into sea walls of long held beliefs. Some parts of the walls were being pulverized into little bits and washed out to sea. Some parts were being loosened, pulled out, and scattered along the shore. I could feel the huge empty spaces within me. Empty places left behind were being filled in as a failed dam might flood a valley in huge, raging walls of water.

I was aware of people walking by me. They were talking to each other as they left Bob's Wednesday night gathering. They walked past me not fifteen feet from where I was rolling in the dirt and grass. They either didn't notice me rolling around on the ground or felt it was too private a moment for them to interfere. I don't know which.

It must have taken at least five minutes of rolling and squirming on the ground before I finally got enough control of myself to stop. I stood up and brushed off the dirt and grass I had picked up and put my shirt back on. Then I walked numbly into the training center and made my way to my CHEC unit. There was one more tape to do tonight, a Free Flow, Focus 21. Free Flow meant there would be lots of time to explore on our own without any specifically selected activities to get in the way. I stood for a moment at the opening to the CHEC unit, feeling how much it seemed like a Gateway into another dimension. Something in me was struggling to hang onto its old identity. I could feel it holding me back. That part of me was trying to prevent my passing through that Gateway and entering whatever dimension of the beyond awaited. I felt a strong urge to stay out and avoid confrontation with whatever powerful force was flowing through me. With gentle pressure and resignation, I pushed myself through the Gateway and into the CHEC unit. I closed the curtain and lay down, put on the headphones, and waited.

Inside I was a jumble of conflicting emotions. I was determined to try to contact myself, my Disk, my Cluster, my I/There. The trainer introduced the next tape over the headphones. Since our session with Bob had run late there hadn't been time to introduce it in the usual pre-tape, large group setting. Had it been done in the usual way I probably would have been spotted as a participant on the verge of something or perhaps in trouble. When the trainer said, "Our next tape is a meeting with Friends in Focus 21," I might have lost control in front of everyone. At the trainer's words through the headphones I felt certain that during this trip to Focus 21 I was going to meet and communicate with my *Friends* who had sent that vision. Too much was happening too fast. I was still struggling to maintain my composure by myself in the CHEC unit.

The trainer's voice in the headphones continued, "You are to go to Focus 21 and try to make contact with friends who may be waiting there to meet you."

A wave of shock flew through me.

Friends! Waiting friends! I was screaming in my thoughts. *These Friends have been waiting to contact and meet with me for almost twenty years!*

As we moved from C-1 (consciousness-1, the level of everyday, ordinary awareness) through Focus 10, 12, and 15, I was silently screaming in every way I could think of, trying to alert my Friends that I was coming. *Be there for me* was broadcast outward in all directions. Barely containing myself, I continued to call out and then quietly wait for a return message. Nothing. . . . Nothing.

During the silences of my waiting I gradually became aware of what sounded like a crude version of a voice coming from the headphones. Focusing my attention on it, I began to hear a single voice, semi-garbled, wavering in the pink sound that masks the Hemi-Sync.

"I . . . Love . . . You . . . I . . . Love . . . You," came screaming back to me through the headphones. A message from me, my Total Self, to me lying there in the CHEC unit. I could feel my Total Self trying as desperately to get through to me as I was trying to get through to It. At the instant of my recognition of the voiced message, my entire being was overwhelmed with joy. I felt an electric, arcing, crackling, spitting, high-frequency vibrational wave moving from the horizontal bottom of me through me to my top. Through it all, in my thoughts, I was screaming back, *I Love You Too!*

Then a second wave of ecstasy blasted through me at my recognition of the chorus of voices off to my right on the same vibrational frequency. In unison, in raised voices, I could hear hundreds, maybe thousands, of them. I could separately distinguish each one in the group shouting in pure joy.

"We Love You . . . We Love You." Repeated over and over to me like a mantra in the strongest message of self-acceptance and love I have ever felt.

An intensity of emotion, pure joy more powerful than I had ever experienced in my life, moved through me. Tears of joy were streaming down my face on my shaking, physical body.

I heard Monroe's voice, on the tape, cutting in to say it was time to leave Focus 21. He was getting ready to take us back to Focus 15.

That brought an immediate *OH NO!!!* to my mind and I silently screamed out in my thoughts, *No!!! I don't want to go back!!! I want to stay, here, with my Friends!* As his voice and the Hemi-Sync tones began to pull me out of Focus 21, I was sending my Friends the message through an overwhelming sea of emotions: *I'll be back.* Monroe's voice on the tape said, "Leave any emotional energies behind."

I did my best to unload the emotional energy of the experience as we stopped briefly at each Focus level on our way to C-1. When I reached C-1, I was still emotionally shaken by the experience. After all, the meaning of my vision of over seventeen years ago had been revealed to me. I knew and understood that I am a part of something bigger, a Total Self which is also me. Words could not express what I now understood myself to be. Grappling with words to try to explain it to myself only led me to confusion. When I stopped the words and felt it, its meaning was clear to me again. The one thing I kept feeling so deeply as I lay there in my CHEC unit was a message of loving acceptance from ALL of ME to me.

After I gathered myself together I left my CHEC unit, washed my face, and went down to the debriefing room. At some point in the discussion I began to divulge bits and pieces of my experience. As I did, I began feeling that something had happened to me that made other people's discussions and complaints petty. I couldn't tolerate the pettiness another moment when someone expressed disappointment at not having had an out-of-body experience up until now, the last full night of the program. Something welled up from deep inside me and I took over the room with my voice.

I remember saying, in a voice that left no mistake about what I wanted heard, "As far as I'm concerned after what I just experienced I don't care if I ever have an out-of-body experience." The crowd around me acted as if I had uttered sacrilege. Most of us, myself included, had come questing after the Holy Grail of OBE.

Poor Rudy, one of the participants, was so taken aback he didn't think he heard me right and said so. I repeated what I had said, word for word, just as firmly as the first time so there would be no mistake. I was sitting in front of the group with my back to most of them. Darlene, one of the two trainers, told me later that, going by the look of shock on every face in the room, what I had said carried a powerful message.

Something about the experience seemed too sacred to share much of it with the group during the debriefing session. Probably they wouldn't have been able to comprehend the emotional impact of what had happened anyway. Their lack of understanding and acceptance of its effect on me might have changed it into something less for me. After the debriefing session I asked Darlene to take a walk with me so I could share the experience with someone to cement it in my mind and this physical world.

During our walk I gave her the whole story. I recounted the vision of seventeen years ago and my shocked reaction to Bob's talk about his cluster. I told her about my experience with the Focus 21 *Friends* tape and my contact with the members of the Disk. I said that I felt myself to be borderline stable emotionally. She remarked that I was doing very well considering the power of the experience.

As we headed up the hill on our return to the Center, a small point of light on the ground, off the right side of the road, caught my eye. It could have been a firefly. Stopping, I bent down to look at it and as I stood back up Darlene commented on the color around me.

"As you bent down," she said, "I couldn't help noticing that you have an incredible blue light surrounding your head, very clear and bright."

"A blue light?" I asked.

"Anybody looking at you couldn't fail to see it!"

Toward the end of our walk I told her some of my impressions of the Diskers or I/There as I had begun to call them. Semantics! When there isn't a word readily available to describe something new it still has to fit into the realm of words. I began using I/There as a name for my Focus 21 friends from the Disk. I/There fit the incongruity of thinking of myself as both an individual and a group. I was one of them and at the same time separate from them. As convoluted as that might sound it describes perfectly the feeling I experienced.

It had been my impression that I/There had as much trouble reaching me to communicate as I had reaching them. I thought these guys were supposed to be some sort of all-powerful beings who could do anything they wanted to, so it puzzled me. I wanted to know from Darlene if this was *normal*.

She confirmed that to her knowledge communication could be difficult from either end. She also confirmed my impression that I/There didn't necessarily know how much their contact affected me. She suggested that if it felt like things were moving too fast I could tell I/There I would like to slow down. Since part of the Gateway Voyage involved learning to communicate in symbols and pictures rather than words, Nonverbal Communication (NVC), she suggested I use this method. By the time we arrived back at the Center I had emotionally cooled down somewhat. I was feeling like I wanted to tell everyone in the group that there are more important things to experience during Gateway Voyage than an OBE. There are parts of ourselves to reconnect with that are far more important. As we approached the Center, Darlene and I joked about a Preacher I could feel in I/There. He was probably enjoying the hell out of all of this.

Later that evening, after our walk, my body felt over-heated constantly. I probably could have melted snow in a circle three feet around me just by sitting in it. I put together an NVC message for I/There about going too fast and the need to slow down a little.

I needed an image or metaphor to represent my body. As I thought about that the image of an open-topped, 1930s-vintage car came to mind. I added the image of a speedometer. I had it show 90 miles per hour to indicate the speed at which my contact with I/There was moving me emotionally. Then I visualized lifting the hood to show the overheating engine to convey that my body was being overworked. I added the image of a gas pedal pushed clear to the floor boards to show that the emotional effects were being pushed too hard. With this stream of images strung together in sequence, I added imagery to ask I/There to slow down.

I showed the gas pedal coming up off the floor boards and speedometer dropping to 15 miles per hour. Finally, I again lifted the hood and showed the engine cooling down. Then to send my message I brought to mind the image of the Disk I had seen in the vision more than seventeen years ago. I relaxed to a Focus 10 and then I remembered and saw, in my mind's eye, all the overheated-car images in their order. That is how I sent my NVC message. Within a minute or two, the emotional overheating I had been experiencing began to cool down. In the next half hour I sent messages using the same imagery to speed up the effect to half its original level, 45 miles per hour. When that still felt too emotionally taxing, I slowed down to 25. At that speed I continued to get insights about what it meant to be an I/There and I could assimilate and integrate them without building up emotional pressure.

It's so strange to experience contacting yourself, from your Total Self, which you are, and at the same time be the self which doesn't know any of this stuff is possible. It's like mailing yourself a letter from another reality and upon receiving it having zero awareness of who mailed it or which other reality the letter came from. What a mind trap! This experience has given me insight into what people with multiple personality disorder must go through. It's very emotionally disorienting! Becoming aware of parts of myself which were previously unknown to me left me feeling, as I had said to Darlene, borderline stable emotionally.

Yet the process of allowing myself to remain in this state of disorientation felt important. As I continued through my acceptance to receive insights, I/There began to subtly change. What seems to come from this acceptance is a whole new set of possibilities for answering the question *Who are you?* I had been screaming that question at someone in my first lucid dream a long time ago. I was beginning to understand that the person I so feared in that dream, the big guy to whom I had been screaming that question, was me!

I understood this process would lead from old beliefs to new ones and then to a new system based on *knowing*. This knowing would be based on more direct experience through communication with I/There and exploration of wheres, whens and whats I could not yet imagine.

The next day, Thursday, was the last full day of my Gateway Voyage program. On the advice of Darlene I decided I had done enough tape exercises. So while the rest of the group continued to explore Focus 21 in their CHEC units, I sat outside on the deck in the sun.

Since my meeting with I/There during the tape Wednesday night I had noticed that if I closed my eyes and relaxed I could feel a gentle but noticeable pulsating flutter between my eyes, about one and a half inches deep, inside my skull. It felt soft and gentle like a small butterfly inside my head, flapping its wings. Sitting in the sunshine, I began to play with it. I found that if I thought a sentence in words as I was feeling the fluttering vibration the sound of the thought of the words changed. Focusing on the fluttering while thinking a sentence joined the vibration and words together, making the sound of the words pulsate. Joined together inside my head, they sounded like talking while gently gargling. When I joined them, the two felt as though they had become entrained together into one vibration. As I played with thinking sentences and entraining them into the vibration, I idly thought a sentence intended to be sent to I/There. After I had finished my sentence I was still focused on feeling the fluttering vibration in my head. All of a sudden I began hearing, entrained with the vibration, words which I had not sent! The words were just as plain as if someone sitting next to me had spoken them out loud.

"Hello, this is Roger, a name you can use to contact I/There. I will act as a point of contact for now," said the voice.

As we carried on a conversation which my memory now fails to recall, I learned to use this new method of communication. This was much simpler than the NVC I had been taught during Gateway. I didn't have to string together images to represent what I wanted to say and then remember them in sequence as I sent them out. Instead, I just felt the vibration and at the same time thought out my message in words. Verbal messages came back entrained on the same fluttering, vibrational frequency. Decoding or listening to the message was a simple matter of tuning in to feel the fluttering vibration in my head. When I could feel it I could send out an entrained message and hear the return entrained answer coming back on the same vibration. The advantage over NVC was that I could hear the return message in words. The disadvantage was that if I couldn't feel the vibration I couldn't do any of it.

Unfortunately, not long after I left Virginia for my home in Colorado, I couldn't feel the vibration any more. This whole episode of learning to communicate via vibration was forgotten within a month and didn't return until February 1996.

There's just one more thing to mention: my Gateway Voyage connection with Dr. Ed Wilson. During a tape exercise, someone had shown me a hardcover book. Whoever was showing it to me opened it up and fanned its blank pages from one end to the other. I couldn't see anything written on the pages, but I did see the face of someone I didn't know. As the fanning pages went by, the face, appearing as sort of a three-dimensional mask, coincided with the image of the book.

During the same tape exercise, after seeing the face in the book, I was shown a device that was identified to me as a magnetic anomaly sensor. This device's purpose was to detect magnetic fields around a human being's body. Its use was intended to allow detection and display of the three-dimensional magnetic field around a person's body. I was shown that sensors were to be placed at the head and feet of the individual. I didn't think much of it until our group took a tour of the Institute's research lab facility the next day.

That tour was hosted by Dave Wallis, a man who worked at TMI, who since then has become a good friend. As Dave led us around on the tour we were introduced to Skip Atwater, who worked in the lab. I recognized Skip's face immediately as the one I had seen in the fanning pages of the book during the tape exercise the day before. I was so dumbfounded at the recognition that I couldn't say a word.

Later that afternoon I told Darlene about this strange experience and asked if she could arrange a meeting for me with Skip. I wanted to explore what it meant to have something so strange happen.

When I got the chance to meet with Skip and talk to him about his face in the book and the magnetic anomaly sensor I got a surprise. Skip and a man named Dr. Ed Wilson had been experimenting with sensing magnetic fields around human beings. The magnetic anomaly sensor information I had received seemed to fit with what they were working on. Not much else came of my meeting with Skip. Unbeknownst to me at the time, this was an indirect introduction to Dr. Wilson, whom I wouldn't meet physically for another year. Dr. Wilson played a surprising and big role in my future explorations beyond the physical world.

The Disk Vision's Meaning

For months after Gateway Voyage, I continued to piece together the meaning of not only the vision from seventeen years earlier but also an understanding of the greater question to which it pointed. While gathering insights, I thought about the Three Great Questions of my childhood: Where did I come from before I was born? What am I supposed to do while I'm living here? Where do I go when I die? Pondering them, I realized they were really different versions of the greater question: *What am I?*

It took me a long time to integrate what I had received during Gateway Voyage through direct communication with I/There, Monroe's Wednesday night talk, and the Disk vision from the Spring of 1975. Even now as I write this, four and a half years later, the only way I can convey what I understand is in the form of a story about who and what I am. A story, because so much of what I understand is in the language of feelings, not words. Listen with your feelings.

A probe called Curiosity

Into Itself Consciousness had launched a part of Its own awareness as a probe called Curiosity. Curiosity moved through the infinite possibilities of Consciousness, transmitting awareness of Itself to Consciousness through an infinitely extendible, fine filament. Time had no meaning. Space did not exist. Yet Curiosity had been launched into Consciousness way back in the beginning with a Purpose. It had been moving through Consciousness forever with the purpose of discovery, gathering whatever it could find in the vast unknown. Consciousness had always been aware of Curiosity's every move.

Curiosity aroused

Faint at first, something unknown had gotten Curiosity's

attention as it moved through Consciousness. It was so strange, it just had to be investigated. It was a jumble of something scratchy, shrieking, and irritating. Curiosity could have described it perhaps as downright uncomfortable. But still, it had the Pull. Curiosity was a sucker for the Pull. This Pull had excitement and the thrill of discovery written all over it. After all, that had always been Curiosity's purpose in Consciousness, the thrill of discovery in the great unknown. Curiosity kept moving straight ahead, probing the Pull with everything it knew.

The Pull gets stronger

The Pull felt stronger now. Curiosity had passed little blips of feeling, uninhabited planets probably, as it had continued to move toward the Pull. The little blips each had some of the same irritating qualities, but whatever was ahead had much stronger attraction, a tremendous Pull!

Curiosity is captured

The Pull was getting weaker now. *Must have passed its source by light years,* Curiosity thought to itself. Curiosity arced around to search for the highest intensity of the Pull again. When the intensity of the Pull reached its peak Curiosity accelerated toward it again, toward whatever this new jumble of feelings was. Back and forth Curiosity went, each time overshooting the maximum intensity of the Pull by less and less. Finally, very near its source, the steady blasting jumble was all there was to feel.

Curiosity closes down

The jumble of the Pull was so intense it felt like a horrendously disorganizing noise. Later Curiosity might describe it as listening to a billion different radio stations blaring all at once. There were patterns in it to be sure, but it was all so loud that picking out one pattern to follow was impossible. Only one method seemed to work. If Curiosity closed down most of its awareness, to a level of just barely awake, it could feel patterns with purpose in the jumble of the Pull. Purpose! Curiosity understood Purpose! Gathering in whatever it could find was Curiosity's

Purpose. The Pull was something jam-packed full of some-things with purposes. With no time in Curiosity's awareness there is no way of knowing when It first found the Pull. No way of judging how long it hovered there, barely awake, taking in everything It could know within the horrendous noise of the Pull.

Curiosity moves in

Once in a while a pattern would stand out in the noise and Curiosity would follow it along until it disappeared in the blaring cacophony again. This began to occur with greater frequency as Curiosity, in small steps, closed down just a little more of Its awareness. Curiosity knew this was the only way to be closest to the horrendous noise of the Pull and still be able to function. Gradually much of the screaming jumble faded into a background hiss that Curiosity could more easily ignore. *True, all that other noise will have to be investigated too*, Curiosity thought back to Consciousness through Its filament. *But closing down my awareness now is the only way I can follow any individual patterns in all the noise of this Pull.* This Pull had by far the most concentrated collection of things to know Curiosity had ever come across. By closing down its awareness to everything else, Curiosity got close enough to investigate individual patterns in the Pull. But in following a pattern in the Pull in this manner, Curiosity, for the first time ever, fell asleep.

The Separation

Curiosity awoke screaming (*screaming?*) in pain (*pain?*) from the pressure (*what's pressure?*) and the cold (*what's cold?*) as it was expelled into a place (*place?*) where Curiosity first experienced The Separation. The pattern Curiosity had been following led to being born in the body of an infant living in the physical world. In time (*time?*) the baby grew, following the pattern Curiosity had unknowingly joined, in a place with hot and cold, dark and light, wet and dry. After it was born, the clashing symbols of everything it experienced soon overwhelmed any awareness of who or what it really was. Its curiosity led it to follow every detail of its pattern so intensely that it had no memory that it had ever been anything else. This physical world had suns and planets and moons and stars and galaxies in a universe so vast it seemed to have no end. The planet it lived on, earth, had air to breathe, food to eat, things to touch and feel. Being Separated from awareness of who and what it really was did have one advantage. It could no longer hear and feel the screech and scratch of the emotional energies of ALL those other beings in the Pull. Concentration on the pattern it had joined was effortless for Curiosity now. Awareness of all that other jamming noise was gone. Best of all, there were other Separated beings there with whom to interact and play.

Curiosity lived this first life, gathering in everything it could find until finally, old and sick, it died. Back in the horrendous noise of the Pull, without the protection of unconsciousness, being dead was quite a shock! Curiosity quickly dove back into the relative quiet of unconsciousness to avoid the noise of the Pull. At death everything it had gathered, all it had come to know while living on this earth, came with it. Of course everything it had gathered remained with it when it dove back in.

An almost endless loop

In that first life, so many things were left undone, unexplored and unknown. But most of all there were the emotional things, unresolved, between itself and other Separated beings. Curiosity, still asleep, had to go back again and again to find those beings it had been with before. There were wrongs to right, debts to pay, and collections to make. You can guess what happened. Each time Curiosity went back again, born into a new body and new circumstances, it became further entangled in a bigger emotional web. New patterns to join, old ones to combine, the possibilities were endless. It's a good thing time has no meaning because Curiosity spent eons in this almost endless loop.

Curiosity wakes up

Almost all the possibilities of that first pattern Curiosity had joined in the noise had played themselves out when it first began to remember who it was. Memory of past lifetimes led to awakening. Floating in space, not far from earth, Curiosity realized what had happened. With most of the noise tuned out by its barely conscious state, Curiosity had been looking down toward earth when it remembered. It saw memory after memory of lifetime after lifetime it had spent on earth. It remembered all the way back to when it had first been following the Pull and why. Curiosity began to understand and know the essence of the Pull.

What Curiosity learned

When Curiosity had first arrived, the noise of the Pull had been a loud, random jumble of too many different feelings at once. Closing down awareness *was the Separation* that allowed one to survive and explore within the horrendously disorganizing noise of the Pull. Curiosity understood that all who lived within the noise had of necessity closed down their awareness level. They were all living in The Separation to one degree or another. If they hadn't closed down they would be constantly bombarded by the horrendous, jumbled noise. They'd feel and hear the thoughts and emotions of every living thing in the entire physical-world universe. Closing down was the only way to explore and it was the resulting Separation which blocked any memory or knowledge of one's true identity.

Separation's effect

Emotional energies and events were so engaging and so distracting, and led to so many different places. Curiosity had been unconsciously gathering these for eons of lifetimes. Consciousness had been aware all along, of course, but with The Separation Curiosity had chosen there wasn't much Consciousness could do but watch. There had been no need for Consciousness to interfere. Conscious or not, Curiosity was still fulfilling its Purpose. It was gathering all the fine details of living in this place called the physical world.

Curiosity becomes a Disk

Curiosity knew when it first closed down to explore one pattern in the noise that all the other noise would have to be investigated too. There was so much more to learn within the Pull. But now, not willing to fall sleep again and become lost in patterns that randomly came along, Curiosity decided to remain aware of who and what it was.

Some of the lifetimes in Curiosity's collection had followed similar patterns of emotional energies. Each had learned more in different time frames about details of a particular pattern. Some had been devils. Some had been saints. There were many, many others everywhere in between. Curiosity began to group together each of its selves who had followed similar patterns in its lifetimes. As it did, each group began to form a basic, coherent personality. When they were all sorted out and merged into their partners, there were ten, maybe twelve, distinct emotional energy patterns or personalities. Curiosity gathered its selves all together in a constellation of Knowing, a Disk, a Cluster. All had become inseparable parts of what Curiosity now knew Itself to be.

A plan

Looking at its collection, its Disk filled with the experience of its lifetimes, Curiosity pondered how to gather more that it didn't know. By combining emotional energies—personalities—on its Disk into new patterns, Curiosity could assemble new personalities. Each one it assembled from itself could be different than any combination Curiosity had experienced before. Each would have the same Purpose as Curiosity. Each would explore the unknown and gather in all it could find. Each would explore wherever its particular set of emotional energies Pulled it. Curiosity would stay at a safe distance away where the Pull was not so strong that it might be tempted to fall asleep again. In this way Curiosity could safely explore the rest of the horrendous noise of the Pull. Curiosity would use these newly assembled, combination personalities to make its own probes!

Probes of Its own

Curiosity was delighted with the simplicity of this plan. Using itself as a model, Curiosity fashioned many probes, all connected to itself by a fine, thin filament of awareness.

Each probe was connected to every part of itself on the Disk of Curiosity's personalities. Curiosity would launch these probes into the cycles of lifetimes on earth. They would follow their paths for lifetimes to wherever their patterns took them.

Curiosity launches its probes

Unhindered by considerations of time or space, Curiosity was free to choose anywhere or anywhen in earth's future, past, or present. These anywheres and anywhens would serve as starting points for the probes. Pinpointing patterns within the Pull not yet fully explored, Curiosity launched its probes into times and places in the physical world. Oh sure, they would be lost in the Pull as they followed their patterns, but they would be gathering all along their way. Through their filaments of awareness, Curiosity would receive knowing of their every move. And of course Curiosity would send, from each part of its Self on the Disk, guidance through the twists and turns of paths. This Guidance was Curiosity's attempt to maintain a probe's focus on its intended purpose. Experienced as feelings, thoughts, visions, intuitions, dreams and such by the probes, with this Guidance Curiosity could suggest places to explore and things to do. Traveling through the filaments of awareness from the Disk, this Guidance would assist the probe. And back from the probe, through the same filaments would come the experience and knowing of more patterns in the noise.

Adding to the Disk

Curiosity had known all along it was bound to happen. Eventually one of its probes would begin to wake up and remember the origin of its curiosity. Once in a great while a probe came back to the Disk during one of its dreams. Probes hardly ever remembered the encounter after they re-entered the distraction of the physical world. In fact, during the dreams of probes was almost the only time Curiosity could communicate directly with them in any way. Even then their entanglement in the Pull usually distorted the communication so badly that such contact rarely added much direction to the lives of probes in the physical world.

It was always a treat when a probe began to wake up. It usually happened when it became curious about who and what it was. Some of them even found the Disk. It was a special treat when the probe had enough awareness to remember the Contact. The more it remembered, the greater the chance it would wake up on its own. When it did wake up, it remembered the origin of its curiosity. That sometimes started a process of remembering that could culminate in a probe rejoining the Disk. When these probes rejoined the Disk they did so as new and distinctly different members of the Disk. They had been assembled as unique combinations of original Disk members and as such returned with unique understandings of the Pull. This was highly prized, as it opened up so many more possibilities with which the noise of the Pull could be probed. As probes returned and remembered their origin, all they had gathered could be used to fashion new probes. Knowledge grew at an ever-increasing rate as probes became capable of encompassing more and more of the Pull. This whole process had been going on for a very long time and the members of the Disk, all the parts of itself Curiosity had become, numbered in the thousands.

Contact

On a spring day in March 1975, another probe found the Disk. He had been in just the right frame of mind to remember when Curiosity sent the Guidance. He was mentally alert and relaxed with not much distraction in his mind. Curiosity had presented a vision of the Disk, and the probe had seen it! It was such a captivating image, so different from anything he had ever seen before. It had a soft, gently beckoning Pull and just like Curiosity, the probe was a sucker for the Pull.

Beginning to awaken

As the probe pondered the meaning of the Guidance Vision, he started to remember who and what he is. It took seventeen years for Curiosity to make direct, conscious contact again. Seventeen years went by for the probe before he heard *We Love You* in the random, pink sound of another Pull. Now he knows he's an I/There. He's a less Separated part of the Total One that Curiosity is becoming. And as he gathers more, satisfying his purpose, he knows that someday he will rejoin the Disk as a new and unique member. He knows he is also One with Consciousness, who launched Curiosity as a probe, way back before there was a beginning. Of course Consciousness has been aware of this exploration of Itself all along, connected as it is by that fine filament of awareness to Curiosity.

Winking Out?

In Bob Monroe's description of his I/There or Cluster, he talked about watching as the last member of another cluster returned. He described that when this happened the cluster would wink out, would disappear. He speculated that such a cluster might decide to create its own reality, somewhere else. Perhaps this new reality would affect the experience of other probes it caught in orbit. Perhaps it would make a better world. I have not yet personally witnessed a cluster winking out so I don't know if that part is true.

I hope you have been able to listen to my story about Curiosity with your feelings. If you listened to the words it probably sounded confusing. As I have continued to explore the New World of the Afterlife I have gained more insight into the vision of the Disk. It seems to suggest that we all exist simultaneously in many different *locations*. The Afterlife contains more than just dead people. We who consider ourselves to be alive *live* there too. I don't yet feel I know all of what that vision means, but I do know that *I am Curiosity.*

IV. Lifeline

The Monroe Institute literature suggested that a participant should let a minimum of six months go by after Gateway Voyage before attending the Lifeline program. In retrospect it was worthwhile to wait. It allowed time to absorb and integrate more understanding of the new who and what I am becoming. But that didn't make the waiting any easier. After hearing The Patrick Tape and learning that the Lifeline program could teach me to explore where people go after they die, I wanted to go *NOW!* I was ready to sail out of the harbor, beyond sight of land and into the New World beyond the horizon of the physical world. One difficulty in arranging to go back to the Institute for Lifeline was convincing my wife that it wasn't some sort of weird, dangerous cult. She was raised as the daughter of a Missouri Synod Lutheran minister. In their belief system, as in many other Christian religions, contact with the *Spirit World* is fraught with the danger of contact with Satan. In their beliefs, such contact carries the very real possibility of being deceived by Satan and losing your soul. This is not a trivial matter. People who hold to these beliefs expect that a person losing his soul to Satan will spend an eternity in Hell. Out of their love for me, my wife and her family were very concerned about my intention to explore the Spirit World. I'm sorry it caused them so much anxiety and concern, but when my curiosity met with the opportunity, I had to explore.

My family's genuine concern and worry that my soul might be lost to Satan and burn in Hell forever makes me think about those early Earth explorers. Surely the beliefs of others had an impact on them. Some probably didn't sail off toward the horizon, fearing perhaps everyone else was right. It's a safe bet many with the curiosity and desire to explore beyond the horizon didn't go for fear of alienating their families or causing them worry and concern. The effect of such widely held cultural belief is a powerful force working for maintenance of the status quo, even when those beliefs force people to live their lives in completely unnecessary fear and limitation.

Fortunately a few early explorers didn't let the fears of those surrounding them stop their quest to know the truth. Perhaps they didn't share the beliefs of most of the people in their culture. Maybe they were willing to take whatever risks were necessary just because they had to know the truth for themselves.

Science-based beliefs in my culture claim there's no proof of anything beyond the physical world. Some from science judge people's sanity and right to freedom to be in jeopardy if they claim contact with the Afterlife. Some religious beliefs that surround me claim there is an Afterlife, some claim there isn't. Most speak of a dragon named Satan who lurks there ready to swallow up the unwary. Science and religion both warn of grave dangers to anyone attempting to explore beyond the physical world. "You'll sail off the edge of the earth and die" has become either "You could end up on medication in a padded cell" or "Your soul could burn in Hell forever."

I had to contend with these forces in my journey. My family tried to dissuade me out of their genuine love and concern for my spiritual well-being. And as a student of science and an engineer, I carried the voice of scientific doubt deep within my rational thinking mind everywhere I went. This baggage filled my cargo holds as I left for my first Lifeline program.

Leaving Denver for The Monroe Institute, I almost missed my flight. In the last-minute rush to get on the plane and into my seat, all my carry-on baggage had to be put in the overhead compartment on the plane. I had a book in my bag I'd planned to read on the long flight, but my seat by the window on the crowded plane made it inconvenient to get it. So with nothing else to do I was reading the boring in-flight magazine when something peculiar happened. A priest, being interviewed about various aspects of Boy's Town, rattled off "several proud stories before settling on the story of one of their most transformed kids, Joshua." I looked away from the magazine for a moment, distracted by something. When I re-read the last line, it said, ". . . settling on the story of one of their most transformed kids, *Marsha*." I remembered seeing the name *Joshua*. I could see it in my mind's eye in the same type face, printed on the page. I looked again. It still said *Marsha*. It was so strange I couldn't believe it happened so I looked away and back several times. Each time I looked back the word *Marsha* was still in the place I had seen *Joshua* printed the first time I read it. This turned out to be I/There planting a seed, again setting me up for an extraordinary experience.

When I landed at the airport in Charlottesville, Virginia, three other Lifeline participants and I waited there for the van the Institute provides for the half-hour ride to their facility. Oddly, I found myself being very judgmental toward the other participants. During the van ride, I felt that none of them were approaching such a momentous journey as Lifeline with nearly enough reverence. They seemed so frivolous in their flirtatious banter and actions. I felt that none of them deserved to be participants. I felt so morally superior; the level of judgment and superiority I felt was exceptionally strong. Usually I'm pretty "live and let live," so the strength of these feelings struck me as odd, very odd.

In my intake interview, I talked about my desire to learn to explore the places people go after they die. The trainer talked about how often times people we retrieve turn out to be parts of ourselves. I briefly flashed back to Bob's image of members returning to their cluster and wondered if I'd meet and retrieve any members of I/There.

During our first gathering in David Francis Hall, we introduced ourselves to the rest of the group, and the trainers gave an overview of the Lifeline program, beginning by describing the various Focus levels we'd be exploring.

(For a more detailed description of Lifeline program information, see Appendix B.)

They described Focus 22 as a level of consciousness where the inhabitants were physically alive, but only partially conscious. These might include people who were dreaming or chemically dependent or anesthetized, comatose or delirious.

In Focus 23 we might expect to find people who have died but are unaware of the fact, can't accept it, or are unable to free themselves and leave. Focus 24, 25, and 26, also called the Belief System Territories, gathered groups of people sharing similar beliefs about the Afterlife.

Lastly, they talked about Focus 27, which they also called the Reception Center and the Park. They described it as a place, created by humans, designed to ease the shock of death for new arrivals. Focus 27 can appear very earth-like, giving an air of familiarity to newcomers. The trainers then moved on to discuss Lifeline as a program of service There and service Here.

By service There they meant that after we became familiar with these Focus levels we would learn how to find the newly deceased in Focus 23 and move them to Focus 27, a process termed *retrieval*. It is considered service There because those we retrieved would then be free to choose what to do from there on rather than being stuck, isolated and alone, in Focus 23. In carrying out these retrievals we might come to know we survive physical death.

The aspect of service Here involved helping others still living in the physical world to know that they survive death. The program trainers suggested, as an example, that this service might take the form of bringing back verifiable communication from departed loved ones.

In wrapping up their overview, the trainers explained that we would each be creating our own place in Focus 27 and that we would be learning to record our experiences by talking out loud into a tape recorder during tape exercises.

Our first tape exercise was our introduction to exploring beyond the physical world of time and space in Focus 23.

I approached this tape with anticipation, looking forward to seeing and hearing those who inhabited this state of consciousness. I wondered what it must be like for them to have recently died and not yet realize it. I wondered how it could be that they would be unable to tell they were dead. I wondered how it could be that they were somehow unable to free themselves from this place. I was excited at the prospect of contacting them and learning answers to these and many other questions. As I moved into Focus 23 this first time, I had only vague impressions of anything. It felt more like floating in the middle of nowhere. I got no answers.

During the second tape exercise to Focus 23, I still found nothing. I couldn't see anything. I couldn't hear, feel, taste, touch, or sense anything at all. Just vague, floating impressions of nothing. I felt disappointed.

The third tape was the same. I kept searching in every way I could think of and I found nothing and no one. While still in this tape exercise I began to feel very upset. I remember angrily thinking, *There is absolutely nothing here; this feels like a rip off!*

Then it was time for our introduction to the Belief System Territories or Focus 25. My experience was the same. I could find absolutely nothing here either. Again in anger and frustration I was thinking, *This is a rip off; there's nothing here. I want my money back and a trip to the airport. This is worse than a waste of time. I paid money to come here and be ripped off!*

I felt even worse during the debriefing sessions after each tape. Many other participants were reporting seeing people and talking to them. They reported seeing buildings, grass, trees, blue skies, and more. As I listened, I didn't know if they were making it all up because they were afraid to tell the truth or if it was real to them. My own experience was like the story of the emperor's new clothes. To my eyes he was parading naked.

During the debriefing sessions it was suggested that if we were having difficulty making contact during any of the tape exercises we ask guidance why. I tried that during the second Focus 25 tape, asking why nothing visual was happening. I didn't understand the answers that came in visual images of blocked lava flows and impending volcanoes.

Then, while returning from Focus 25, as I was passing through Focus 12, I asked again why I couldn't see anything in any of these exercises. What I saw next is an example of a visual pun. Whoever sent it has a great sense of humor. I saw a large metal bolt bent into a circle on one end, with coarse threads like a wood screw on the other end. In perfect three-dimensional color, right before my eyes floated the brightest, shiniest, chrome-plated screw eye imaginable. It looked just like a large chrome-plated screw eye you'd find in a hardware store. As I thought about it later during the debriefing session, I got its message: *Bruce, screw the eyes! There are other senses available in these levels of consciousness!*

Darlene, my trainer from Gateway Voyage and now one of three trainers in Lifeline, remarked after I shared this experience, "I seldom interpret experience for participants but I'd say that's a pretty clear message to lighten up."

I wasn't sure exactly how to go about lightening up. I didn't have any idea what other senses might be available, and I was still angry that nothing was happening. It wasn't that I was unable to see anything; the image of the screw eye had been perfectly realistic. During the previous debriefing sessions the trainers had listened to my barely veiled anger and advised that I open up to whatever may be There. This just kept increasing my frustration as I kept opening up to nothing!

So during the next excursion into Focus 25 to explore, in my frustration I again tried to open myself up to whatever might be There. I didn't have any idea what that meant. Not much happened except that at one point I thought I heard something in the pink sound of the Hemi-Sync. I remembered that was how I'd first made contact with I/There during Gateway Voyage, so I focused my attention on the sound. As I listened, the sound of a choir of female voices became distinctly audible. I listened as they sang a hymn I remembered from my church days. I could hear all the voices singing together and I could focus on single voices in the choir and hear them amongst the other voices. They were singing:

Holy, holy, holy, Though the darkness hide thee,
Though the eye made blind by sin thy glory may not see,
Only thou art holy; there is none beside thee,
Perfect in pow'r, in love and purity.

So, I could hear under some circumstances in Focus 25, that was at least something. But I still felt frustrated that I wasn't able to see anything. For me, *seeing is believing*, and if I couldn't see it I couldn't believe it. I didn't realize at the time how powerful such beliefs can be. I'm certain that part of the reason I had such difficulty during these early tape exercises went back to beliefs I'd taken in and accepted over the years. Guess I accepted a lot more of these kinds of beliefs than I realized. I know that during the Focus 25 exercise in which I heard the choir I saw brief glimpses of cathedrals and churches. But I discarded them as figments of my imagination and not real images at all. Funny how beliefs can blind us to so much.

Next we were ready for our introduction to Focus 27. I saw nothing, heard nothing, and felt nothing. As far as I could tell this area was completely uninhabited and I was pissed! On the way back from Focus 27, passing through Focus 15 or 12 I saw a clear image of a man and a woman with their arms around each other, kissing. This was accompanied by humming tones and the feeling that what I was watching represented the joining of masculine and feminine within me. I had no idea what this meant, just the feeling of the masculine (rational) and feminine (intuitive) parts of myself joining together.

At the next small group debriefing session I again complained about sensing absolutely nothing during the tape exercise in Focus 27. Rebecca, one of the trainers, laughed out loud and instead of feeling insulted I felt relieved. I swear her laugh could break through any wall or barrier to reveal whatever was being hidden. As she laughed it felt as though thick, glacial ice somewhere inside me was being pulverized and swept away. After our debriefing session, Rebecca took me aside and suggested that the energies of Focus 27 were indeed subtle energies. I had the immediate impression that what I was learning to perceive was different than what other participants were working with. That somehow it was more difficult for me because what I was attempting to connect with was inherently more difficult to perceive.

Looking back from where I am now, as I'm writing this, I understand it differently. The truth was, my own beliefs about the Afterlife were blocking my perception perhaps more strongly than other participants' were. The trap I was in needed direct experience of the Afterlife to dispel my beliefs that blocked just such experience, a Catch-22.

During the next Focus 27 tape exercise, I experienced several odd body sensations. My entire body felt as if it sank into a deep, deep sleep, then my arms and legs began to feel prickly heat. My whole body would heat up until I thought for sure I was going to break out in a sweat. Once at Focus 27, my fingers—not my physical fingers but nonphysical fingers—began moving and wiggling in the air. After the tape exercise I felt as though some part of my nonphysical body was not fully back in the same place as my physical body. I left my CHEC unit feeling a little disoriented and disassociated.

The next Focus 27 tape exercise was to be the one in which we made our own place There. After arriving There I decided to give in to the temptation to pretend and imagine. I'd been holding out against this temptation in the belief that if I allowed myself to pretend or imagine something was happening it wouldn't be real. Whatever I might experience as a result would be purely a figment of my imagination, something I had completely made up. But I was also beginning to feel desperate. Nothing at all was happening, so I didn't have much to lose. After all, this was Tuesday and the program ended Thursday night. If something didn't start happening soon it probably never would.

I started by pretending my place in Focus 27 would have a beach hut look to it. I imagined, pretended to visualize and see, even though I couldn't, a beach hut roof. It would, I decided, be made out of palm fronds and would be shaped like a funnel with the point up. Looking down from above the scene, I was shocked when that image came clearly into view! I stopped actively imagining anything and watched, dumbfounded, as the entire structure materialized in front of my eyes. From a point in space palm fronds extended themselves radially outward and down to form the funnel shape. I moved my vantage point down, below the roof, and, looking upward, I watched as a support pole extended itself downward from the center of the roof and into the ground. Then thin wooden poles appeared and placed themselves in a suitable structure under the roof to support it. The whole thing was not much bigger than a large beach umbrella.

How about a table for cool refreshing drinks? I thought to myself. Moments later a round table formed with the roof support pole at its center. I hadn't imagined it; I just asked for a table and one formed itself in the proper place.

And someplace to sit? A strong-looking pole appeared, bent itself into a circle, and attached itself to the outer rim of the roof. Seven canvas hanging chairs appeared all by themselves, suspended by ropes from the outer rim pole. I recognized these chairs as a design called *Sky Chairs*. Each chair was a different solid color—white, purple, green, rose, yellow, red, and blue. I recognized the colors as the ones in a visualization exercise used to move from Focus 15 to Focus 21 back in Gateway Voyage.

I think I'd like this place to be high up in the mountains, I thought. The ground around the center support pole of my beach hut roof began to change. The change spread outward in all directions at once from this center. I stood up and looked around. I was standing on a high rock outcropping looking down at deep valleys all around me. These valleys rose into huge, rocky mountains in the distance that ringed my place in Focus 27. Everything was illuminated by bright sunlight shining down from a deep, clear blue sky above. All of this scene just formed itself after my initial thought without any further conscious input by me.

I wonder if it might be nice to have a lake here too? As I thought this, a section of the deep valley over to my right began to take the form of a lake. It was round and probably a quarter to a half mile across. It seemed a little out of place and I wasn't sure it would look right where it was. As I tried to decide if I liked the lake in the place it was forming, I realized there were Beings sitting in some of the hanging chairs around the table at my place. I would have said they were people. They did look like human people, but there was something about them that was different enough that I have to call them Beings. I couldn't quite put my finger on what was different about them. I wondered who they were. With my attention diverted, I left the question of the lake and decided I'd have to come back to it later.

I assumed the Beings must be what the trainers had been calling Guidance. I told them I'd be grateful for any knowledge of my purpose they could tell me. Without words they showed me by first bending forward and then stretching downward, reaching far down below my place in Focus 27. Then unexpectedly:

I was above the ocean, no land in sight, looking down from above at a ship. In a series of brief, fleeting images, impressions more than pictures, a story unfolded below me. I felt a name—Elsen or Elsor or Ensen (Ensign?). I saw large, spent shell casings scattered on the deck near a gun emplacement. I saw a huge explosion. I could see men standing on the deck near a railing on the port side, amidships. I was watching the Navy ceremony of a burial at sea. Men stand on either side of a flag with their hands curled around it at the edges. They lifted up one end of the flag and a wrapped body slid out from under the flag, dropped to the water, and disappeared under the sea. Then I heard Monroe's voice on the tape suggest it is time to return to C-1. The images of the burial at sea were gone so I followed the Hemi-Sync tape sounds back to C-1.

Imagination

In the debriefing session that followed, I realized I'd used imagination as a tool for communication and interaction in Focus 27. I also realized that imagination is not the same as fantasy. I didn't have to fantasize or plan my place in Focus 27 into existence. I didn't have to actively direct any of the details as I would have had to using fantasy. Just the thought that it would be nice to have my place high up in the mountains was enough on my part. Several square miles of authentic-looking mountains, valleys, trees, rocks, and cliffs had formed in exquisite detail without another single thought about it from me. My previous belief had been that fantasy and imagination were the same thing, and therefore neither one of them was real. I realized that belief was one of the major blocks to my perception in Focus 27. This was one of the most valuable lessons I learned during this Lifeline program.

Imagination, used this way, reminds me of using an old-time hand pump to bring water up from a well. You can pump the handle up and down all day long and never get any water from the well. But if you pour just a little water in the pump to prime it, pretty soon you could keep pumping the handle and fill a swimming pool. By pretending just a little, just that I could see a beach hut roof at the beginning of this exercise, I had somehow primed the pump of imagination. Once primed, with each thought about what my place in Focus 27 should be, the well of imagination kept flowing it into a reality I could perceive.

I can't stress enough how important a concept this was for me to grasp. By learning to pretend at the beginning of the exercise I engaged the creative power of imagination. Imagination opened up the entire nonphysical world to my perception.

To clarify further, it might be helpful to read the definition of imagination taken from *The American Heritage Dictionary of the English Language*, Third Edition, © 1992 by Houghton Mifflin Company:

Imagination:

1. a. The formation of a mental image of something that is neither perceived as real nor present to the senses. b. The mental image so formed. c. The ability or tendency to form such images.

2. The ability to confront and deal with reality by using the creative power of the mind; resourcefulness: *handled the problems with great imagination.*

3. A traditional or widely held belief or opinion.

4. *Archaic.* a. An unrealistic idea or notion; a fancy. b. A plan or scheme.

Translating this definition for use in the reality of Focus 27, imagination is the formation of images which are not present to the normal physical senses but which are instead present to the senses appropriate to the nonphysical reality of Focus 27. Imagination in this context is the ability to confront and deal with the reality of Focus 27 using the creative power of the mind. Rebecca had been right; these are indeed subtle energies which are not perceivable using one's normal physical world senses. When we engage the power of imagination, the subtle energies of Focus 27 are every bit as real and perceivable as the physical world. If you're interested in exploring beyond the physical world yourself, using imagination is a key ability to develop and utilize.

Learning to do so did not happen in a flash. I struggled to accept and utilize the power of imagination for quite some time after this first successful tape exercise. Part of me continued to fight against it with the admonishment that I was making it all up and it therefore wasn't real. Gradually, over a period of years, I learned to accept and use imagination as a tool, a window or a gateway through which to perceive. By peering through this gateway, it is possible to perceive levels of human consciousness which are different from the physical world and just as real. Accepting that I wasn't just making this all up in my head was the longest voyage across open sea I had to make before reaching the shores of realities beyond the physical world.

Impressions

Another very important tool I learned to use from this first successful tape exercise is temporary suspension of disbelief. This is a very powerful and useful tool which I used to work my way past long-held beliefs that blocked my path. Even in my work as an engineer, an image in my mind of the solution to a design problem wasn't real until it was brought into the physical world in the form of a sketch, drawing, or working model. I thought of it as fantasy, not realizing it was instead imagination. So my belief that things I saw or heard or felt during tape exercises weren't real because they were only in my head was tough to get past.

Rather than continuing my struggle with this seeming paradox and continuing to perceive absolutely nothing in these new levels of consciousness, I used a semantic trick on myself. I told myself that what I had perceived were merely impressions. I could conceive of the possibility that none of what I had seen, felt, or sensed was real, or maybe it was. They were only impressions of whatever might have been there, if anything was really there. I could allow myself to continue exploring using my impressions of what might be there. Impressions didn't have to be real or true. Tricking myself in this way dissolved the paradox and allowed me to temporarily suspend judgment as to the truth.

So I no longer had to worry about being tricked by my imagination into thinking I was actually perceiving what was really in Focus 27. After all, I was only perceiving impressions. These impressions could be something I made up in my mind or they could come from somewhere else. Their source didn't matter anymore. I'd just play along with whatever happened and see where it led.

Later, during debriefing sessions, I went so far as to stop saying I saw, heard, felt, or sensed anything after a tape exercise. Instead, I coined my own word, shortening *impression* into *Imp* to make it easier to describe my experience. For example, to describe what occurred when I asked the Beings sitting in chairs around my table for guidance as to my purpose, I would have said: I Imp'd Beings sitting in my hanging chairs. I Imp'd a question to them asking for guidance as to my purpose. Got an Imp of them bending forward and reaching down, far below my place in 27. Then I got an Imp of a burial at sea.

My Imps didn't have to be in three dimensions, full-color and stereo sound to be real, as they would in the physical world. They could be in black and white or shades of gray. Imp'd sounds didn't have to be in a language I understood. They could be totally unintelligible to the ear and I could still feel their meaning. Suspending judgment and disbelief using the concept of Imps opened up my perception. An Imp could be anything I could perceive: a flat-screen picture; a grainy, high-contrast, 3-D image; the feel of someone moving in close to me; a ball of light that talked; anything.

I know all this mental gyration must seem pretty silly to some of you, but I was such a hard case. I was so trapped in a paradox of my own making that I needed this level of rational explanation to accept my own direct experience. Before I began using Imps as a vehicle of perception, I know my frustrated complaining must have worn on all three trainers' nerves. Imping primed the pump, so to speak. Once primed, the flow of information sustained itself in ways I could not have imagined on my own. I knew I was really starting to get somewhere when things began to happen that I knew I hadn't consciously pretended. Best part of all this mental gyration is that it worked! I didn't have much to complain about any more—which must have been quite a relief to the trainers.

If you don't already know what I mean by an Imp you can experience one using the following exercise. Remember, these are very thin, vaporous, ethereal things, so you'll have to be on your toes. Here goes:

Close your eyes and relax for five or ten seconds.

Then, intend to remember something or someone. Pick one: a friend; your cat; your dog; your first car; your first love. Don't try to picture it, just intend to remember it.

Then, when you remembered whatever you chose, you might have experienced what I describe as an Imp. You saw it and yet you didn't. You didn't really see it with your physical eyes, yet you saw its image in your mind's eye.

If this makes sense to you, then you know what I mean by an Imp of someone or something. If you didn't get anything after many tries, then you know how I felt before I had even the faintest of impressions to go by. I felt confused and frustrated and was certain the Lifeline program was just a big rip off.

If you didn't get an Imp in this exercise, you might try pretending you're seeing a friend or pet or whatever. Keep at it; you'll get it.

I discovered later that the same Imping process works with my eyes open. You can try this too. Pick a different someone or something and with your eyes open intend to remember it.

Again, if you got an Imp, you saw it yet you didn't.

I hope this little diversion worked for you. I hope you see what an utterly simple, everyday, ordinary, garden-variety thing it is to get impressions of things—or Imps. It's something we have probably all been doing without giving it a second thought. It was so important for me to realize and accept that this simple, ordinary human ability is a key to perceiving in the realities beyond the physical world. Coupled with curiosity, this simple human ability has led me, an ordinary human being, into extraordinary experience.

After learning to prime the pump by initial pretending and to allow imagination to continue the flow of information through impressions, I had the tools necessary to begin exploration of the Afterlife.

So, What's a Retrieval?

Learning to explore the great unknown of human existence after death was my reason for attending the Lifeline program. With my telescope, compass, and maps in hand I was ready to sail out past the edge of physical world reality to explore this great unknown.

Exploring there during previous tape exercises, I had found very little evidence these Focus levels were inhabited by anybody. The next part of the Lifeline program would change all that.

As our group sat listening to the briefing by the trainers before our first attempt at retrieving, I felt a mixture of excitement and worry. I had been waiting for this moment since childhood, wanting to know where I would go after I died. I was excited by the prospect of learning answers and worried that I would still find nothing. During our briefing the trainers went over some of the details of what retrievals are, what to expect, and what to do.

Focus 23, they reminded us, is a level of consciousness inhabited by the recently departed. Some of these people have not yet recognized or accepted that they are no longer living in the physical world. Some may be aware of their death but are unwilling or unable to let go of certain aspects of the physical world. In either case, these individuals tend to be isolated and alone in Focus 23. In essence they are stuck there. Stuck because they are unable, through their own efforts, to move on from Focus 23 to a level beyond. We were now going to learn how to find people who are stuck in Focus 23, get their attention, and move them to the Reception Center in Focus 27.

Waiting to assist us, it was explained, would be Guides, who had an interest in our learning this process. A Guide would handle the move to Focus 23 and bring us into the vicinity of the person we were to retrieve.

This brings up an aspect of the retrieval process that I didn't understand at first. I could accept that there might be Guides or Helpers in the nonphysical world. I could accept that these Helpers were, perhaps, human beings who had lived physical lives on the earth and now lived in a nonphysical realm. My early religious training had spoken of beings called Angels, so it wasn't too far a stretch to accept beings called Helpers. But I couldn't understand why it was easier for me to get the attention of the recently deceased than it was for these Helpers. Our trainers told us it was easier for us because we still lived in physical bodies and the Helpers didn't. People who become stuck in Focus 23 tend to focus their awareness at the level of physical world reality—our C-1. They can oftentimes still see and hear activities going on in the physical world, adding to their confusion about their situation. Their thinking processes, even at subconscious levels, are in physical world terms. They continue to operate as if they are still living in the physical world. They still walk instead of fly, subconsciously accepting the influence of gravity even though there is no gravity in the nonphysical world. They walk through doorways rather than walls because they subconsciously accept the solidity of matter. This has a subtle but powerful effect on their awareness.

Nonphysical beings, therefore Helpers, do not exist within their awareness level. So the stuck person cannot see or hear the Helper (or Guide, or Angel, if you will) who is trying to assist him. To the stuck person such a Helper is just like a ghost to us in the physical world.

We who are still in a physical body, even when we focus our attention into nonphysical levels, still have a portion of our awareness at the physical world level. Therefore, both I and someone I encounter who is stuck in Focus 23 have a portion of our awareness focused at the level of physical world reality. To the stuck person I appear real and can be seen and heard. I can simply walk up to the person, introduce myself, and communicate with him within level of awareness in which we both exist. So it's easier for me to make the first contact with someone stuck in Focus 23 than it is for a Helper. This is the critical role physically-alive people fill in the retrieval process.

The trainers reminded us that at several times during the tape exercise Monroe's voice would prompt us to report verbally on our activities. At that time the tape recorders in our CHEC units would be turned on and we could take the opportunity to make verbal notes. We could also use the call buttons in our CHEC units to request that our individual tape recorders be turned on if we wanted to record at any other time during the exercise.

Throughout our briefing the trainers emphasized that those we retrieved could be anyone: a friend, a relative, a total stranger, or even parts of ourselves. Every time they mentioned that last possibility, I would see an image of the Disk and wonder if that might happen. When we had completed the briefing we all left to attempt our first retrieval.

As I was getting into my CHEC unit I was feeling both great anticipation and some worry again. I was looking forward to the experience of retrieving someone who was stuck in Focus 23 and still worried nothing would happen. I lay down, covered myself with a light blanket, and slipped on the headphones. Then I flipped the ready light switch to *on*, indicating to the trainers in the control room that I was ready to proceed. Lying there waiting for the tape exercise to start, I felt a little nervous about what would happen next. Deciding to just trust that all I had learned to do so far would be enough to allow me to experience the retrieval process, I waited in the darkness of my CHEC unit to begin.

I followed the Hemi-Sync sounds to Focus 27 and headed for my place there in the mountains. I can't say I had any clear impressions that I had arrived there, but I trusted I was there nonetheless. It felt more like I was floating in a three-dimensional blackness as I arrived. This was the same 3-D blackness I had experienced a few times before. There in the blackness I asked for a Guide to assist me with a retrieval. Didn't really see anything but I felt something moving toward me slowly, coming from some distance away. Whatever it was moved to my left and stopped very close to me. I took this feeling of a presence to be a Guide coming at my request for assistance.

I pretended to myself that a Guide had arrived, and responding to Monroe's voice on the tape suggesting I do so, I Imp'd a move to Focus 23 with the Guide. As we arrived I couldn't sense anything in particular around me. Then I felt a strong, electrical-charge-like surge move through my body. The surge felt like the body feeling that sometimes accompanies a strong emotional feeling such as pride. That feeling built up to a fairly high level and then faded away. I took this surge to be an indication that I was very near the person I was to retrieve.

Monroe's voice on the tape suggested making contact with the person, so I rather sheepishly Imp'd the beginning of the following conversation:

Bruce: "Hello?"

Person: "Hello?"

Bruce: "My name is Bruce; what's yours?"

Person: "Bill."

Common name, I thought to myself. *I am probably just making this up. I'll just keep playing along.*

Bruce: "Hi, Bill. My last name is Moen. I am Bruce Moen. What's your full name?"

Bill: "Bill Watkins." (Or maybe he said Watson?)

Yeah, sure, I thought to myself again. *An old friend of mine's last name is Watson; that's probably where this made-up name came from.*

Bruce: "What happened, Bill? How did you get here?"

Bill: "A fall. I . . . a . . . I fell off a roof."

Bruce: "Where are you from, Bill?"

Bill: "Arkansas."

Bruce "What city?"

Bill: "Little Rock."

Too easy. I probably made that up too. I don't know what Little Rock looks like; maybe Bill can tell me.

Bruce: "What's the terrain like around there where you fell off the roof, Bill?"

I got an Imp of three tooth-shaped mountains. They were large at the base and tapered to a necked-down area about two thirds of the way to the top. Then they tapered to a point at the top. They looked a little like three Hershey's chocolate kisses but spread out much wider at the base. The three mountains were side by side in a row.

Bruce: "What's your Social Security number, Bill?"

Bill: "373 . . . 0778 or 7078 . . ."

Yeah, right, I said to myself. *I couldn't allow myself to make up the whole number. If I did then it could be checked out and I would find out I was faking this whole thing, so I'm BS'ing myself here.*

Bruce: "Bill, I have come to take you to a better place. Would you like to go there with me?"

Bill: "Oh . . . ah . . . okay."

I got a strong Imp of a man standing in front of me, facing me. I reached out my hand toward him, as if we were going to shake hands. He reached his hand toward mine. As we clasped hands I nodded to the Guide I could feel still standing at my left.

"Let's go to the Park," I thought out to the Guide quietly, so Bill wouldn't hear me.

I could still feel I was holding Bill's hand as I began to feel a sense of movement. The movement lasted for only a short time, during which I was pretending we were going to the Park in Focus 27. I pretended we landed there and I saw waiting there someone who stepped forward and greeted Bill.

Hmmm, I don't remember pretending that someone would be here waiting for us.

Bill seemed to recognize whoever it was who was waiting for him. I watched as they turned and walked away from me, side by side, talking to each other.

Imp from the Guide: "Let's go back to your place."

I didn't expect this statement at all, I thought. It was coming from someone else. There was a short feeling of movement and then I was sitting in one of the hanging chairs around the table at my place.

After a short relaxing rest, Monroe's voice on the tape said it was time to go back to C-1. He instructed us to leave any emotional energy we had experienced there in Focus 27 and not bring it back into C-1 with us. I pretended to remove any emotion there might have been that I wasn't aware of. Then I followed the tape sounds and Monroe's voice back to C-1 and my CHEC unit.

At the debriefing I shared what I remembered of the experience with Bill. Most of it felt pretty bogus to me. Still, I was curious about whether there were any mountains in Arkansas that looked like the three Bill had shown me.

If there were, I reasoned, it might mean that some part of the experience might be real. And it was unexpected when the Guide had taken me back to my place in Focus 27. I had an unexpected feeling of movement and was surprised when I found myself sitting in one of my chairs. But overall, I was pretty well convinced I had made it all up in my head.

After a break we were ready to attempt our second retrieval. Using the same procedure as before, I went to my place in Focus 27 and waited for a Guide to arrive to assist me. This time, as I felt a Guide approaching, I Imp'd a fuzzy, elongated ball of light moving toward me and it felt like that was the Guide. The fuzzy, grayish ball of light was about my size and I could feel and see it standing next to me. I addressed it as if it was the Guide, explaining that I was there to do a retrieval in Focus 23 and would like his assistance.

"Yes, I know." The thought seemed to come from the fuzzy ball.

That's funny, I thought to myself, *I don't know why but that fuzzy ball of light is definitely male. It's definitely not female. How do I know that? And I don't remember making up that part where he said, "Yes, I know," but I suppose he would know why I was here if he came to help.*

"Well, okay, let's go to Focus 23," I thought out to the Guide as I looked toward him.

"Okay," the fuzzy ball thought back to me.

Shortly after we arrived, I felt the same electrical-type surge rise up in my body and then fade away. I decided that must be a signal from the Guide that I was near the person I was supposed to retrieve. I decided to start a conversation as I did last time with whomever this was.

Bruce: "Hello?" I waited awhile, ten maybe fifteen seconds. No response, so I said a little louder, "Excuse me, is there someone here?"

Old Woman's Voice: "Yes, yes, I am here," with a feeling of not wanting to be rushed in her voice.

Bruce: "Good, I am glad to meet you. I am Bruce Moen. Who are you?"

Imp'd an old woman, very old, wrinkled, and somewhat frail.

Woman: "My name is Mary, Mary White."

To myself: *Too common a name. I will bet I am making this all up.*

Bruce: "How old are you, Mary?"

Mary: "I am 81."

Bruce: "Well, Mary, what happened to you? How did you get here?"

Imp: Mary was a very old woman. I saw her in an institution, old folks home, a nursing home. She was walking slowly, shuffling really, toward me in a hallway at the nursing home. Mary stopped walking. Her body stiffened and straightened up. She stood stiffly for a moment with a look of great pain in her face. With both hands she reached up, clutching at the center of her chest. Then she fell forward, still stiff-bodied, landing face-first on the floor.

Where did that come from? I wonder. *I expected her to answer me in conversation, to tell me what happened to her. Instead, I just saw a series of images like she thought the story out to me and I got it all at once. I thought I would have made up that she explained it to me in words. I am not so sure I made that part up. But if I didn't, who did? Maybe she will give me something I can try to verify later.*

Bruce (trying to maintain my composure): "I see, Mary. When did this happen?"

Mary (gruffly): "April.".

Bruce: "What year was it?"

Mary: "1984." *(Or did she say 1894?)*

Bruce: "I am sorry, Mary, I couldn't hear you. What year did you say it was that happened?"

Mary: "1984!" She shouted loudly at me with aggravation in her voice.

She is upset at me for asking all these questions and then not paying enough attention to her to hear the answers. . . . How did I know all that about what she was feeling and why she shouted at me?

Bruce: "Where were you living at the time?"

Mary: "Tucson, Arizona." She raised her voice again to answer.

I can feel she is getting more aggravated at my incessant

questioning. I want any potentially verifiable information I can get. Maybe just a few more questions.

Bruce: "What was your address there in Tucson?"

Mary (shouting at me): "Pine, on Pine."

She is getting so irritated at my questioning that I feel I better get on with the retrieval before she gets mad and won't listen to me anymore.

Bruce: "Mary, I have come to take you to a better place. Would you like to come along with me?"

Imp: She didn't want to leave the safety and comfort of her home when she had to move to the nursing home. She didn't want to leave the nursing home after she died either. It too had become a familiar place where she felt safe and comfortable. She didn't really want to leave with me now. She might come with me if she knew there were people to visit with where I was taking her.

Bruce: "Mary, the place I can take you to has lots of people to talk to and visit with."

I don't know how I know this but I know she has been very lonely since she died. None of her friends in the nursing home can see or hear her so she's been feeling isolated. The loneliness is something she doesn't like. The prospect of being around people she can talk to and visit with might be just the thing that gets her to leave with me.

I assured her again that where we were going there would be lots of other people she could visit with.

Bruce: "There are lots of people you can visit with there, Mary."

She reluctantly agreed to leave with me.

Mary: "Well, okay. I'll come with you."

Bruce (as I turned and nodded to the Guide): "Let's go before she changes her mind and decides to stay. In her confused state of mind I could I lose her."

Imp: She was definitely confused and she didn't trust me at all.

Imp: Mary, the Guide and I were still in transit to the Park. We were about to come in for a landing, when potential trouble started.

Bob Monroe's voice cut in on the tape, saying it was

time to report our activities out loud for the tape recorder. I had hold of Mary by the hand and I was afraid to start talking out loud to someone she couldn't see. I knew she would hear me and in her confused, mistrustful state of mind I was worried she might freak out and run. Fearing I'd lose her, I waited to begin my reporting until I could see that we were approaching a garden in the Park and that people were waiting there. I pretended to be introducing Mary to this group of people as a ruse; actually, I was reporting out loud into the microphone of the tape recorder as we landed near the waiting people. In my introduction of Mary I recorded every detail I could remember of the experience since I met her in the nursing home. I was careful to be diplomatic and vague about her frailties so as not to offend her.

Bruce (addressing the waiting people): "Hello, this is Mary White . . ." I gave all the details of my activities up to that point and the transition went smoothly as I handed Mary off to them.

Imp: Those people who met Mary were Helpers, people who do volunteer work in Focus 27. None of them were friends or relatives of Mary's, just Helpers who came to make an old woman's arrival a more gentle experience. As I left her there I got a clear impression of Mary being attended to by the Helpers who had been there to meet us when we landed in Focus 27.

It took me a long time to finish my introduction of Mary to the waiting Helpers as I recorded all the events. Since I stood around watching their interaction with her so long, Monroe's voice on the tape took me by surprise. It was his prompting to once again leave any emotional energies there in Focus 27 and return to C-1.

In the debriefing session that followed, most of the other people reported carrying out retrievals too. I felt envy as I listened to those whose experiences were full-color, 3-D, and stereo sound. My own experience felt pretty insignificant by comparison. All I had were just impressions and conversation I probably made up in my head. True, some things that happened came unexpectedly. Still, I was pretty sure I was making this all up in my head. I told myself I just had a really good imagination.

In Focus 27 the third time, I again saw a fuzzy, oblong ball of light approach me after I requested the assistance of a Guide. I couldn't tell if it was the same Guide as last time but it was definitely a male again. We moved to Focus 23 again and I waited there in the blackness for something to happen. The now-familiar surge moved through my body.

Bruce: "Hello there . . . excuse me . . . is there someone here?"

Little boy's voice: "Hi mister. I am over here."

Imp: A little black boy about four or five years old. He was standing on a concrete sidewalk facing a paved street. He was standing near the curb. He spoke with the accent of someone from the middle South, not the deep southern drawl, more like Missouri.

Bruce: "Hi, my name is Bruce. What's your name?"

Little boy: "Benjie. My name is Benjie."

The thought of Ben, the only black person in our Lifeline group, popped into my mind. I wondered if he had some connection to Benjie.

Bruce: "Hi Benjie. What happened? How did you get here?"

Imp: He didn't know what happened. He just found himself standing here on the sidewalk. He was alone and waiting for someone. At times he seemed to be looking around as if he was expecting to see someone he knew.

Bruce: "I see, Benjie. You're here by yourself. Benjie, how old are you?"

Benjie: "I'm four."

Bruce: "When is your birthday?"

Imp: No answer but I got he was born in 1949.

Bruce: "Where do you live, Benjie?"

Benjie: "Des Moines, Iowa."

Imp: Clear image of a large white house with a fenced-in grass lawn.

Bruce: "Benjie, I have come here to take you to a better place."

Benjie (in a very firm voice): "No! My mamma and daddy said to never go anywhere with a stranger. I don't know you. You're a stranger!"

This was completely unexpected. I didn't know what to do. *This isn't supposed to happen,* I thought. *This is a retrieval. He is supposed to come with me. He has got to come with me!*

Bruce: "But Benjie, it's okay, honest. If your mamma or daddy were here they would tell you it was okay to come with me."

Benjie: "NO! NO! NO! You're a stranger and I am not going anywhere with you!"

This can't be! I was trying desperately to think of some angle to convince Benjie to come with me. Several different ideas quickly ran through my mind. *Maybe if I leave and come back, pretending to be his father. Maybe if I pretend to be his dad I will look like his dad to him and he will come with me. Maybe if I pretend to be his uncle, one he has never met, maybe that would get him to come with me. I can't believe he won't come with me. I have been brought here by a Guide to retrieve Benjie from a place he is been stuck in, alone since 1953, and I can't get him to come with me?* I was beside myself feeling the anguish of my failure to retrieve this poor little boy, but he was adamant in his refusal. He was not going to do something he had been told not to do. He was going to wait there for his mom or dad to come for him and that is all there was to it! Emotionally, I was bouncing all over everywhere. *I've got to find some way to get Benjie to come with me. Time is running out. I can't just leave him here, poor little guy.* But nothing I tried convinced Benjie to come with me. I gave up. I couldn't figure out what else to do.

Bruce: "Okay, Benjie, you stay here and your mom or dad will come for you in a little while. You keep looking for them and they will be coming soon, okay?"

I was having a hard time thinking my words out to Benjie. I was feeling a strong sense of failure and sadness at being unable to help him and leaving him where I had found him.

Benjie: "Okay, mister. I am gonna wait right here until they come."

Guide: "Let's go to your place in 27."

I had forgotten the Guide was with me. I was so involved with trying to get Benjie to come with me that the Guide's voice in my thoughts startled me.

Bruce: "But what about Benjie? I've failed. Poor little guy is still stuck in Focus 23."

Guide (very firmly): "Let's go."

I was crying. I could feel the tears streaming down both sides of the face of my physical body. I was feeling overcome with sadness and grief at leaving Benjie stuck in Focus 23.

Bruce: "Okay, let's go to my place."

CLICK: Without any sensation of movement or time I was back at my place. I was sitting in one of the hanging chairs, at the round table under my beach hut roof.

(Note: I use CLICK here and elsewhere to indicate a change so sudden, so immediate, there is no awareness of movement or time. One second I am in one place, in the next timeless instant I am somewhere else. It feels like someone pushed the button on a TV channel changer and I am instantaneously moved to a different program on a different channel. In less than an instant every clue about where I am is changed. It happens so fast the original location doesn't even have time to fade and disappear. It's just CLICK, and I am somewhere different.)

Imp: There was a crowd at my place in 27. All seven chairs had individuals sitting in them. There were tall glasses of cool drinks on my round table. Everyone felt like a friend I had known for a long time, yet I couldn't see any of them. If I could have seen the faces maybe I would have known who they were but I could see only their hands as they reached for their drinks on the table. I felt that all of them were there to assist me in some way, but I was not sure exactly how.

Guide: "Bruce, I would like you to smooth yourself and relax now, please."

Bruce: "Okay." I pretended to lean back in my hanging chair and relaxed. I found that the Guide's request to smooth felt very good. I wasn't sure exactly what he meant but as I relaxed it felt like many hands gently stroking my entire being in long soothing strokes. The rippling, bumpy emotions evoked by the experience with Benjie were smoothing out and fading away. I got an Imp that the crowd had formed a ring around my place. They were standing in a circle several feet larger in diameter than my beach hut. Whatever they were doing gave me a strong sensation of heat in the area where my physical hands were resting. I relaxed there, continuing to smooth myself until I heard Monroe's voice on the tape prompting us to leave the emotion there and return to C-1. This time I definitely had emotional energy to try to leave in Focus 27 before I returned.

Darlene opened our debriefing session by saying that in other Lifeline programs participants had reported that retrievals got successively more difficult or complex. Several others in our group related similar experiences. I was still emotionally upset and had to hold back my tears as I related my experience with Benjie. My heart ached as I told everyone I could not get him to come with me and I had to leave him there. After sharing my experience I asked for ideas about how to handle a situation like this in the future. I wondered how many other little kids are stuck, lost and alone in Focus 23, because they won't leave with a stranger. The best idea for dealing with this sort of thing in the future came from Darlene. She suggested that most children have some religious training and perhaps that can be used to advantage.

Ben, the only black in our group, remarked that some of the details I had related matched some of his own childhood experiences. It was pretty clear that he felt that I may have been attempting to retrieve a part of him from his childhood. That concept was still foreign to me at that point and I was still too emotionally shaken to focus on what he was saying.

Later that evening I begin to wonder if it is really possible that we split off parts of ourselves that become lost and stuck. The concept of retrieving parts of myself still sounded a little strange to me.

As I wrote some notes in my journal that night, I realized

that the increased difficulty I experienced trying to retrieve Benjie had been part of the training. Bill's retrieval had been a simple matter of asking him to come with me and he did so without any resistance. Mary White had to be convinced that there would be other people to visit with to end her loneliness before she would come with me. In Mary's case I had been able to use logic to take the information I received and give her a good reason to leave with me. In Benjie's case I had become so emotionally involved I couldn't use logic. I realized as I thought about it that part of Lifeline training involves learning to maintain emotional stability both during and after a retrieval. I hadn't done so with Benjie and as I wrote in my journal my eyes stung every time I thought of him still lost and alone in Focus 23.

Who Is Joshua?

During the Lifeline program there is a lot of free time set aside in the afternoon for participants. The trainers suggest the time be used to record experiences in a journal, talk with other participants to learn by sharing, and do other things to encourage grounding—re-establishing connection to the physical world through physical activity. When you spend so much time *out there*, focusing your awareness in the nonphysical world during tape exercises, it is easy to start feeling spacey. Without grounding, a feeling of disassociation from physical-world surroundings can give a dream-like, surrealistic quality to everything. While it is a rather pleasant sensation to be ungrounded, a lot like floating in the air, it is not conducive to integrating nonphysical awareness into memory. One of the best forms of grounding is a long walk on the dirt roads that surround The Monroe Institute facility. Something about walking barefoot along a dirt road brings the feeling of connection to the earth and physical reality back into one's awareness. Maybe it has something to do with the feel of dirt against the bottom of your feet. What ever it is, I found that long walks were a great way for me to get back in touch with the physical world and integrate experience.

For several days I had been taking long walks with a woman named Elizabeth during free time in the program. We used the time to talk about our experiences in the program and about our lives in general.

Thursday morning, right after breakfast on the last full day of the program, Elizabeth and I were walking. We had just passed the llama farm and were talking about how we had each traveled to the Institute for the program. She had had a long flight from The Netherlands and had arrived early to allow herself to become accustomed to the time change.

I was telling her about almost missing my flight from Denver when I remembered reading the Boy's Town article. I related the strange event in which I had first seen the name *Joshua* printed in the article and then *Marsha* in its place. As I told Elizabeth the story, I began to get the feeling that the name *Joshua* was a clue about something I was supposed to explore during Lifeline. Walking back to the Institute facility, I wondered who this Joshua might be. As I wondered, I got clear impressions of a young Hebrew warrior. I could feel spears flying through the air and feel the sound of men's voices in battle. Before we reached the building I decided to see what I could find out about this Joshua person during the next tape exercise. He had the feel of a part of myself I'd somehow left behind.

When I reached Focus 27 during that first tape exercise of the day, I had already decided to ask any Guide who came to assist me in finding out about Joshua. In response to my request for a Guide, a by-now familiar oblong, fuzzy ball of light began to approach me from the distance. He moved next to my left side and stopped close by. I asked the Guide for his name but its pronunciation was so twisted I couldn't even repeat it, much less remember it. So, dispensing with his name, I opened my conversation:

Bruce: "I would like your assistance in finding someone named Joshua, if there is such a person."

Guide (calmly): "Yes, Bruce, we know."

With the Guide's assistance I moved from Focus 27 to Focus 23. I felt a sensation of movement as we made the trip and as usual I sensed next to nothing upon arrival. I stood there in the blackness, waiting for that familiar feeling of the surge to let me know I was in the vicinity of the person with whom I was to make contact. When I felt the surge I didn't want to take a chance of connecting with the wrong person.

Bruce: "Joshua?"

I had the immediate impression of someone answering my call.

Male voice: "Yes? . . . Who is that? . . . What?"

Bruce: "Joshua, my name is Bruce . . . Hello? . . . Hello? Joshua, what happened to you?"

It's hard to describe the feelings that flooded through me as strong, clear, visual and audible impressions came, rapid-fire, in response to my question. I immediately *knew* that Joshua was part of me. I recognized and remembered myself as him. His experience was not something he was telling me about. It was more that I was remembering my own experience from long ago. I knew Joshua and I were the same I/There, from the same disk, the same cluster. The realization that I was in contact with a part of myself that was stuck in Focus 23 brought me to a state of hyper-alertness. My focus of attention expanded to take in every detail available that might help me retrieve Joshua. I didn't want a repeat of the experience with Benjie while trying to retrieve this part of myself. I struggled briefly to remain calm, focused, and alert.

Impressions, all arriving at once in a package of thought: Joshua, a young man, was standing on a walkway near the top of a wall during a battle. The wall was part of a fortified position which resembled a castle or a city wall. It was a thick wall made of field stone standing perhaps ten or fifteen feet high. It surrounded a small village as a defensive barrier against attack by men on foot. Standing where he was at the top of the wall, Joshua could see the invaders' movements as they directed their attack against the walled fortress. He was waving his arms and yelling to other defending villagers, pointing to places along the wall where forces needed to be concentrated to repel an attack. He had a short, broad sword in his right hand and he pointed with it as he shouted out orders to the others. In this battle he and the others were fighting to defend their village from an attacking enemy who would kill them all and take everything. As I was watching him point to an area where enemy troops were concentrating for an attack, I saw a spear come flying through the air toward him. It plunged deep into Joshua's right side, just below his rib cage. I could feel it slice through my flesh, through my liver, and emerge out my back. Joshua stood for a moment, looking down in disbelief at the wooden shaft of the spear sticking out of his body. In shock he fell, unconscious, at the wall. The battle raged on around him and I saw that when it was over, the attacking enemy was defeated and left empty-handed. The image of the wall, Joshua, and the retreating enemy faded and I found myself floating in the air looking down.

Below me I saw Joshua lying on his back on some sort of bed. It was a low wooden platform raised above floor level by short posts at each of its four corners. Wooden planks formed a frame between the posts with wide planks laid over the frame to serve as the bed platform. There was nothing I recognized as a mattress on this platform. He was lying on a thin blanket which covered the wooden planks.

Joshua was writhing in excruciating, unbearable pain. In his turning and twisting he had become tangled up in the light-weight blanket on the bed with him. I could clearly see the incomprehensible level of pain in the grimace on his face. Through his tightly clenched teeth I could clearly hear the terrible agony in his moans and screams. I knew as I watched him that Joshua's village was successfully defended and that it was a very long battle. I knew that the initial spear wound did not kill him. Joshua survived the bleeding and trauma long enough to die from the infection the spear wound caused in his liver. He died before the outcome of the battle to defend his village was certain. It was a long battle for his village and a long, horribly painful death for Joshua.

CLICK: I was lying in the recovery room after surgery during my present lifetime. I feel the same level of pain Joshua experienced in the same area of my body during my present lifetime. In 1987, after a long, drawn-out process of inconclusive medical tests, my doctor recommended exploratory abdominal surgery. In the recovery room I reawakened after surgery in pain so intense that I was stunned and at first unable to move. I remember not being able to scream because a large tube was in my throat. I remember thrashing my head from side to side trying to dislodge the breathing tube so I could scream. I remember the nurse calmly telling me not to do that as I might vomit and suffocate. I remembered thrashing around as the pain built up to such a high level I blacked out. I remember reawakening and blacking out from the pain, only to reawaken in repeats of the cycle. I remember the anesthesiologist came into my room the next day to ask me if I had been in much pain after surgery. When I described the intensity of pain I experienced he remarked he had thought as much from my reaction in the recovery room. He said I had been given enough morphine for my body weight that I should not have been able to regain consciousness. He was so surprised when I did that he continued to increase the dosage up to the point where he was concerned I might not regain consciousness at all. At that point he said he had to stop increasing the dosage and yet I continued to reawaken and thrash around, seemingly in pain. I will never forget the consciousness-gripping nature of that pain which prohibited anything else from entering my awareness.

The result of this exploratory surgery was a diagnosis of sarcoidosis in my liver, gallbladder, and lymph system. Sarcoidosis is a very rare disease for white American males, with an incidence rate of about 1 in 900,000. It is a disease which causes inflammation within body tissue much like an infection would but it is not an infection. It is just inflammation, but like an infection it can form scar tissue and something called granulomas within healthy tissue.

For eighty percent of all people diagnosed with sarcoidosis, it just goes away on its own within two years. The remaining twenty percent are divided between chronic and degenerative cases. Many in this latter category die of the disease. It had been five years since my diagnosis, so I knew I was in one of the last two categories. When my sarcoidosis would flare up I was treated with steroids to suppress the inflammation. Steroids made me feel like a paranoid wacko. On steroids I always felt as though there were someone right behind me that I had to find and attack before I was attacked. It was seldom fun. Sarcoidosis has no known cause and no known cure.

CLICK: I was back in the air hovering above Joshua. He was still writhing in unbearable pain I could now remember as I watch him on the bed below me.

Bruce: "Joshua. I see you were wounded in the battle defending your village. I can tell you that the battle was successful. Your village fought off the enemy."

Impression: He couldn't focus on what I was saying due to the intensity of his/my pain. It was so intense it took great effort on his part to focus his attention anywhere else. I remembered that feeling. I realized Joshua doesn't know he died as a result of the infected spear wound. The pain had such a grip on his awareness when he died that he hadn't noticed the change. He was in such a struggle with it as he died that he continued to fight against its memory afterwards. It felt just as agonizingly real to him after he died as it did before. He was locked, stuck in Focus 23, in its grip. He had been writhing in pain on the bed I could now see below me since the day he died. I knew that my sarcoidosis was somehow connected to the fact that Joshua, a part of myself, was stuck in the pain of a liver infection that killed him. His constant experience of that infection was somehow responsible for the rare disease in the same area of my body. I knew that if I could manage to retrieve Joshua my sarcoidosis might halt its advance. It might even go away. I also felt that if I couldn't retrieve Joshua, the shadow of his fatal infection cast in my body during my present lifetime, my sarcoidosis, would eventually kill me. This retrieval suddenly had my full, undivided attention.

Bruce: "Joshua, when did this happen to you? How long have you been here?"

My impression, 1300, felt more like a year in the Hebrew calendar then the number of years he had been writhing on that bed. I decided to try a tactic Darlene suggested after my experience with Benjie.

Bruce: "Joshua, what has your religion taught you about Heaven—Nirvana—Paradise—The Afterlife—The Kingdom of God?" I projected every image of the Afterlife I could think of into my question. I wanted to be certain Joshua knew I was asking him about his image of life after death. Not knowing much about the Hebrew religion, I wanted to be sure to cover every possible base.

Joshua (Imp'd back): "The Garden!" I felt something in him well up in recognition of the memory of teachings about The Garden and about what it was like. It was a paradise in which food and water were plentiful. Milk and honey were everywhere, free for the taking. It was the promise of his God to His people for a life beyond the Earth.

Bruce: "Joshua, I have come to you from The Garden. I was sent to bring you from this place to The Garden. In The Garden there are many who will tend to your wound. You will be healed and free from your pain."

My impression of Joshua's response was that he would have gone to Hell with the Devil if freedom from his pain was the promised reward.

Joshua (excitedly): "What's that you say? Am I to be taken to The Garden?"

Bruce: "Yes, Joshua, that is why I have come to you. I have come to take you to The Garden. Joshua, give me your hand."

From my position above his bed I reached down and got a firm, locking grip on Joshua's wrist. I could feel his hand and fingers getting the same grip on my wrist. Holding on to him firmly, I pulled upward, intending to lift Joshua up to where I was hovering over the bed. When I did, what looked like a flimsy, clear sheet of multicolored cellophane lifted up out of his body. It had the outline shape of Joshua's body but it seemed to have very little substance. As the last of him came up out of his body, his pain level immediately subsided. I got the clear impression that Joshua's new body looked the same to him as the old one. He hadn't noticed any difference except that the pain was gone.

I turned and nodded to the Guide, "Look, I am putting all my attention into holding onto Joshua. I am not going to lose him no matter what. You drive us back to Focus 27."

The scene which previously included the bed below us faded into the blackness and disappeared. I could feel it as we started moving through the blackness, slowly at first and then with increasing speed.

Joshua (very excitedly): "I am flying. I'm flying through the air!!"

Bruce: "Yes, of course, Joshua. We are flying. Do you remember anything from your religious training that could explain this?"

Joshua (still very excited): "Oh yes! I remember. Angels/Spirits can fly. My Hebrew religion teaches that Angels/Spirits can fly."

Bruce: "Well, that explains it then, doesn't it, Joshua? I was sent like an Angel/Spirit from The Garden to bring you there. Because you are with me you can fly too."

I wasn't above a little subterfuge if it would help make certain I didn't lose Joshua before we got to The Garden, wherever that was.

Joshua: "That makes sense. I understand."

My impression was that he was not completely certain he should be able to fly just because he was with me. Fortunately he was still dulled somewhat from his long ordeal and maybe a little confused by what was happening to him then. I didn't feel like pushing my luck by explaining he could fly because he was dead. That knowledge might have come as a shock to him and I didn't want anything to interfere with his retrieval.

"Very soon, Joshua, we are going to be arriving at the Garden. Very soon you will be seeing The Garden. The doctors/healers are waiting there to heal your wound. There will be Helpers/healers there to meet us when we arrive."

Just as I finished sending this thought to Joshua, Monroe's voice on the tape cut in, requesting that I report into the tape recorder on my activities. I completely ignored his request. I didn't want even the slightest chance of my talking out loud to someone Joshua could not see. I didn't want any chance of losing him. Healing of my sarcoidosis depended on retrieving Joshua. I just concentrated on holding on to him and let the Guide do all the flying. We seemed to be circling in a holding pattern until Monroe's voice stopped on the tape. As we circled I could feel very strong, emotional feelings building up in me. With Monroe's voice gone the three of us—Joshua, the Guide, and I—turned and began our descending approach for a landing at The Garden.

I could see green grass and trees below and ahead of us as we glided gently to a landing on a wide footpath that stretched out in front of us. On either side of the path, which was as wide as a single lane road, lush green grass and low rolling hills extended as far as I could see. Further along the path in front of us I could see huge, stately trees which reminded me of the sequoia redwoods in California. It had the feeling of an ancient forest. The wide spacing between trees and their lack of branches close to the ground gave a clear view of the green grass spread like a carpet beneath them.

The path on which we had landed led through a green pastoral setting beyond the trees and off into the distance. Joshua's Garden was spectacular! There were buildings surrounded by vertical shafts of light such as I have never seen before. There were huge, magnificent buildings with towering spires reaching hundreds of feet into the air. Soft billowy clouds, in pastel pinks, yellows, and golds seemed to emanate from the buildings and illuminate the entire area. It reminded me of those outrageously beautiful pink and gold sunsets over mountains. From the buildings, columns of soft, gentle, and diffuse light rose into the sky. I wish I could paint and do justice to the Heavenly glow of those buildings and spires in the distance.

As my eyes followed the path to the edge of the trees I noticed two men had appeared. They were standing on the path facing the place where Joshua, the Guide, and I had landed. As I watched them they began walking at a slow, determined pace toward us. Long, full, whitish-gray beards extended almost to their waists. Glowing, radiant, all-knowing smiles graced their faces. They were somewhat balding, with white-gray hair flowing down the sides and backs of their heads. Both wore heavy, flowing robes woven of thick white strands of material in a coarse weave. Their robes nearly touched the ground. Though not exceedingly tall, they were big, hearty men with a well-fed look to them. Each carried and used a long wooden staff as they took their own sweet time walking to where we were standing. Their slow, stately pace added to the majesty of the moment. They may have been walking slowly to intentionally give Joshua enough time to soak in the full view of his surroundings and stir memories from his religious training.

The two men approached a wide-eyed Joshua, one on either side, and turned facing toward the buildings in the distance. I let go of Joshua's hand and each of the men reached out and cradled one of Joshua's arms in his. He was overjoyed and overwhelmed. Absolutely ecstatic awe of this experience comes closest to describing the feeling he was experiencing. Then the three of them started walking the path through the trees toward the pasture and the magnificent buildings beyond.

As I stood there watching the three of them leaving I became aware of the strong emotion I had felt building up earlier. I had been holding it in since I first felt it and it began to surface quickly now at almost overwhelming levels. It's difficult to express in words the intensity of relief and gratitude pouring through me. As I spoke into the tape recorder, I had to stop several times to let the choked-up feeling of gratitude pass enough to speak some more. I recorded what had happened until my emotional expression of gratitude toward all the Guides and Helpers who had assisted me overwhelmed my voice. With tears streaming down my face I completely choked up, crying in joy. I couldn't say any more. I lay just lay there crying.

Guide: "Let's go to your place."

Bruce: "Okay."

CLICK: We were there. No movement, just there. The group I had seen before was there waiting for me. They were sitting in hanging chairs around my table.

Guide: "Just relax now. Just let yourself relax."

I allowed myself to begin relaxing and felt a change in myself and my position. No longer sitting in my hanging chair, I was instead flat on my back and had changed into what felt like a two-dimensional being. It felt like I had my eyes closed and was lying on a huge turntable with the sensation of continuous, curved motion moving to my right. It was like I was on a huge merry-go-round with my head pointed toward the center and my feet at the outer edge. It felt like I was slowly, constantly spinning as I was lying there on my back. As I slowly spun I began to calm down.

I continued talking to the tape recorder until my voice broke down in tears of joy and gratitude. Then Monroe's voice came in on the tape saying it was time to leave the emotional energies behind in Focus 27 and return to C-1.

Guide: "Just relax, Bruce. Make no effort to do anything. Let Bob's voice and the tones on the tape do that for you. I will stay with you all the way back to C-1. Just allow yourself to continue spinning the entire way there."

Bruce: "Okay, glad to." The spinning sensation continued to have a deeper and deeper calming effect on my emotions.

I followed the Guide's instructions and made no effort to return or pay any attention at all to the process of getting back to C-1. As I continued slowly spinning, I began to see the connection between my sarcoidosis and Joshua's death due to the infection in his liver. As this information came to me I gained insight into the process or rules by which this works.

Joshua, a part of me, had been left behind on that bed, writhing in pain and unaware of his death for centuries. Since we are parts of the same being, we are connected in a way that allows our individual experience to affect each other. Sarcoidosis is a medical mystery. It has no known cause and no known cure. I had seen the spear wound and resulting infection which explained the inflammation in my liver. The memory of that wound and infection were expressing through my physical body. I had carried into this lifetime the memory of that infection from a part of myself left dying long ago. I had carried that memory into my present physical body. Lacking an actual wound or infection as expression of that memory, I had developed this rare, unexplainable disease called sarcoidosis.

By the time I reached C-1 I understood that part of learning to be of service Here in Lifeline could help my physical existence during this lifetime. By retrieving parts of myself, bringing them back into memory and expressing them, I had the opportunity to heal myself. This healing could be physical, mental, or spiritual, depending on what each part of myself that I retrieved needed.

I was still quite shaken by the experience of retrieving Joshua as I left my CHEC unit. I briefly shared some of my experience with my roommate until I emotionally choked up and was overcome again. I sat through the large group debriefing session without saying much. I was feeling emotionally unstable and a little numb.

When we moved into our small group debriefing session, I sat quietly and listened to what the others had to say about their experience until one of the other participants asked a question.

"What's the sense of doing this? I go to Focus 23, grab a bunch of them and drag them off to Focus 27. There is a never-ending supply of them. It's like going to Focus 23 with a wagon, shoveling in shit until it's full and then hauling it back up Focus 27."

I was appalled and enraged at seeing the experience of retrieving parts of myself as shoveling a never-ending supply of shit into a wagon. The preacher in me wanted to jump up into the pulpit, take over, and start preaching. In the ensuing discussion within the group I gently butted in and asked if I could have a crack at answering his question. I nodded toward Rebecca, the trainer facilitating our small group debrief. I knew she could see the fire in my eyes.

Without saying a word she nodded and Imp'd back, "Have at it, Bruce."

I looked intently into the other participant's eyes the entire time I shared my story of retrieving the part of myself named Joshua. As I ended I told him I had absolutely no doubt my sarcoidosis was already beginning to heal. I could feel the swirling movement of energy throughout my liver and the right side of my chest. The preacher inside me was fired up and taking no prisoners.

Small wonder the poor guy felt like he was being attacked. In defense he said he had done past life regression therapy for that kind of stuff and found it easier and less complicated than retrievals. I remember looking through him as I told him, with sarcasm in my words, that if I were as far along as he was maybe I could do that too. But that in any event what I had done and was doing was working just fine for me. Poor guy. I took such offense I really unloaded on him. But really, thinking of the parts of yourself you've left behind as a never-ending supply of shit! I am sure they would feel offended too!

After a short break our group assembled in the large conference room for a briefing about the next tape. This exercise would be another visit to Focus 27 in which we could further explore the Afterlife. I expected to either go back and be put in a spin cycle again or perhaps retrieve another part of myself. My thinking was that perhaps there might be another part of myself to retrieve for a complete cure of my sarcoidosis.

This time I shifted to my place in Focus 27 with antic-ipation of meeting a Guide to continue some aspect of the previous tape experience. This was the first time I had any sense of continuity from one tape experience to the next. As the Guide moved toward me and stopped at my left side, I thought about the symbolic nature of my left side.

The left side is the feminine side in some esoteric teachings. The Guide stopping on that side struck me as having something to do with the way I was receiving information. Information seemed to come through the feminine side of me (the left) to reach the masculine side (the right). All kinds of *feminine is intuitive, masculine is logical* thoughts were running through my mind before I opened up communication with the Guide standing on my left.

Bruce: "So what's it going to be this time, more spin cycle or go retrieve another part of myself?" I somehow wasn't surprised to hear the Guide ignore my question with his own suggestion.

Guide: "Follow me from here to the Garden. We are going to check on Joshua."

CLICK: No sensation of movement or time, we were just at the Garden after the next timeless instant.

We were about thirty feet above the ground, flying over tan-colored buildings below. I could see paved streets in the same soft beige earth tones. Everything was illuminated in shadowless brightness as if by the noonday sun from a cloudless sky. We were approaching a building with a large dome-shaped roof structure that felt like a temple of some kind. We stopped, directly above the center of the domed roof of the temple, and I was looking down through the dome. It was as if a large area of the dome had somehow become transparent. Looking down through the dome I could see inside the temple.

The two old men who met us on the path when we landed in The Garden earlier with Joshua were standing near a raised sandstone-colored altar. They had placed Joshua on this altar. He was lying on his back and the two old men were talking to him. I watched and listened as they explained that there in The Garden all the latest advances in medicine were available. He was told that doctors there had knowledge and abilities beyond the wildest dreams of doctors Joshua knew back on earth.

They explained that a special team of the finest doctors in The Garden would be coming soon to completely heal his wound. As I looked at Joshua's body I could clearly see the oozing pus-filled gash in on his right side, just below the rib cage. The old men told Joshua that when his wound was completely healed there would not even be a scar to remind him of where it once was. It would be so completely healed, they told him, that it would be as if it had never happened. As I listened to them and felt Joshua's reaction to their words, I could feel his utter amazement that such a thing was possible.

The two old men explained that they had anesthetized him in a way that he would feel absolutely no pain. They encouraged him to watch as the team of special healers did their work and his wound was repaired and healed. As I listened, I could feel that the old men were doing everything in their power to convince Joshua of the reality of this healing process. As far as Joshua was concerned, he had a real wound which had to be dealt with. His experience, living as a physically alive human on earth, dictated that wounds must go through a long healing process. I was certain that the old men could have just as easily made the wound completely disappear right before Joshua's eyes. But such a miraculous healing would not have fulfilled Joshua's expectations and beliefs. There might have been remaining inner scars of doubt. By healing in the way they had chosen, the old men would heal not only the outward signs of the wound, but the inner, mental wounds as well. I was fascinated at the level of understanding of human nature these two old men possessed. They knew that all of Joshua's inner feelings about his wound were just as important to heal as its outward manifestation.

Suddenly a set of double doors near the foot of the altar flew open with a bang. Marching side by side in two rows of three, a team of six modern gowned and gloved surgeons burst through the doorway into the room. Like a precision drill team, marching in formation, they moved toward the altar. The surgeons stopped, lined up side by side, on both sides of the altar as if it were an operating table. By the look on Joshua's face I could see he was utterly amazed by their sudden entrance. As he watched they began to carefully clean, irrigate, and suture his open wound. They took great care to make sure Joshua could see everything they did as he watched in astonishment.

I was so engrossed in watching the procedure below me that I had forgotten all about the Guide who had brought me there. I was startled when he spoke.

Guide: "Do you understand?"

Bruce: "Yes. Joshua must believe the wound has been completely healed in his own frame of reference before it is truly *healed*. It must be done in a way that is convincing to him in a physical body sense. When he can look down at his own body and see the smooth, unscarred surface without any evidence of the former wound, his *healing* is complete. It has to happen in the same way he has seen wounds heal during his physical life. It must be believable. The lack of a scar he can accept as possible because he is in The Garden or Heaven where all things are possible. The act put on by the surgeons and old-time healers is done to provide structure and support for his belief. In a sense he is being tricked into allowing the healing to occur because in Joshua's mind he is in Heaven and anything can be done. There is a connection with my sarcoidosis. If, for example, Joshua were to incarnate again before completely healing he would carry the memory of the wound into his next or some future physical body. Any residual memory of the wound would affect that body. My own body and this rare, no-known-cause, no-known-cure disease is an example of what would happen."

Guide: "Back to your place."

CLICK: We were at my place in Focus 27. The group was there, sitting in my hanging chairs.

Guide: "Relax now. Make no effort to go anywhere. Let the tape sounds do all of that for you again."

Bruce: "Okay." *Boy, these guys sure don't mince any words.*

As I began to relax, this time I didn't experience the same two-dimensional sensation or the same spinning as last time. This was a completely different spin cycle. I felt instead as if I had become a ball of light with many different colors running through me and I was spinning on my own vertical axis. My axis was fastened somehow to the outer edge of and perpendicular to a large disk. The large disk was also spinning on its own central axis and the overall sensation was very odd. It felt as though I was constantly counter rotating but I had no concept of what my rotation was counter to. There wasn't any dizziness that accompanied all this spinning as a ball on the disk. There wasn't any the time before either, when I had the sensation of being two-dimensional and on the spinning disk. At times I sensed that I was not the only ball of colored light spinning on this disk. I couldn't see them, I just felt and knew there were several others spinning on the disk with me.

I rather enjoyed this odd sensation of spinning and remained relaxed in it even after Monroe's voice on the tape called me back to C-1. As we moved back through the focus levels on the way to C-1, I noticed some physical pain. At about Focus 15, the area of no time, the pain settled into the right side of my chest. It was considerably above Joshua's wound, more like the upper part of my right lung. I had the distinct impression of having been in a house fire where smoke and heat had damaged my lungs. In my present lifetime I have never been in a house fire. My impression was that whoever I was in the house fire lifetime needed to be contacted and retrieved also. Heeding the Guide's instruction not to attempt to go anywhere, I made a mental note to pursue this later. When I reached C-1 I felt on the great side of normal. Once in a while I would intentionally focus my attention on the area of my body where Joshua was wounded. When I did I could feel patterns of energy moving and crisscrossing throughout that area. It felt like a healing process and I was just as certain of the outcome as Joshua. I knew my sarcoidosis was being healed.

Later that evening, lying in bed, I recalled the pain I had felt in my chest in Focus 15. I decided to send Dolphin Energy to find and heal whatever part of me the pain was coming from. I call my dolphin healer Decky: As I drifted off to sleep I pictured Decky swimming off to find and heal that part of me wherever I was.

During the last large group debrief of the program, sitting

in the front of the room as usual, I became overwhelmed by the feeling that everyone in the Lifeline group was perfect just as they were. Remembering the oddly strong, judgmental feelings I'd felt during the van ride from the airport before the program began, I began to understand that what had irked me most was the triviality and singles-bar flirtation they engaged in as we approached what was for me a sacred, spiritual quest. Sitting there, I realized that my own religious baggage tended to isolate spiritual endeavor from other, merely human activity. I had been watching others play out very real parts of my human self I had always suppressed and isolated from spiritual experience. My own religious ritual had kept me from integrating what I saw as my spiritual self with my human self.

The thing I most despised about Fundamentalist religions turned out to be a part of me I had refused to acknowledge. Living by rules which became blinders, I had refused to allow my merely human self access to spiritual knowledge or understanding. It's no wonder I could feel my spiritual connection to the universe only during my ritualized spiritual activities. Outside of those rituals I could lie, cheat, steal, and plunder the planet with impunity. Since I'd never seen fit to welcome those disgusting, merely human parts of myself into spiritual awareness, they had none. In a flash, as I sat there in our final gathering, I realized that all the other participants mirrored myself back to me by just being who they really were. They were all just parts of a greater self of whom I was beginning to become aware.

My strong, judgmental feelings about who did and who did not deserve to participate in the program completely dissolved. I told everyone of my earlier feelings. How I had picked out those who were worthy and those who were not. I told them how my feelings had changed. In a tearful, emotional experience I expressed my love and gratitude to all of them. I thanked them all for being who I felt them to be at that very moment, parts of myself.

After returning to my home in Colorado, I looked back at my experience in the Lifeline program I had just completed. My hope had been to learn how to explore human existence in the Afterlife. The only barrier I had foreseen before the program was learning to reach the new Focus levels taught in the program. The real barrier I had discovered was, instead, my own acceptance of the reality of my own perceptions within those Focus levels. Perception there was little different than the exercise of well-developed powers of imagination would be anywhere. It was difficult to shake the nagging feeling that I was just making it all up. Yet, it was different than my ordinary use of imagination in which I supplied all the details. Unexpected things had happened in great detail—things that I felt no part of generating within my own mind. But, when the only place something happens is within the thoughts of your own mind it's very difficult to know what is real and what is fabrication.

Long ago those who thought the Earth was round might have had little supporting evidence. What they had was really just a theory. Like any theory, it existed only in the minds of those who imagined it. To prove a theory requires experiments providing supporting, repeatable, verifiable data. I had come home from Lifeline with a little (rather flimsy) evidence suggesting the possibility of human existence beyond the physical world. All the evidence came from perceptions within my own mind of people such as Bill, Mary, Benjie, and Joshua. By the end of the program my direct experience with them felt very real to me, but I was the only one who had experienced them.

So, I had come home to Colorado not with solid, verifiable data but with a consuming hunger to find it. Still carrying my feelings of doubt, thinking I could have fabricated it all, I now craved verification. Finding a way to verify the reality of my perceptions became a howling gale, a storm of obsession.

Benjie Again

Following my return from Lifeline, I built a small-scale version of a CHEC unit in the basement of our home to have a quiet place to carry out my activities. It was nothing fancy, just a small enclosed space with a foam mattress, blankets, and sound isolation. Amid my wife's growing concern that I had become the victim of some strange cult in Virginia, I pursued my obsession for knowing the truth.

About two weeks after I completed my home CHEC unit, I decided to look for Benjie again. Leaving him lost and alone in Focus 23 where I had found him was difficult to bear. So I climbed into my CHEC unit one night with the intent to find him and try again.

I had intended to start from my place in Focus 27 and was somewhat surprised to see it there when I arrived. For a figment of my imagination it was at least persistent, and it looked just like I left it on my last trip there during the program. I could even see my group sitting once again in the hanging chairs around the table. Still couldn't see their faces. I could see only their bodies from the shoulders down as some of them reached for their cold, sweating glasses of ice tea and fruit juice. As with each time before, it seemed they didn't want me to know their identities. My request for a Guide to assist me in the retrieval of Benjie was met in the now-familiar way. A bright, fuzzy ball of light approached from my left side and stopped close by. I could feel the sensation of movement as we pulled away from my place in Focus 27 and headed into darkness on our way to Focus 23. I could feel when we stopped and then I felt a muted version of the surge. As I stood there in the darkness, the image of a small, black boy gradually came into view. It was Benjie, and he was still standing on the sidewalk near the curb, waiting for his mom or dad. I stood there quietly in front of him, waiting for him to notice me. This time I had a plan.

I could tell by his puzzled, inquiring look that he thought he knew me from somewhere but couldn't quite remember. Then a look of recognition swept over his face as he remembered meeting me before.

"Hi, Benjie. Remember me?" I asked.

"Yeah. I remember you. You're a stranger. My mommy

and daddy told me not to ever go anywhere with a stranger. And I am not going anywhere with you!" he responded.

Benjie had a strong look of determination on his face as he announced his intention not to disobey his parents.

"Your mommy and daddy are right. You should never go anywhere with a stranger, Benjie, but I am not a stranger."

"I don't know you, and if I don't know you that makes you a stranger," he snapped back.

"I'm not a stranger, Benjie. I'm an Angel," I said to him very matter-of-factly.

He stared at me in complete disbelief and shrugged my statement off as just the sort of lie a stranger would tell to trick him into coming along. Smart boy!

"You ain't no Angel. I don't see no wings and I don't see no halo around your head. That's what Angels look like so you can't be no Angel," he said, his face showing pride at exposing the obviousness of my lie.

"Tell me some more about Angels, Benjie. What can Angels do that a stranger could never do?" I asked, smiling warmly into his eyes.

He thought about it for a moment, with the blank look of every little kid who has been asked a question to which they don't know the answer. I thought about pictures I had seen in Sunday School of winged, glowing Angels. I imagined them hovering in the air above frightened shepherds. Benjie's face suddenly brightened. He had seen the hovering Angels too. The bright, self-satisfied look on his face told me he knew the answer.

"Angels can fly, mister! That's what they can do that no stranger could ever do. Angels can fly!" Benjie said, with great pride in his accomplishment.

"That's right, Benjie. A stranger could never fly. Only Angels can do that," I said. "I am an Angel. You just watch me, you'll see."

I had been standing in front of Benjie, perhaps six feet away, since I arrived. Keeping my eyes fixed on his, from my standing position I slowly rose straight up in the air about eight feet off the ground. Then, focusing my attention on him continuously, I did three vertical figure eights in my standing position in the air right in front of him. By the end of the third figure eight his jaw had dropped in amazement. I slowly, gently, landed again on the sidewalk in front of him on the spot where I had started.

"See, Benjie. Like I said before, I am an Angel," I said with a smile.

He was speechless. He just kept looking at me in wide-eyed amazement.

"Sometimes, Benjie, Angels come to bring little boys and girls to Heaven so they can be with their families again. That's why I'm here. Would you like to come with me to Heaven now, Benjie?" I said, amazed I got through it all without showing him my tears.

Benjie was still speechless. Never stopping his wide-eyed gaze directly into my eyes, he nodded his head slightly to indicate he was ready to leave with me. I reached out my hand toward him and he reached out with his. Taking his little hand in mine, I smiled warmly at him, then I turned my face away.

"Good. Benjie, you just hold onto my hand. Heaven is over that way," I said, pointing off into the blackness in the distance. "We will be there in just a minute."

"Okay, I am ready," Benjie said, finding his voice again.

I turned to the Guide and nodded, "Let's go."

We slowly began to move in the direction I was pointing. After picking up speed, we continued along at a moderate pace for perhaps ten or fifteen seconds. Then the blackness began to fade like dispersing clouds and a low hill covered with grass came into view. I could see a black man standing on a footpath through the grass that led to the top of the hill. As we approached him I got the impression he was one of Benjie's uncles, one that Benjie would recognize. We landed on the grass not far from Benjie's uncle. They looked at each other for a moment and then Benjie's face brightened as he recognized the man.

"I got to fly to Heaven with an Angel," Benjie shouted, as he ran toward his uncle's open arms. His uncle picked Benjie up off the ground and hugged him. Then he stood Benjie on the path next to him. His uncle took Benjie's hand and they started walking along the path, up the hill, away from where I was standing. I had held it in as long as I could to trick Benjie into leaving with me. Now I had to let the emotion out. In deep racking sobs my body shook as tears ran down my face. I cried off and on for several minutes and then I felt the voice of the Guide who had assisted me.

"Let's go to your place."

CLICK, I was at my place then, sitting in one of the hanging chairs around the table. I sat there for a while smoothing the emotional ripples still coursing through me. When I felt I could leave all the emotion there, as Monroe had always instructed, I returned to C-1. Back to my physical body, back to my little CHEC unit in the basement.

This experience was certainly no more verifiable than those during Lifeline itself. Nevertheless, I felt better for having found and moved Benjie to Focus 27, even if it was all just in my mind.

V. Second Lifeline

At this point, I had been working at one place as a mechanical engineer for years in Research and Development, the one place in engineering that really felt like home because of the creative expression and problem solving it required. But in the previous year, changes in the management structure had turned that wonderful job into a frustrating situation. The new regime jumped from one short-term, got-to-have-it-now project to the next, each time scrapping the previous project for something else, just as hot as the last one. After about the sixth cycle of putting my heart and soul into solving the latest hot problem, only to have to leave it unfinished because they had changed their minds in midstream, I was burned out. I negotiated a month off at work and set out to spend a month as a volunteer at The Monroe Institute. I flew to Minneapolis, borrowed my parents' minivan camper, and drove to Virginia for the month of October.

The first two weeks I did all sorts of odd jobs around the facility. I did maintenance on CHEC unit tape recorders and electrical wiring, fixed leaky toilets, and just generally had a ball. The laid-back pace of working as a volunteer with no pressure, for people who appreciated my efforts, washed the feeling of burnout away.

There was a Lifeline program scheduled during my stay and, as it approached, my desire to attend began to climb, but my shoestring budget couldn't handle it. A surprise phone call took care of that.

The woman who ran the training center kitchen called me on Tuesday wanting to know if I could fix their dishwashing machine, which had just broken down in the middle of a program. The factory repairman from Roanoke wanted six hundred dollars to fix it and couldn't get to it until the following week. Providing thirty meals, three times a day, meant she couldn't afford to be without the machine for a few hours, much less a week.

Three hours later it was running. I had fabricated and installed temporary repair parts, had new replacements on order, and had traded my repair job for half the Lifeline program's cost, which meant I could now afford to attend. Being an engineer has its advantages.

I entered this program without my previous superior, judgmental frame of mind. I found myself accepting everyone else as if they were a part of me who had come to explore too. Since being in this Lifeline program came as somewhat of a surprise, I had fewer expectations built up and felt more relaxed.

During the first few tape exercises, five experiences stood out as new and different. I feel they describe islands with hidden treasure, islands worth exploring should your curiosity lead you to undertake this journey of self-discovery.

The first involves seeing other physically alive people in the nonphysical world. In my two previous programs, I had never seen one of the other program participants nonphysically, during a tape exercise. It came as a surprise, then, when Rita popped into view in Focus 10. Rita is a young woman enrolled in this Lifeline program. When I saw her I was not focusing on anything in particular. I was just floating in blackness when suddenly I heard a woman's voice giggle. In a grainy black and white image, there was Rita, standing in front of me giggling like a happy, mischievous kid. As soon as she realized I could see her, she let out a delighted squeal, turned to my left, and ran away laughing and giggling. When I mentioned this to her during a break between tapes she had no conscious memory of it. After I told her which CHEC unit I was in, the encounter did make sense to her in a strange kind of way. During a previous program Rita claimed she and two other participants had intentionally, nonphysically, visited the person who had been in that same CHEC unit to cheer him up.

Off and on throughout the rest of our program Rita would suddenly pop into view, usually giggling, and then run away as soon as I saw her. I attempted several times to say or do something she might later remember, in an attempt to verify the experience, but that never worked. My hunger for verification was not satisfied; had Rita and I both remembered our communication during these non-physical meetings at least nonphysical communication between physically alive humans would have been verified for me. I felt disappointed at not being able to successfully verify even this small step, but the experience turned out to be a seed planted for future growth.

The second island appeared on the horizon during the second tape of the program. I was lying in the blackness with my physical eyes closed when I saw a tall, thin woman enter my CHEC unit. She walked in through the wall on my right. I use the term *woman* here rather loosely, as she in no way resembled a human female—or a human at all, for that matter. Female was something I *felt* rather than saw. She looked more like a tall, skin-and-bones body made of light. She was at least six feet tall and strode in through the wall as if it weren't there. She turned, facing me, crossed her legs, and sat straight down Indian style at my feet. I continued to see her sitting there throughout the rest of the tape exercise. During the remainder of the program I could feel her sitting there but couldn't see her. As far as I know she never communicated with me directly and I am still puzzled at who she was and why she was there.

The third island's hidden treasure was 3-D blackness. With the privacy curtain of my CHEC unit closed it was quite dark inside, dark enough that I couldn't see anything more with my eyes open than with them closed. But that kind of blackness isn't a pure blackness, more a fuzzy, grainy mixture of black and various shades of gray. It might even resemble the snowy screen on a black and white television tuned to an open, unused channel. You might say the grainy blackness you see with your eyes closed resembles the television screen's flat, two-dimensional quality. It has height and width but it doesn't have any depth dimension to it. It is just a flat, grainy black. Flat, grainy, and black is what I normally see when I close my eyes in the dark. The hidden treasure of the third island is a similar grainy blackness, but it has the feel and appearance of depth.

All of a sudden I felt an internal shift of awareness; the blackness before my eyes took on a feeling of depth. It felt as though I was looking into the depths of a grainy, black and white hologram. During debriefing sessions I used the term *amorphous black* to describe this strange 3-D blackness I found myself shifting into, trying to describe the sense of formlessness this dark, holographic blackness had. As I traveled to this island of 3-D amorphous blackness during tape exercises, I discovered that I could interact with it, particularly as we began to carry out retrievals. I found that if I shifted my awareness to this amorphous black state and expressed my intent to do a retrieval, vague shapes would begin to coalesce and form within its depth. If I then intended to move toward one of these shapes within the blackness I would enter a passageway that led to the person I was to retrieve. The process of shifting my awareness to the 3-D amorphous blackness and then expressing my intended activity became my method of opening my perception to the nonphysical world. From this point on, when you read that I opened my perception to the non-physical world, I mean what I have just described. I mean that I shifted my awareness to the 3-D, amorphous blackness. It led me to the *flying fuzzy zone*, the fourth island.

I was experimenting with the 3-D amorphous blackness when suddenly it felt as though the top of my head was pushing against something elastic. I mentally pushed upwards, against the stretchy barrier, and then I felt my head pop up through something like a thick soap bubble. When it did I saw thousands of little fluttering lights. They looked like fireflies or wingless little butterflies made of light flying in a black night sky. They were each flying in small arcing circles, corkscrew fashion, like moths around a bright light at night. Almost as soon as I realized what I was seeing, just as I began to try to figure out what these flying things were, my head moved down with a popping sound and the scene disappeared. To this day, three and a half years later, I still occasionally pop into the flying fuzzy zone. The result is always the same. I am there for a second or two and then the scene is gone. The flying fuzzy zone feels like a nonphysical reality of some sort that actually exists separate from my experience of it. It feels like a real, definite place with its own reason for existence, but where and what it is, is still a mystery to me.

My curiosity about the flying fuzzy zone and my efforts to stay in it long enough to figure it out led to the most important thing I learned during this Lifeline program. The Balance that leads to Knowing was the fifth island I encountered. Learning to achieve this Balance is the most important landmark of this portion of my journey.

During the early tape exercises I began to notice a recurring, frustrating pattern. After moving to the Focus level I was to explore I would prime the pump of my imagination by pretending the first thoughts of my intention. Then I would relax and shift my awareness to the 3-D, amorphous blackness, opening my perception to whatever might be there. Vague, small swirls would begin to form in that blackness and I would begin to examine them. My perception would open and I would begin to get impressions of what was going on around me. My perception would begin to change to the point that I could see and/or hear whatever was going on. Just as I began to get clear, visual images, my perception would stop suddenly, as if someone had shut off the switch. I would be back floating in flat-screen, two-dimensional blackness. Frustrated but realizing that getting angry would be a waste of time, I decided to observe this whole process carefully.

I found a real key to understanding when I realized I was talking to myself. These *thought conversations* were not at all connected to the impressions I had been seeing and hearing. I could usually remember what I had been perceiving before I realized I was talking to myself about something not at all related to it. This same pattern happened repeatedly. I began trying to become aware of what was happening at the exact instant my perception shut off. As I did, I became aware of two components of my awareness, one I call the Perceiver and the other I call the Interpreter. It took several tape exercises just to figure out the part my Interpreter played in shutting down my Perceiver.

I found that opening my perception to nonphysical realities is a process of allowing the Perceiver to supply information to my awareness. Examining the vague shapes forming in the 3-D blackness somehow allows the Perceiver to connect with a nonphysical reality and supply impressions—images, sounds, feelings, sensations and communication—to my awareness from that Focus level.

The Interpreter, I discovered, supplies information to my awareness from a completely different source. The Interpreter takes whatever impression is within my awareness and relates it to information previously stored in my memory. For example, suppose the impression of a cat came into my awareness as my Perceiver examined one of the vague shapes in the 3-D blackness. The Interpreter would then bring into my awareness some image stored in my memory that is associated with cats. The Interpreter would continue supplying related, associated images to my awareness until it was consciously stopped or until my awareness was diverted for some reason. So the Interpreter might supply the following train of thoughts in response to the image of a cat in Focus 23.

Cat, I had a cat once that was accidentally locked in a sewing machine case overnight when I was about nine years old. We lived in a trailer house then. House, I built a house on a lake once, what a job. Job, oh yes, my job. I will soon be sharing my cubicle with that new guy from Brazil. Brazil, I wonder if they grow bananas in Brazil.

One clue as to why my perception had shut down came when I remembered that the impression of a cat in Focus 23 had somehow left me thinking about *bananas in Brazil.* And so I discovered and identified the Interpreter, which can only bring to awareness information stored in preexisting memory. The Interpreter tends to jump through memory from one item to the next, making associations between stored memory and new information it *sees* in awareness. Once the new impression has been associated with enough existing images in memory, that new impression becomes part of memory. It is cross-referenced, so to speak, to enough different places in memory that it can be found again later by thinking about any of the other associated images. The Interpreter's function is to build memory. But with the Interpreter filling my awareness with images from my memory, there wasn't any room left in my awareness to perceive anything else.

The key to solving this problem was the fact that the Interpreter supplies these distracting trains of thought in the form of conversation. Verbal commentary on the images and associations it was making seems to be a vital component of its process. As the tape exercises continued, I began to listen for the voice of the Interpreter as it began to talk about the impressions supplied to my awareness by the Perceiver. At first I wouldn't notice that voice until my perception had shut off and I was thinking about *bananas in Brazil* again. Through force of will I began to consciously stop the Interpreter's jabbering as soon as I detected it. Gradually I began to hear its voice and shut it off earlier and earlier in the process of my perception shutting down. As I continued I discovered I could shut off the Interpreter at the first hint of a feeling that it was about to make its first verbal comment about my Perceiver's impressions. That is when I discovered the Perceiver's limitation.

The Perceiver is just that—pure perception and only pure perception. It has no associative function or ability with which to anchor its perceptions in awareness or memory. When I became really good at shutting down the Interpreter at the first hint of its presence—I clicked out. I became *unconscious to the experience.* I would completely shut off the Interpreter as I began to experience the first impressions coming from the Perceiver and the next thing I was aware of was that I had been seeing a cat in Focus 23, for example, and had then been clicked out for an unmeasured amount of time. Three seconds or three hundred years could have elapsed during these click-outs. I had absolutely no way of knowing. This led me to understanding the Balance necessary to both perceive and remember my experience while exploring the Afterlife through my impressions. Through that Balance I discovered Knowing.

Clicking out was just as frustrating as talking to myself about bananas in Brazil. I might have been perceiving clear, full-color, 3-D and stereo-sound impressions—but I had no memory of them. I began to experiment with allowing the Interpreter to jabber in short bursts, three to five seconds or so, as my perception began to open to the nonphysical world. After allowing it to comment for that short amount of time I would begin to shut the Interpreter off. At first, as I could hear the Interpreter start talking, the images and sounds of impressions from my nonphysical surroundings would fade into blackness. When I shut the Interpreter off the images and sounds would fade back into my awareness. When they faded back into my awareness the impressions would be a little later in the sequence of events I had been observing. My perception was shut off during these fade-outs and I would miss that part of the story. As I got better at stopping the Interpreter quickly, the length of these fade-outs shortened. I then began to see, hear, and remember enough impressions to understand the whole story I was receiving.

At first this process of shutting off the Interpreter was a struggle involving vigilance and will power, often taking half a minute or so to accomplish. I had to maintain awareness of the impressions supplied by my Perceiver while listening for the voice of the Interpreter. Once the jabbering associations started, I had to stop them by force of will. Stopping them could not be done in the form of arguing with the Interpreter. That just continued the stream of associations off into even more divergent areas. Stopping the Interpreter had to be done by relaxing it. Relaxing the Interpreter is the best way I can describe what it felt like to stop it. I would feel it beginning to talk and then I would relax it, moving my attention or awareness away from the Interpreter and back to the Perceiver. Continued experimentation with this process led to the Balance.

Over a relatively short period of time I began to be able to move back and forth between the Interpreter and the Perceiver in shorter and shorter periods of time. This moving back and forth between perceiving the images, sounds, and feelings of my impressions and then making associations to preexisting memory was like riding a bicycle on a high wire. Leaning too far to either side meant either I would fall off into long trains of thought having nothing to do with the impressions or I would click out. Continued practice made it easier and easier to ride that bicycle without falling off the high wire. The path of Balance on that high wire led to Knowing. Gradually I became able to allow both the Interpreter and the Perceiver to be switched on and off in a faster and faster cycle. Once the fade-out times were short enough, I didn't miss any of the story. It was as if, while watching a television program, I opened and closed my eyes. Opening my eyes would be like perceiving. Closing them would be like interpreting. At first my eyes were closed so long that I missed too much to connect the sequence of events into a coherent story. As I learned to open and close my eyes faster and faster, I saw enough to see the whole story and made enough associations to preexisting memory to be able to remember it. Using this process, I learned not only to remember the story I had seen but also to Know what the story was about. Riding a bicycle well on a high wire takes confidence and practice. If I haven't done it in a while, at first I fall off again on one side or the other. But I always know I once knew how. I always know that Balance on the high wire leads to Knowing.

During one of the early expeditions to the Belief System Territories, I saw several previews to coming attractions. Each of these short snippets of impressions occurred between long, faded-into-blackness jabbering from the Interpreter. I opened my perception in the 3-D blackness and looked for something on which to focus my attention. An area became more densely black. The blackness faded and I was flying high over a huge, magnificent cathedral with towering spires and beautiful architectural lines. Then that image faded and I could hear the faint sound of singing in the pink noise of the tape. I focused attention on the sound and distinctly heard a male choir singing *Onward Christian Soldiers*. It sounded so real that I wondered if they were actually singing on the tape. I could hear the entire choir and I could focus in on a single voice within the choir and hear it and the rest of the choir together. Then the sound stopped and I was thinking about *bananas in Brazil* again.

Relaxing the Interpreter, I waited in the 3-D blackness, feeling my perception once again opening. This time I was standing on an open prairie and could see hills or low mountains in the distant background. It was dawn and I was standing with my back to the sun, watching a Native American man in front of me performing a ritual of some sort as he faced the rising sun. He was dressed in clothes made from animal hides and held something in his hands as he moved them from side to side and up and down. I had the impression he was worshiping, carrying out the ritual of his belief system, there in Focus 25. Then I realized the Interpreter had taken over and I was thinking about *bananas* again.

I again relaxed my attention away from the Interpreter and waited, looking into the 3-D blackness. This time, after a vague image formed in the blackness and then faded, I was watching a man pacing, out in an open grassy field. His hands were clasped behind his back and he had a pensive look on his face. I was keeping pace, observing as closely as I could his manner and expression. He seemed to be deep in thought and searching desperately for the answer to a question. Then he too was gone in a flurry of jabbering about associated thoughts.

By the time we started doing retrievals in Focus 23, I was alternating between shutting down the Interpreter too soon and letting it run at the mouth for too long. As a result, sometimes I was clicked out too long and didn't remember quite a bit of the show or I wondered off into associated thoughts and had no perception of it. All I remember of one such retrieval started out with me flying directly under an Air Force C-130 aircraft. As I watched it flying above me, it took a direct hit and something exploded about midway along the fuselage on its right side. A man fell out of the huge hole in the side and bottom of the aircraft. As I watched him fall past me I got a name, Major David Hasenburg or Hashburger, something like that. Serial number 531065 . . . something, something and he was an electronics specialist. This time it was the Interpreter that ran on too long but the associations it made were interesting.

CLICK: In the 1970s I had been experimenting with automatic writing—being in a sort of meditative state and writing with a pencil on paper—as a means of learning about what came after physical death. I was certain that I was making it all up, but I communicated with a young man named David who claimed to have died in the Vietnam war. He claimed to have been an electronics specialist, and claimed to be responsible for the strange fact that lights started going on and off by themselves in my house. My friends would poke fun at me about having a ghost in the house until after they had been to one of my nighttime parties. "Bruce, I hear there's a ghost in this house and you think you can talk to it and that it talks to you," someone would walk up to me and say, usually laughing.

"Yeah, his name is David. Would you like to meet him?" I would casually ask.

"Sure, of course I would," was the usual, snickering response.

"Okay, I will introduce you to him. David, please turn off the lights," I would say, loud enough so everyone in the room could hear me above the noise of the party.

Others who had already *met* David knew what would happen next. Within one or two seconds every light in the entire house— upstairs, downstairs, and outside—would go out in the same instant. I would stand there, in the dark, in front of the person ribbing me and wait for at least fifteen seconds.

"David, turn the lights back on please," I would say after waiting to let it sink in that we were standing in complete darkness. The look on the person's face was always a treat when the lights came back on. A mixture of shock, disbelief, and awe usually described it.

CLICK: Right after I saw the aircraft explode in flight above me and got the name David, the Interpreter started remembering those party episodes. I don't know if it was the same David or not. I followed the associations and missed the rest of the story my Perceiver was seeing about the David who fell out of the aircraft. I remember the surprised look on the partygoers' faces and the sound of laughter from the rest of my guests who had met David before. But I didn't see or remember any more of the story from the retrieval.

In the next retrieval I found a little boy named Timmy. I had picked up a Guide in Focus 27, as usual, and followed him to this place in Focus 23, materializing on a driveway in a suburban setting. An ordinary ranch-style house stood behind me and I could see a large tree in the neighbor's yard next door. I was facing the street, watching the reenactment of the accident that had killed Timmy. He was on a scooter, one of those two-wheel contraptions you stand on with one foot and push with the other. He was looking back toward the house smiling at someone and didn't see the fast-approaching truck. I turned to see who Timmy was looking at and saw his mother at first waving at him. Then her hand went up to her mouth and her face registered horror just before I heard screeching tires and a thud as the truck hit Timmy. He died moments later to the sound of his mother's voice, shrieking in horror.

It wasn't clear to me why he was stuck here in Focus 23. I walked over to where he was standing and introduced myself. The truck was still there, along with the bent and twisted scooter. His mother was gone. Timmy looked unharmed. An impression from the Guide brought the knowledge that Timmy's father and mother would be waiting for him in Focus 27 when we arrived. I tried to get information that might have some possibility of verification. But I fell off the high wire on the side of the Perceiver and felt lucky Timmy was still standing there when the Interpreter restarted after I'd clicked out. All I remembered of his answers was the number thirty-seven. I don't know if it meant he died in 1937 or thirty-seven was part of his address.

When I asked Timmy if he would like to leave with me to see his mother and father he agreed right away. We didn't really fly from where he was standing in the street. The scene just faded into darkness very briefly and then brightened up again. The scene faded out and back very quickly. I could feel we had shifted from Focus 23 to Focus 27. The scene looked very much the same as before except that Timmy was standing with his scooter the way it looked before they were both mangled by the truck that hit and killed him. The truck was gone too, nowhere in sight. Timmy's mother was standing in the doorway again calling his name and waving to him. He waved back and called, "Mom!" then jumped on his scooter and pushed it up the driveway toward where she was standing. He had arrived in Focus 27 rejoining the scene in the neighborhood with his family as if the accident had never happened. Mom, the Guide, and I exchanged looks of gratitude and a surge of emotion pushed through my body.

"Bruce, let's go back to your place," I felt the Guide say.

I was getting pretty good at maintaining the Balance necessary to Know the story of my perceptions when I found the man pacing in the open field again. I had been in Focus 25, peering into the 3-D blackness, when I felt a subtle sensation of movement toward one of the vague images in it. I entered it and there he was. It was the same guy, but this time the images of him and his surroundings were clearer, brighter, and in full color. The man was wearing the white collar and black clothes of a priest. As I watched this time, I could feel every thought going on in his mind. He felt something he had done during his life had landed him in Purgatory. He had been pacing this field so long he had worn a path in the grass. As he paced back and forth he was trying to figure out what he had done to deserve such a fate. I could tell that was why he was stuck in Focus 25. In his belief system there were rules given by the teachings of his church that could warrant time in Purgatory. It was not Hell, but rather a place where he would be alone with his sins until somehow he was released to Heaven. He had been here for a very long time, trying to remember what it could have been that he had done.

"Excuse me, Father," I blurted out, "but I have come to take you to Heaven." It seemed like a reasonable approach given his circumstances.

"But what did I do to deserve to be sent here in the first place?" he asked.

"I was shown your papers before they sent me," I replied, "but I wasn't told anything about that. All I know is you've done your time here and now they sent me to bring you to Heaven."

"But . . . .but . . . why?" he asked again.

"I don't know why. They didn't tell me. They just sent me here to retrieve you," I said, sticking to my story.

"Who sent you?" he asked.

"Come with me and I will introduce you to them," I said, hoping whoever they were they would actually be waiting for us.

"Very well, what do I do?"

"Just listen to the sound of my voice and have faith, Father," I said, as I placed my hand on his shoulder. As we dematerialized into the blackness I was telling him my name. In a moment or two I could hear the voices of a group of men very close to us. As the scene materialized in front of us, we were standing in a grassy open area not far from a few small stone houses. There were eight or ten men, dressed as priests, standing in a group looking our way and welcoming the priest with me into Heaven. All smiles and happy voices, they called to him, beckoning him with their hands and arms to come closer to where they were standing. He joined their group to the sound of "Welcome home, Father!" spoken to him by each one of them. Then another man dressed in tall hat and white robe with fancy gold embroidery approached the group. He looked like pictures I have seen of Catholic bishops or Popes. He approached the priest I had just brought there and ceremoniously welcomed him into Heaven. Several times the bishop- or Pope-looking guy reassured the priest all his sins had truly been forgiven. He seemed to be in good hands, so I left the priest, went to my place, and waited for Monroe's voice on the tape to say it was time to return to C-1. As I waited there I began to wonder if maybe this priest I had just retrieved was a part of myself. Over the past several years, in past life readings by psychics, I'd been told I had lived many lifetimes as a priest. As I wondered whether or not this priest was one of those past lives the *right* side of my body lit up with a crackling, tingling sensation which I took to mean, *right*.

New Tools of Perception

Interspersed with the retrieval experiences were exercises in which I was introduced to new tools of perception. Learning to use these tools carried my ability to perceive to levels I had previously only dreamed of. Two Guides whose gifts stood out were Shee-un and White Bear. From Shee-un I learned a new method of perceiving the non-physical world which brought dazzling, 3-D, full-color and sound displays. The technique he taught can be used by anyone to improve perception. From White Bear I learned to communicate with animals.

The method of nonphysical perception taught to me by Shee-un involved learning to perceive from a different location within my body. Instead of feeling my perception to be located in my head, I learned to perceive through a specific location in the center of my chest.

During a tape exercise I arrived in Focus 27 and asked for a Guide to assist me in doing a retrieval. The big, fuzzy ball of light that approached me identified itself as Shee-un and said it had something to show me. I became aware of a sense of pressure in the center of my chest, about three inches down from the top of my rib cage. The sensation of pressure built up quickly and then began to feel warm. Shee-un explained that he was showing me a place on my body on which I should focus my attention. As I focused there I had the sensation that my awareness (located in my head) became the shape and size of a golf ball, but soft and fuzzy like a cotton ball. It had a mild, electric buzzing feeling to it, not the least bit uncomfortable. As I focused on the spot in my chest, the *ball* of my awareness moved downward into the spot in my chest.

Following Shee-un's instructions to maintain my awareness in that spot, I placed my intention on doing a retrieval. My perception opened and a small, dark, black swirl formed in the 3-D blackness. I felt myself accelerating toward the swirl and then I entered it. In a moment I felt myself rushing through the 3-D blackness at incredible speed. I broke out of it into the light, cruising along above a clearly visible countryside. I could see a carpet of deep green leaves below me as I flew perhaps a hundred feet above densely packed trees. It was a cloudy day and the trees looked so deep green and real that I felt as though I were watching a 3-D movie. Before I realized what had happened, a small castle or chateau came into view and went by below me. I was traveling so fast I must have gone another mile or so in the next few seconds. It took that long before I realized I had flown over the stone building and decided to turn around and go back to it. I turned in a long, upward sweeping arc in the sky and headed back in the direction from which I had come. Before the castle came into view again I found myself standing in a large bedroom with a huge canopy bed set up against the smooth stone block walls on my right. The walls were hung with oil paintings and tapestries. Tall wooden posts at each corner of the bed held up the silken and lace fabrics of the canopy. Cord sashes were draped from post to post at their tops. It looked like a very, very expensive bed. I could clearly see a woman lying on her back on top of the bed coverings. She appeared to be sleeping in very fine clothes, a long ornately decorated dress, stockings, and shoes. I could see her face through a thin white veil she was wearing. When I saw the position of her hands and arms, lying crossed at the wrists over her chest, I realized she was not sleeping. Actually she was dead.

As I stood there watching her, in full living color, I knew that when she was alive she believed dying was like going into a sleep from which she would never awaken. She had held so firmly to this belief during her life that she was now stuck in Focus 23. Nothing and no one had been able to penetrate that belief to inform her otherwise since she died.

"Just dreams," she had told herself when Helpers had come to try to reach and retrieve her. "Just dreams in my endless sleep."

She had been lying on that bed for hundreds of years, ignoring the approach of everyone who came trying to help her. I had no idea how to approach and awaken her. I had never come across a situation like this before and, as in my first encounter with Benjie, I didn't know what to do. Fortunately for both of us, I didn't have to wait long before help arrived. A door behind me and to my right burst open and slammed loudly against the stone wall. I turned to see what was happening and there was another woman, dressed in the apron and cap of a servant, standing in the open doorway. She was a plump woman with a ruddy face and the manners of a river barge. In the next instant I was suddenly pulled inside the body of this servant woman, waving my arms and raising my voice as I moved toward the woman lying on the bed.

"My lady, my lady!" I shouted with a loud, hurried urgency in my voice. "My lady, you must get up right away or you'll be late!"

At the loud, crashing boom of the door the woman's eyes had snapped open and the urgency in my voice had her stirring slowly on the bed. She wasn't sure what was going on. Still groggy from sleeping, she felt a little disorganized and disoriented. The audacity of a maid disturbing her sleep, yelling at her so loudly, triggered thoughts of having the maid punished for her insolence. As the maid, I kept at her in a raised, irritating voice to focus her attention on me.

"My lady, you must hurry now," I shouted emphatically at her. I reached over and jostled her body lying on the

bed. "My lady . . . you . . . must . . . get . . . out . . . of
. . . that . . . bed . . . this . . . instant or you are going to
be late."

Now she was feeling genuinely angry! She turned her
head and looked at me through rage-filled eyes. She was
still somewhat dazed. She was confused about what it was
she was going to be late for, but she was certain this maid
must be punished for having the audacity to touch and
jostle her so. I kept up my loud ranting, raving, and
hand-waving until she was fully awake, standing on the
floor beside the bed. She was positively furious at me.
Fuming. Then I turned on my heel and headed for the
door I had just come in. Just as I reached for the door to
close it behind me I jumped, or rather was expelled, from
the maid's body. I was left standing in the room as the
maid left. The door slammed with the sound of a cannon
behind her. The woman, still standing near the canopy
bed, was just regaining her composure when another door
opened, this time on my left. This one was opened with
care, much more quietly than when the maid sent her door
crashing into the wall. In the next instant I was catapulted
into the body of the man walking through the opening
doorway into the room.

"My dear. I am happy to see you are ready to leave," I
said, with the voice of an old-school gentleman. "We haven't
a moment to lose if we are to arrive on time."

As she stared at me I knew she recognized the man
whose body I was in. I walked, rather ceremoniously, toward
her and extended my arm. Still confused as to where we
were going in such a hurry, the woman took my arm and
we walked out the doorway and into a hall. The hallway
was on the second floor and open to a high-ceilinged foyer
all along one side. We strode together a short distance
down the open hallway to a huge, curved stone stairway
leading down to the main floor of the foyer. There were
two of these stairways, mirror images of each other, leading
from opposite ends of the same second-floor hallway down
to the main floor. We took the stairway on the right side
of the doorway we had used to exit the bedroom. We

walked slowly down the stairs to the main floor and outside through two huge wooden doors at the base of the stairs. The doors must have been at least twelve feet high and there were two servants, doormen I supposed, standing there as we walked through the doorway. The view outside was spectacular.

A wide stone stairway at least twenty feet across led from the main floor of the castle or chateau to a roadway in about eight or ten steps. I could clearly see a horse-drawn carriage waiting for us at the bottom of the stairs. The driver was seated in front of the carriage, holding the reins of two horses who were standing quietly. The road or driveway was in the shape of a "U." The carriage was parked, waiting at the bottom of the "U" and the legs of the "U" extended off into the distance for a quarter of a mile that I could see. A garden of flowers and shrubs filled the inside of the U-shaped driveway and on the outside of the driveway tall, fully leafed trees lined the roads.

With *my lady* still holding my arm with her right hand, we descended the stairs and approached the carriage. I reached for the handle, opened the door, and assisted her into the back seat. I stepped up inside, closed the door, and sat down beside her on her left. I felt the carriage jerk slightly as the driver coaxed the horses into taking up the load and moving. I could hear the jingling sound of metal chains that were part of the horses' harness and the sound of their hooves meeting the ground. I engaged the woman in conversation, distracting her from the fact that we went only about twenty yards down the road before the scenery changed.

The carriage was now moving over smooth, short-cropped grass that covered a vast open field. We were headed toward a group of people standing on our right, perhaps thirty yards away. They were all dressed up in party clothes that could have been worn by local royalty in the middle 1400s. (I don't know much about such clothes; the period could have been earlier or later.) The men wore white wigs, tight pants, and fine jackets with wide lapels over ruffled white shirts. The women wore dresses that were low-cut, tight at the waist, with puffy sleeves ending just above the elbow. Their dresses spread out so far at the bottom that they must have had hoops in them. As I looked over the crowd in the distance I became alarmed at seeing the man standing nearest our approaching carriage. He looked exactly like the man whose body I was occupying. I was worried the woman sitting next to me would realize there were two of us in this scene and fall back into the only explanation, a dream.

This small detail was taken care of just as she saw him standing there and started turning her head to look at me sitting next to her. Before she had finished turning to look at me sitting there beside her, I disappeared into thin air and jumped forward into the body of the carriage driver. A bit confused, she looked for several moments at the empty seat next to her. From my vantage point in the driver's seat I heard the man call to her as he reached to open the carriage door.

"My dear, it's so wonderful to see you here. Let me help you step down out of the coach and you can join our party," he said as he opened the door. Several others called out to her and waved, inviting her to join them. Several of these others were people she recognized. I sat quietly, looking straight ahead, holding the reins, until she was out of the carriage and walking away with the group toward the party. Then I drove the carriage out of sight over a small hill and moved out of the body of the driver. The scene faded to blackness and I felt myself moving through it, heading back to my place in Focus 27. When I arrived Shee-un was there waiting for me.

"Bruce, you must practice the movement of your awareness from your head to the spot I have shown you in the center of your chest until you are called back to C-1 by Bob's voice. Feel it as it moves down to that spot and then let it move back up into your head. Repeat this as many times as you can before you must go back. It is most important to feel it as it moves from one location to another. Remember this technique I have shown you. Use it as often as you can as a means of perception in your exploration. It is a useful tool of perception in any reality."

I followed Shee-un's instructions and practiced feeling the movement of my awareness from one location to the other and then back again. It seemed like a rather odd thing to be doing, but the results of using this method the first time were rather spectacular. Hard to argue with such amazing results. I continued to practice this method off and on during the remainder of the Lifeline program. I was experimenting with and practicing so many different things I couldn't always remember to do them all each time I entered a tape exercise. But focusing on the Shee-un spot, as I later called it, is a method I still use today, three and a half years later. It is very effective.

Whereas Shee-un taught me to perceive in a new way in the nonphysical world, from White Bear I learned new perception and communication abilities for use in the physical world.

I had gone to Focus 27 in the usual way and as the fuzzy ball of light approached I saw a brief flash image of the Native American at sunrise again. After the Guide stopped at my left side, I asked if he had a name I could call him.

"White Bear," was his reply.

In our ensuing conversation, White Bear explained that I could call on his abilities at any time by saying his name in my mind and inviting him to come. He explained that the perception techniques he would teach me could be used anywhere, including the physical world. He gave examples such as walking through a forest at night. If I wanted to know what was around me, or along the path I was walking, I could call him. My perception would be changed in a way that would allow me to feel the presence of any living thing near by.

White Bear suggested that after this tape exercise I take a walk outside and call him. He talked about being able to join into the world of the animals in a way that they would not fear my presence. I could learn to communicate with them through his presence and need not fear any animals who might cross my path. Such communication, he explained, would be done by opening my perception and—without using words—expressing what I wanted to say. He explained that the perceptual method I could learn through his assistance would put me at the same level of consciousness as the animals. Being at their level of consciousness, I could communicate with them but he could not explain how, as I hadn't yet learned to communicate without words. Unfortunately, he explained, he couldn't teach me to communicate without words by using words. I said his explanation sounded pretty convoluted to me, to which he replied, "Such is the way of communication with words."

This was quite beyond my comprehension, a point to which he readily agreed. I didn't understand why White Bear had come or what role his knowledge would play in my exploration. Several years later I would be reintroduced to White Bear at my place in Focus 27. Another seed planted for later sprouting.

After group debriefing, I decided to follow White Bear's suggestion. As I stepped through the exit door into the warm afternoon, I said his name in my mind and invited him to come. I felt a calmness come over me, like a cool fog filling my body, then I heard White Bear's startled voice. I felt him say, as I stepped outside through the doorway, "What's that sound?"

"An air conditioning unit. See those white boxes on the ground over there? The sound is coming from them."

"What are they for?"

"They make cold air to cool the inside of this building we are leaving. Nothing to worry about."

"I see," he said.

As I closed the door behind me and started walking toward a small stand of evergreen trees not far away, I noticed something very odd. The gait of my walk was different. It had a smooth, flowing glide to it. I was paying close attention to this different way I was walking as we approached the trees. This walk was so smooth and silent that it was hard to believe my feet were touching the ground. They landed on the ground in a way that produced almost no sound.

I heard the chirping of small birds in one of the trees and walked over to get a closer look. Three or four sparrows, near eye level, were flitting here and there in the branches of the tree. It was as if the birds didn't see me as I walked slowly closer until they were chirping less then two feet from my face. I stood there looking at the birds so close to me that I could have reached out and touched them. Over and over in my mind I kept saying, *This can't be happening. They should have been frightened away as I walked toward them. How can it be that they're acting as if I am not standing here?* I was sure they must be able to see me since occasionally one would hop close to my face and look right at me. I stood and watched for several minutes. None of the birds became frightened and flew away. Then I walked backwards in the same smooth, flowing glide, away from the tree and the birds. When I left they were still chirping and hopping from place to place in the branches. I just couldn't fathom how such a thing could happen. *Was I invisible to them? Had the change in my perception moved me into a level of consciousness in which they could not perceive me? Or was I one of them, at their level of consciousness?* Those were the only things that seemed logical to me, but logical doesn't mean I thought it was possible!

I continued to walk along at the edge of a small forest, then up a low hill and across an open field. I experimented with White Bear leaving and coming back and marveled at the change in my gait. Each time I called his name and invited him again, the same calm stillness would fill me and my walk would change to that smooth, silent glide. After a while I headed back to the training facility. It was getting toward dinner time and I was feeling hungry. I entered the building, walked into one of the restrooms, and closed the door.

"What are we going to do in here?" I felt White Bear ask.

"Watch and you'll see," I replied.

He had evidently not seen or used a toilet before. As I lifted the lid he had no idea what it was for.

"That's quite a contraption," he said with surprise, as I stood there watching the last of the flushing water disappear.

After washing my hands (the source of water was a little puzzling to White Bear too) I left the restroom and walked in his smooth, silent glide to the dining room. Over half the participants were already seated as I joined the line to fill my dinner plate.

"What are we going to do now?" White Bear asked.

"I am going to eat."

"Eat? Eat what?" I could feel his genuine surprise at my reply.

I had the distinct feeling there wasn't anything nearby White Bear recognized as food. Even after I had filled my plate with fettuccine Alfredo it didn't register as food until he realized there were mushrooms in it. He hadn't recognized them at first because they were sliced so thin.

Later that evening, after dark, I decided to take a short walk to experiment with the perception White Bear was teaching me. While walking across an open field I said White Bear's name in my mind and invited him to come. Like a cool, dense fog I felt his presence flow into my awareness and my walk abruptly changed to his. As I continued to walk I could feel my awareness expanding outward beyond my body. It felt like a circular bubble expanding out over the countryside. It felt like everything within that bubble was within my awareness. I could feel deer behind me perhaps eighty yards away. I turned around to walk that direction to investigate. Instead of walking directly to where they were standing, I diverted my path and walked in White Bear's smooth, flowing glide onto the deck on the south side of the training facility. I walked far enough along the deck to be away from the lights coming out through the windows. I stopped and looked over to where I felt the deer to be. There, standing about twenty yards away, at the edge of the grass, just in the trees, was a young fawn. She had been curious about the lights, sounds, and smells coming from the building and had come to see what it was. As I watched her I knew there was another deer standing a little further into the trees. I couldn't see her but I could feel the doe standing there, a little to the left of the fawn and back out of the light. She was staring at me, unafraid for her fawn, picturing the spot in her mind where they would bed down for the night. I stood there watching the fawn and feeling the presence and thoughts of the doe for four or five minutes. Then I went inside to eat popcorn and snacks and gab with the participants. I continued to experiment with the presence of White Bear off and on during the rest of the program and for the remaining week of my stay in Virginia. After I returned home to Colorado I couldn't talk about White Bear to my family. In their eyes it would have smacked of some sort of sinister, demonic possession. Gradually I forgot about White Bear. I didn't remember him until he came back several years later.

Retrieving the Colonel

On the last full day of the program, during the last tape exercise retrieval, Shee-un met me at my place in Focus 27. I had been experimenting with perceiving through the Shee-un spot in the center of my chest since the first time he had shown me how.

"We've saved the best for last," Shee-un said with a beaming brightness. "This one will be on your own. You don't need my help much right now. Just open your perception in the way you've been practicing and head to Focus 23 on your own. I will be nearby if you should need me but I don't want to interfere. We want you to know you are capable of doing this on your own now. You've learned well. Enjoy!"

I focused my attention on the ball of awareness I could feel up in my head. I allowed it to move downward, feeling it pass through my body first along my neck, then down my spine. It came to rest in the center of my chest at the Shee-un spot. A slight sense of pressure and warmth built up as my perception opened into the 3-D amorphous blackness. As I peered into the depth of that blackness a vast array of fluffy, white clouds materialized. I was moving toward these clouds from quite a distance away and could see them in clear, brilliant detail. I could see hundreds of them against the backdrop of a black, starless night sky. They were arranged in a grid-work pattern in a single layer that stretched off in every direction as far as I could see. The clouds, all about the same size and shape, were separated from each other by empty, black space of about three or four cloud diameters. With nothing else in view I couldn't tell if they were as large as the moon or as small as the fluffy, white cotton balls they looked like. I seemed to be heading for one cloud in particular and as it got closer I stopped looking around at the overall scene and focused my attention on the one cloud straight ahead. After I penetrated its outer fringes and continued deeper into the cloud, a full-color, 3-D scene began to materialize in its haze. I was in a desert, flying just a few feet above the ground.

Not a cloud in the sky. The sun, burning brightly overhead, lit up this desert. I could feel the heat and dryness in the air. The rolling expanse of sand dunes extended to the horizon with no signs of life. Not a tree or shrub or blade of grass was in sight. Just miles and miles of hot desert sand in low hills and dunes sculptured by the wind. The air was completely still and stiflingly hot as I continued to fly along less than five feet above the sand. I gradually overtook a tank racing along at full speed across the desert.

I matched the tank's speed, keeping pace with it, as I flew along on its right side. Then I moved to within fifteen feet so I could carefully look it over. It was World War II vintage, painted a tan color not much different than that of the sand over which it continued to race at full speed. The tank seemed a little small in size and its single gun was in a level position, pointed straight forward. I didn't see any markings or insignia to indicate which of the World War II combatants this tank belonged to. It must have traveled a quarter of a mile across the desert before I began to extend my perception inside the tank. I was trying to determine who might be in it. I didn't see inside the tank. It was more as though I felt around inside it with my perception, feeling around for any occupants. There was only one person inside. My first impression of him was *the*

Colonel. I felt an immediate sense of recognition and emotional connection in my gut to the Colonel. Some part of me knew who he was, but that part wasn't talking to me.

I extended my perception to determine who the Colonel was, why he was there, and what he was doing. As I did I received a *package* of information about him that came into my awareness all at once. Monroe called these packages thought balls or Rote. The information didn't come in a serial, sequential fashion like a series of words that formed a sentence. It was more like all the information was printed on a large movie screen in my mind all at once. I could look at any portion of it at any time and remain aware of all of the rest of it at the same time. Some of this information was in words, some in still photographs, some in feelings and some in little movies. It was all available for viewing as a whole. The story it told was this:

The Colonel was unaware that he was dead. I watched a scene, before he died, in which his tank had been moving at slow speed along what passed for a road through the desert. Without warning a projectile struck the left side and exploded with such ferocity the tank had been partially lifted up off the ground. It rolled over on its right side. It ended up almost completely upside down, resting on its right side and a portion of the gun turret. Every one of the crew members, including the Colonel, had been killed instantly. He had died so suddenly and so unexpectedly that his intent to keep his tank moving had created a thought form of the tank. His thought form of the tank was moving through his thought form of the desert. The other crew members had all been retrieved before I arrived. Perhaps the Colonel's rank and sense of duty to mission and country had not let his awareness be diverted from the thought form environment of his own making. He was trapped, stuck in Focus 23, in a dream of his own making and would not be diverted from his duty.

He was racing across the desert, trying to find and rejoin his unit. Some part of me was emotionally joined in his effort and hoped desperately he would find them. He had been racing across the desert for a very long time. Over forty years of our earth time had passed since he had been killed. He had no sense of how long he had actually been searching for his unit. It seemed like hours to him. He was perplexed as to why he hadn't yet found the rest of his unit or been spotted by the enemy and attacked. He could not understand how he could have crossed so many miles of desert without seeing another living thing.

At times he thought he might be unknowingly driving around in a large circle. That at least could explain why he never seemed to get anywhere. Alert to that possibility, he had been looking for the tracks of his own tank in the sand but had not seen any tracks at all. Not knowing what else to do, he continued driving at high speed across the desert sand, hoping to find his own unit as soon as possible. He was afraid that the enemy might find him first. He knew that his single tank, with only him as the crew, wouldn't be able to fight off an attack.

That was something else that puzzled him greatly. He was the only man in the tank. He seemed to remember that there had been more in the crew but somehow they were gone. He spent considerable time rationalizing why he was alone while he scanned the horizon for his unit. I felt that I had enough to go on to open a conversation with him. I felt a strong emotional desire to successfully retrieve the Colonel from his Focus 23 situation. I began my conversation as a voice within his thoughts that he at first took to be a conversation with himself.

"Well, I've been in tough spots before. It's going to work out okay. I'll pull through," I thought into his awareness using the sound of his own voice.

"Yeah, I'm gonna make it," he said back to himself. "I'll find my unit. They've got to be around here somewhere. Maybe just over that next hill up ahead."

"Seems like I've been driving for such a long time I should have come across at least tracks in the sand," I said, inside his mind.

"Yeah, if I find some tracks at least I could follow them and maybe see somebody. Even an enemy unit would be somebody," he replied, still thinking he was talking to himself.

"Maybe the war is over and everybody left to go home," I said, still using the sound of his voice to talk to him.

"Yeah, wouldn't that be something? The war is over and I am lost out here in the desert trying to find my unit, and they've all gone home," he said back to himself, laughing.

"Colonel, that's exactly what has happened. The war is over," I said, switching to my own voice and using a firm tone.

"What? . . . Who said that?" he asked. He was so startled at hearing a different voice in his own mind that he snapped his head around, looking to see where else it could be coming from.

"I said it! I am a friend. I have come to tell you, Colonel, for you the war has been over for a very long time," I replied, still in my own voice, direct but very calmly.

"Where are you and what are you doing here?" he asked, still looking around inside the tank.

"I'm right outside the tank. I've been sent to return you to your unit. If you would like I can take you to where they are right now." I could feel some confusion building up in his thinking.

"How is it possible that I can hear you if you are outside the tank?" he asked.

"I have got some news for you, Colonel. It might come as a bit of a shock, but I assure you it's good news," I said, trying to break it to him as gently as I could.

"What's going on here? Shocked about what?" he asked, a sense of fright and bravado in his voice.

"The truth is, you are not physically alive right now," I said straightforwardly.

"Not physically alive? You mean . . . I am dead?" he asked incredulously.

"Yes, Colonel, that's right and I have come to bring back you to your unit."

As the shock of the realization that he was dead sank in it stunned him. I took that opportunity to reach in and put my hand on his right shoulder.

"Close your eyes so you can concentrate and listen carefully to the sound of my voice. Focus all of your attention on the sound of my voice," I said, in the most soothing, hypnotic voice I have.

I could feel his awareness narrowing as he closed his eyes and focused all of his attention on the sound of my voice. I continued talking in unending, run-on sentences as I began to dissolve the images of the tank, the sand, and the desert around us into blackness.

"Very soon we are going to be rejoining your unit. They are waiting for you," I said, my hand still on his shoulder. I felt a surge of love and respect for the Colonel move through me.

A scene right out of old war movies of Army buddies reuniting began to materialize in the blackness around us. His crew, the ones who had died in the tank with him, stood crowded together six feet in front of us. They were dressed in military uniforms, looking at us as we materialized in front of them. When the new scene took on solid enough form his crew began cheering and calling out to him to get the Colonel's attention.

"He's back, guys. Look! It's the Colonel—he made it back!" one voice shouted.

"Colonel, boy am I glad to see you, sir!" came from another.

I felt the Colonel's recognition of the men's voices rise up in his awareness. I could see the images of each of them forming in his mind as he heard their voices. He was seeing each of their faces and remembering their names, standing there with his eyes still closed. After he recognized all their voices and remembered all their names, he opened his eyes. They were all smiling, waving and cheering as they moved toward and surrounded him. Pats on the back, handshakes, and "Great to see you again, Colonel!" came at him from all directions as his men welcomed the Colonel to his new home. Smiling and happy, he greeted each of his men by name in a genuine show of affection. His stunned shock at the realization that he was dead faded away quickly in this reunion.

After he had opened his eyes and his men had begun moving toward him, I had lifted my hand up off his shoulder and stepped backwards, moving away to give them more room. I watched for few moments longer, taking in the joy and relief of all concerned. They started to walk away as a group, laughing and telling stories about experiences they had been through together during the war. I knew the Colonel was indeed feeling that he had rejoined his unit. I knew in their hands he would do just fine. A surge of emotion moved up to my throat without me knowing why. Then I de-materialized, leaving the scene, and re-materialized, sitting in one of the hanging chairs at my place in Focus 27. Shee-un was waiting there for me. Other members of my group had gathered around also. I still couldn't see their faces and had no clue as to their identity.

"You did very well with the Colonel on your own, Bruce. We all knew you could handle it alone and now you know that too," Shee-un said.

"Thanks. That was a pretty spectacular view. It all looked, sounded, and felt so real," I responded.

"We're pleased you picked up on the reason the Colonel was stuck. You correctly deduced it was all a thought form of his own making. Helpers from Focus 27 had tried many times to get through to him but his sense of duty held his attention firmly within his own thought form," said someone else who was sitting at the table.

"Shee-un, is the Colonel an aspect of myself who was stuck?"

"No, he is not a part of yourself. It was a commitment."

"A commitment? What kind of commitment?"

The look on Shee-un's face told me that was as much of a clue as I was going to get. I thought about a couple of possibilities, people to whom I might have made such a commitment. All I could figure out was that somewhere in the distant past I must have known the Colonel. I must have promised the Colonel or someone else to find him and free him if he was ever stuck in Focus 23. My Interpreter kept feeding images into my awareness, groping around in my memory for something, anything associated with the

Colonel. There were so many images flopping around in me at once that all I seemed to do was get further and further away from any answer. Then Monroe's voice came in on the tape reminding us to leave the emotional energy there and return to C-1. I left that last tape exercise of the program still not knowing who the Colonel is or the nature of my commitment to him. As I write this, it is over three and a half years later. I still don't know the answers to those questions. But I know how this process works, and someday, somehow, I will remember and a whole new episode of learning will begin.

In those days Bob Monroe was still living among us and he would often come down to the training center Friday morning to share in the last breakfast participants ate together. This time he arrived late, after everyone else was seated. Some were nearly finished eating. He carried his plate to an empty table across from where I was just finishing up and sat down by himself. After a minute or so a trainer sitting at my table suggested I move over and talk with Bob so others might feel more comfortable joining him also. In the two or three minutes he and I sat there alone talking, he posed a odd question. As he sat there he pointed at a light fixture on the wall, across the room from us.

"Bruce, why is it that someone hasn't come up with a way that I can mentally draw a circle of light around that light fixture and turn it on or off?" he asked.

I turned my head, following the line of his index finger, to see what he was pointing at. It was one of those cheap brass-plated fixtures with a small, cone-shaped, frosted glass shade. As I looked at it a vision of two narrow ribbons, like the old paper ticker tape, emerged from the fixture. They remained side by side, parallel and close together, as they continuously came out of the fixture and moved in an undulating motion through the air and across the room. Just like ticker tape, they had small, black marks printed in a single line along each of them. I could see as the tape went by me that in some areas along its length these marks on each tape were side by side. In other areas of the tapes one might have a mark and the other didn't. Sometimes there were side by side marks consecutively on both tapes followed by long stretches where only one had a mark and not the other. I continued to watch this apparition of ticker tape ribbons, continuously emerging from the light fixture and undulating through the air for at least fifteen seconds. As strange as it might sound, I intuitively knew what I was seeing held the answer to how to accomplish what Bob had asked.

"You mean, you wonder why you can't turn a physical world light fixture on or off just by thinking about doing it?" I asked, turning back to look at him.

"Yes, why hasn't somebody figured out how to do that?" he asked in all seriousness.

"I don't know exactly how to do it, Bob, but somehow I know after seeing what I just saw that it's possible," was my reply.

Others joined us at the table and struck up conversations with Bob. I sat there puzzled about what I had just *seen* and what it meant. It felt so strange sitting there contemplating the meaning of such an outlandish experience and at the same time accepting that it had actually happened. Later I took my hand-held cassette recorder with me and went for a walk outside. I was still pondering the question Bob had asked. I was wondering what the *vision* of the ticker tapes had to say about the answer. As I started walking I opened my awareness with the intent of connecting with that answer.

For the next fifteen minutes or so I spoke off and on into my recorder, making notes, as I pondered the question and thoughts came floating into my mind. Condensing the bits and pieces of my verbal notes down into something coherent, here is what I found:

The thing in the physical world most easily affected by human thought is pure randomness. The more purely or perfectly random any given event in the physical world is the more easily it can be influenced by human thought. The physical world forces which cause an event to be most purely random require an extremely delicate balance of all the forces involved. The least perturbation of these forces will shift the purely random event toward a less random event. Any physical world event which is purely and perfectly random can be used to demonstrate this effect. Experimentation will show that, for such events, human thought has sufficient force to disturb the extremely delicate balance of forces required to cause an event which is purely random. To build a prototype device which will demonstrate the soundness and feasibility of this information is a relatively simple matter. All that is required are random events for which shifts in relative randomness can be detected and correlated with attempts to influence them using human thought.

You would think that as an engineer I would have thought this was all a lot of nonsense. On the contrary, it made perfect sense to me and I decided to build such a device to experiment with the theory. I wrote up a patent disclosure for the idea, a process I had done many times previously as part of my work in Research and Development. My description contained all the elements above along with a proposed embodiment of the device.

I left the Monroe Institute a week later, driving my parents' borrowed minivan camper back to Minneapolis. As I drove, I thought about all that had happened before, during, and after the program. I had taken this month off hoping to cure a case of burnout with my job. Driving back I felt refreshed, renewed, and excited about spending some spare time perfecting a thought switch device most people would say was impossible. Somewhere inside me I knew it was completely reasonable and could be built from components I could probably buy at the Radio Shack store half a mile from my home in Colorado.

I arrived at my sister's house in Minneapolis two days later in the mid-afternoon, tired after driving straight through from Virginia. She has had some unusual, unexplainable things happen in her life and is pretty open to talking about these strange things that I do. We talked about Lifeline, retrievals, and such until I started to run out of gas to the point I needed to lie down for a nap.

"As long as you've just finished this course where you learned to deal with ghosts, why don't you nap in the bedroom upstairs no one will sleep in?" my sister suggested with a laugh.

"Why, what's wrong with the room?"

"All of my kids have had that room as their bedroom and they say there's a scary lady in there," she replied. "They refuse to sleep in there, they're so frightened of seeing her. They're so scared they would rather sleep outside the room on the floor. They call her the *scary lady*."

"Okay, if I see any scary old ladies I'll send them on their way," I laughed back, and I headed upstairs to take a nap.

The kids were right! No sooner did I lie down and close my eyes to go to sleep then the image of a wrinkled old woman appeared above me. It looked like she wasn't wearing her teeth, if she had any to wear. She was looking down, making disgusting faces, and reaching toward my face with long wrinkled fingers. She was doing her best to scare the holy whatever out of me. With my eyes still closed I looked up, directly into her face, and smiled.

"Hi, may name is Bruce. What's yours?" I said to her, in a light, singsong voice in my thoughts.

She yanked her hands up to her face, let out a screech, then turned and ran into the closet next to the head of the bed. She ran through the back closet wall and into a bathroom two rooms away. I guess what I said must have really startled her. I remained awake, waiting for her to come out of the closet again. I didn't have to wait long. In a minute or so she came out of the closet doorway. She tried the same grotesque facial expressions and waved her hands at my face.

"You know, it's really not very nice to be scaring little kids like that," I said to her, looking directly into her eyes. She let out a scream and hot-footed it into the closet, through the wall and back into the bathroom again. I waited for her to come back. When she did she walked out very slowly with her arms hanging limp at her sides. She looked down at me again, but this time she wasn't making hideous faces. She was curious more than anything else.

"I am not going to hurt you. Don't be afraid," I said, and as she ran away again I finished with, "I am here to help you if you'll let me."

She came back more quickly this time and stood over the bed, looking down at me. I asked her why she was here, and without her saying a word I understood. She had lived and died in this house a long time ago. She didn't realize she had died and kept trying to scare away all these strangers who kept coming into her house. She couldn't understand why they were in her house, but it was her house and they didn't belong.

"What's your friend's name? You know the one. She used to come over for coffee all the time and to visit. What was her name again?" I asked, thinking maybe I would get a little help from someone she knew when she was alive. She didn't say a word. She just stood there looking down at me with a blank, befuddled look on her face. Then I felt someone else standing in the closet doorway. It was a woman about the same age as the scary old lady. The scary old lady felt her standing there too, and she turned to see who it was. A smile came over her face and the other woman reached out and took the scary lady's hand. Then the image of both of them faded out and I drifted off to sleep.

Since that day no one at my sister's house has seen the scary old lady again, but no one likes to sleep in that room. None of them wants to take the chance of seeing her again. She was a very scary old lady.

The next day I boarded my flight back to Denver and flew home to an uncertain future. I knew my job would be the same frustrating ordeal and my relationship with my wife was suffering. Besides my interest in what she felt was a cult, we had other problems. Our relationship was deteriorating and our marriage was heading for divorce. We were staying together, trying to maintain a two-parent family for our kids, but we both knew it was a losing battle. I was feeling repelled by my job and incredibly drawn to Virginia. There was so much there for me. I felt that it was only a matter of time until I would go.

VI. Further Journeys

After I returned home, life in general took over, muting my desire for verification with the distraction of other things. I couldn't shake the nagging feeling that I was just making it all up.

But before I left Virginia something had happened that would open the path to verification of my experience in the nonphysical New World. I had the great fortune to have dinner with Rebecca, a trainer I had met during both Lifeline programs. We gabbed about experience and how I might somehow satisfy my hunger for verification. Rebecca offered to help by working with me after I returned home.

We would start trying to meet nonphysically, in Focus 27, at a place called *the flowers*, and then later compare notes about what we had experienced. I was to use my imagination to picture Rebecca, then picture the flowers and then picture myself going to the flowers. After that I was to use something called the eye switch method as a signal to myself that I was ready to proceed with the exercise. Then I was to *let go* of my intent and be open. These instructions sounded a little vague but I decided I would figure it out as I went along.

The Flowers, Rebecca, and Coach

After I got back home to Colorado, I began practicing the procedure Rebecca had suggested. I didn't really know what the place called the flowers looked like, so in my procedure I just pictured a bunch of flowers growing in a garden. On my first attempt I relaxed and shifted my awareness to Focus 27. I felt a strong pulling sensation on the top of my head and thought I should try to go with it. Lying there on the living room sofa, I focused on feeling that pull, but that was all that happened. During some attempts I would find myself in a version of the flying fuzzy zone where the surrounding environment was much lighter than I had seen it before. At other times I experienced entering a completely darkened room. When that happened I would mentally call out Rebecca's name but I didn't hear any answers. When I would phone Rebecca to tell her my experience, she often claimed she had seen me but couldn't get my attention.

During one attempt someone suggested I use the Shee-un spot technique, shift my awareness there and then begin the procedure. I didn't find Rebecca during that attempt but I was getting closer. I woke up the next morning feeling I had found the flowers in a dream. There had been a woman with red lips, dressed in white, standing in a garden of bright flowers in the dream. There had been a group of people standing next to the flowers and in the dream I had gone over to talk to them.

When I called Rebecca on the phone later that day to report on my progress, she said she had seen me in Focus 27 but I walked right past without seeing her. She said she saw me walk over to a group of people nearby and talk with them for a while. She reminded me again of the four steps to contacting Guidance: get comfortable and relax; ask a question once then let go of it; expect an answer; and open to receive it, opening like a flower. I continued to ask for assistance from Guidance in finding Rebecca at the flowers.

Then during one of my attempts I found some flowers! They were not what I had been expecting to see. They looked like a carpet of flowers which completely covered a very large area. Their colors were not only in the flowers but also in the air surrounding their petals. They were light and bright and shorter than I had expected. I had tried something different this time. I'd pictured the flowers first and then Rebecca. I pictured each once, expected to see them, let go, and opened to receive. I had felt a slight pull on the top of my head and had gone with it. Then there they were! I was standing on the ground looking at the carpet of flowers.

Immediately I thought of Rebecca and thought she should be nearby. A strong, tingling sensation surged through my right side just like the one I'd experienced during Lifeline when I was close to someone I was supposed to retrieve. I tried to find Rebecca by feeling for her in my nearby vicinity. Then I thought to ask Guidance how I should try to attempt to communicate with her. I got that the tingling was connected to communication somehow and that I should sort of focus my attention on it. I did that and felt several strong, tingling surges move through my body but I wasn't able to find and talk to Rebecca before I fell asleep.

I called and spoke briefly with Rebecca and she said the flowers I described were the same ones she was waiting at for me. It wasn't verification yet but at least I had found and seen the same flowers that she was seeing. I felt excited at having found them and that I was getting closer to verifiable experience.

Three nights later I tried again to find Rebecca at the flowers. I used the same new order of picturing, putting the imagined images of the flowers before Rebecca instead of after. I didn't see the same flower image, but while I was looking for them two other images did come into view. The first was of a hooded figure, the second was of Rebecca.

In the first image I encountered a woman wearing a long black, hooded cloak. In the 3-D blackness I couldn't see her face; the hood came too far forward and covered it. The cloak covered her entire body and was long enough that it reached the ground all around her. As I looked at this cloaked figure I remembered having seen her before but couldn't remember exactly where or under what circumstances. She was not the least bit threatening, just there standing in front of me.

The second image or series of images were of Rebecca. It was just a brief glimpse of her, really. I felt that I was walking around in a huge, crowded restaurant trying to find the table where a friend was seated. Looking across the length of the restaurant, over the crowd, I caught a glimpse of Rebecca! I saw her for only a moment with her arms raised above her head waving her hands. Her actions fit into the feel of the restaurant scene. She appeared to be standing near a table waving to get my attention. I knew I was supposed to walk over to join her but before I could the scene faded into blackness again and I couldn't see her any more. I'd seen her for only a second or two and then she was gone, but she had been there!

When I phoned Rebecca the next day to check on what she remembered about this attempt to find her, she told me she had seen me. She had been at the flowers and had seen me there looking around. She had raised her arms and waved as I had described. She knew I had seen her but realized I'd lost her when I resumed looking around for her. I felt I was getting close to the time when I would find her at the flowers. I was a little frustrated at coming so close and then losing her again but was encouraged to have seen her at all. My next attempt to find Rebecca at the flowers opened an entirely new chapter in my exploration and in my life.

About a week later I decided to look for Rebecca again at the flowers. She had been training a Lifeline program in Virginia and, since it would not be easy to reach her by phone to compare notes, I'd waited. Now that she was back at home I thought I'd go looking again. After looking for her at the flowers and finding neither, I decided to ask questions and wait for answers, thinking perhaps I could learn something that would make my efforts more success-ful. After I had asked a few and received answers, I asked a question I had asked several times before. It's an open-ended kind of question intended to allow the answering party to select the content of the answer.

"What is the most important thing for me to be knowing right now?" I questioned. In response, I felt a surge of tingling along the right side of my body.

"I'm receiving. I feel a tingling surge on the right side of my body. I'm in contact but I do not understand the meaning of this tingling surge. Who is this contacting me?"

In response, I received an impression of the Disk from my vision some eighteen years earlier. I had communicated with my group, my cluster, my I/There from the disk a little over a year and a half before during my Gateway Voyage program.

"What information do you have for me?" I asked, excited to have made contact with them again. In a clear chorus of many voices, I heard the same message I'd heard in the pink sound of the tape during Gateway Voyage.

"We love you . . . we love you," called out in my mind from I/There, like the chant of a mantra.

"I love you," I chanted back, feeling a charge of emotion surge throughout my body.

I thanked I/There for this message and asked what else, if anything, they had for me by way of answering my question. I seemed to lose contact for a little while; perhaps I fell asleep briefly. Then as I woke up a stronger impression of I/There began to form.

"Who of my I/There is communicating with me?" I asked, in more of a visual, impression way then with words thought in my mind. I began to receive strong, clear visual impressions. The Disk came into view, looking as it did during the original vision on that long ago spring day in Minnesota. I felt surprised and excited at the clarity of the visual image I was seeing. Its blackness blotted out stars in the background. The concentric rings of yellow dots were clearly visible. I could see it all. Being some distance away at first, I began moving closer to the Disk at a leisurely pace. As I moved closer I could see fewer and fewer of the yellow dots. I knew each had a picture on it. I remembered each of these pictures represented a single, fully developed personality of mine in the I/There I know myself to be. Moving closer yet, I began to see I was heading steadily toward one of the yellow dots which were beginning to look more like small, yellow circles. Closer yet and I could see the image of a face on the yellow circle I was approaching. Closer still and I could see it was the face of a man.

He looked to be in his fifties. His wide, bulldog face looked scrunched up and wrinkled. Prominent, round cheeks and a thick heavy brow made his eyes look more like slits than eyes. His hair was cut in a short flat-top like you sometimes see on old men who have served in the Marines. The blackened, squared-off end of a fat cigar stub protruded no more than half an inch through his lips. From the set of his jaw, I could see he held the cigar clenched tightly in his teeth. Probably chewed it more than smoked it. If it weren't for that cigar, his face would look entirely at home on the sidelines of any college football team, barking out instructions to players on the field. But that stubby cigar, held tightly in his teeth, spoke volumes about a lifetime spent in a gym, at ringside, coaching boxers.

Coach—that's who he is, I thought to myself. *The Coach.*

"That name will do nicely," he said, as his image moved out of flat yellow circle toward me. His face took on a three-dimensional, holographic form that came into view more sharply as the image of the rest of the Disk faded into the background.

Looking at his face, without his saying a word, I began to gain understanding of Coach's role in the relationship between me and the rest of myself on the Disk, I/There. As a member of I/There, whose most recent lifetimes and overall character were closely aligned with coaching, he would act as liaison and Guide. My limited understanding of myself as an I/There made it difficult for me to conceptualize communication with so many different aspects of myself. Coach would serve as funnel for such communication, providing a single *individual* upon which I could focus my attention. I knew that, in the future, by placing my intent on the Disk image and Coach's face, I'd be in contact and communication with all of them. The electrical surge feeling I experienced in my body before would, I knew, be an indication Coach was nearby and available for communication.

The next morning I remembered a dream in which I had been in a telephone conversation with a voice that sounded exactly like Bob Monroe. I didn't remember much of the content of the conversation but I remembered the voice had identified itself as my great-grandfather. He seemed to want to disguise himself by identifying himself as such but I knew it was Monroe and he knew I knew.

The following evening I attempted to contact Coach but was too tired and kept drifting off to sleep. I remember drifting around in the 3-D blackness trying to focus on seeing him again. Then, just as I dropped off to sleep, I heard him very clearly.

"Bruce!" I heard him say, not in my thoughts but in a loud, sharp voice that snapped me back awake. From the tone of his voice I knew he was trying to get my attention. I tried to enter into a conversation with him but was so tired I kept drifting off. Later the next day it occurred to me that Coach's intent was probably that I drift off to sleep physically and remain mentally awake and alert at the same time. It seemed he was using the same technique on me, when he called my name, that I used during retrievals. I better understood the awakening, shocking quality of someone unexpectedly calling your name in such a loud, sharp voice. I decided to try to remain calm should this happen again. By remaining calm I hoped to awaken into an alternate reality in which Coach and I could see and converse with each other directly. That never worked out. Hearing my name called out in that way always snapped me awake in the physical world. Two nights later I was again ready to try to find Rebecca at the flowers and connected with Coach to ask for his assistance.

I imagined going to the Disk and meeting with Coach. I pretended the first part of my conversation with him. Moments later I felt a strong tingling surge move through me and I took it to mean he was near.

"I know you and Rebecca have been thinking about working on a remote sensing project," he said. "I encourage you to go ahead with it."

"You mean where she puts objects into numbered envelopes and I try to sense what's inside them?"

"Yes. It will be good practice and will give a slow, verifiable technique by which you can accept that your awareness can sense things remotely. Some of your beliefs about such things need direct experience in order to change."

"Okay, when I talk to Rebecca next time I'll suggest we

go ahead with that project. Speaking of Rebecca, I'd like to ask you to accompany me to the flowers tonight to assist me in connecting with her there. You up for that?"

"Sure," Coach replied. "It will be good practice for the same reasons as the remote sensing project. Lead the way."

I pictured the flowers in my mind and then I pictured Rebecca. I placed my intent on meeting her there and then let go, being open to receive. A few moments later I felt I was standing on the ground and the image of the flowers began to materialize into view. As the image gained strength, there she was! Rebecca was standing right in front of me, smiling. As I looked at her, an exhilarating feeling of love and gratitude built up in me. I felt overjoyed to have finally found her. In our exuberance, one or both of us shouted out, "Let's play!" and we shot up off the ground like rockets.

We flew straight up in intertwining spirals and arced back down toward the ground. Level flight barrel rolls, twisting and turning through the air, we were laughing with glee in our hearts. We'd found each other at the flowers and now it was time to have fun. We must have flown, enjoying our aerobatics, for a couple of minutes before I felt the call. *Call* is the only way I can describe it. It's like the pull of something you need to be doing that occurs to you in the middle of something else you are doing.

"Do you feel something, Rebecca? Like there's something we are supposed to go do?" I asked as we pulled up and stopped for a moment.

"Yes, it feels like a call," she replied. "You want to go do it together?"

"Sure, I'll follow you to wherever it is." I think she took my statement as a challenge to a game of follow the leader. As we zoomed off together with Rebecca in the lead, I thought we'd fly to wherever it was in a straight line. That didn't happen. As soon as we got up past break-neck speed, she suddenly veered of in a sharp, snapping turn to the right. I could see her looking back, giggling at my attempts to keep up, and the game was on. It reminded me of scenes from the movie *Top Gun* as she'd dart straight up, down, and sideways in front of me. It wasn't long before I couldn't see her any more as we rocketed through blackness at incredible speed. I had to switch to feeling my sense of where she was up ahead of me to follow her zigzag trail through the dark. She could reverse direction in an instant and make ninety-degree turns without slowing down at all, like light reflecting off a mirror. What a wild ride! When we both came to a stop, Rebecca was still giggling. As I looked around I realized we were standing in a hospital room.

The little boy, maybe six or seven years old, was standing near a hospital bed in the room. He had died just minutes before we arrived. He was frightened, not knowing what had happened or how he'd come to be standing beside his bed. He was scared and the thing he wanted most was his mommy. Rebecca moved over in front of the little boy and spoke with him briefly. I could see she was doing something funny with her hands as she spoke to the boy. Then she turned and looked at me.

"Bruce, maybe you'd like to take over. It might be good practice. I can observe your technique," she said.

"Sure, that would be fine with me."

Then Rebecca swooped around behind me with a whoosh to watch.

"Hi, my name is Bruce. What's yours?" I asked the boy after moving closer to him.

"Albert; they call me Al," he replied. In his response I felt the certainty that both his parents were still alive. I would not be able to bring him to them. I'd need to find somebody else.

"Al, do you know what the name of this hospital is?" I asked, impulsively trying to get information I could verify later. Al didn't know, but after asking, my impression was *Jewish* or *St. Jude's*.

"Al, is there someone we could go visit with instead of your mommy or daddy?" I asked, hoping he could give me a clue where to take him. Al didn't really understand my question or why I was asking it. Still, I got the impression that old friends of the family were available. They were neighbors, friends of the family. They weren't really relatives, but they were called aunt and uncle so-and-so. I was wondering if the "aunt" was available as I was looking at Albert trying to formulate my next intelligent question. That's when I noticed the scene in front of me begin to shimmer and fade in and out. I felt Rebecca swoop around in front of me and take over. The scene restabilized back to a solid image of the hospital room.

I must have been doing something wrong, I thought to myself.

"Albert, would you like to come flying with me?" Rebecca asked the boy.

"Flying? We can go flying? Sure, that would be great. I'd love to!" Albert responded.

"Okay," Rebecca said with excitement in her voice, "hold on to my hand and here we go!"

They moved up into the air, slowly at first, and gradually picked up a little speed. I followed quietly a short distance behind them. We flew much more slowly this time, without the zigzagging. Watching Rebecca and Albert from behind, I could see the two of them talking. Albert and Rebecca were both "Ooooing" and "Ahhing" as we made our way toward Focus 27. Half a minute or so after we left, the blackness began to dissipate and the scene ahead of and below us began to materialize. On a short footpath ahead of us a woman was standing and waiting. It was Rebecca's mother. The aunt was unavailable for some reason so Rebecca's mother had come to meet Albert. This was the first time in all the time I had known Rebecca that I knew she and her mother sometimes worked together on retrievals. I had known she died a few years ago but I never suspected I'd see her, much less that she worked as a Helper in Focus 27.

We landed and Rebecca introduced Albert to her mother. She explained that his mommy couldn't come right now so instead her mommy was going to help. In the few moments between Rebecca letting go of Albert and her mother establishing good contact with him, Albert felt a surge of loneliness for his mom. Rebecca's mother did something similar to what I had seen Rebecca do earlier with her hands. As she moved her hands in a peculiar sort of way and talked to Albert, he calmed down, relaxed, and was fine. He and Rebecca's mom turned and started walking up the path, holding hands and talking to each other.

"Okay, how about some fun?" Rebecca giggled out, and she took off flying again. We flew together in big loops and rolls, enjoying our flight just for the pure joy of flying together. After we had been flying for a while, Coach cut in.

"I think that's enough fun for now," he said. "Bruce, let's go to your place."

"Rebecca, before I go I want to thank you for such a great time. I'm so happy to have finally found you here. I'm grateful for all the effort you're putting into helping me learn. I'm going to write all of this down in my journal, of course, and I'll be phoning you tomorrow to compare notes. Rebecca, thanks again."

I headed back to my place in Focus 27 and found Coach sitting in one of the chairs waiting for me.

"Since I've got you here, Coach, I've got a question," I opened.

"Sure, go ahead. Let's hear it."

"The past few times I've been out trying to find Rebecca at the flowers, I noticed some pain in the upper right side of my chest. I feel it only when I'm aware in the various focus levels; as soon as I come back to C-1 it disappears. I remember Bob Monroe claimed this kind of thing was something worth looking into. You got any ideas?"

"You remember in your first Lifeline after you found and retrieved Joshua you had a similar pain?" Coach asked.

"Yeah. Now that you mention it, I remember. Supposedly connected to a previous lifetime when my kids died in a house fire." And with that I was brought back to a scene I had remembered seeing before.

CLICK: It was night time and I had awakened in the second-floor bedroom of our house. Choking smoke filled the room and I yelled to my wife to wake up. She went to the window and hollered at me to help her get it open.

I moved through the smoke toward where I knew the door to the hallway had to be. The kids' bedroom was at the other end of the hall and I had to get there to get them out. Struggle as I might, the last thing I remembered feeling was the heat of the flames and choking and coughing in the smoke.

The scene shifted to after the fire. My wife had gotten out through the window and someone had come in after me. Later I saw the charred remains of my two children under the twisted, burned-up mattress springs and wires that had been their bed. I wished then I had died in the fire. I hadn't, but there was enough smoke damage to my lungs to lay the blame on when I died over a year later, depressed and brokenhearted. *I should have been able to save them; it should have been me and not them who died in the fire,* I remember thinking as I stood in the ashes of that home.

CLICK: The scene shifted again to my present life. Shaela, my daughter, was four. I awoke to her screaming in terror and ran down the hallway see what was wrong. She was sitting up, looking at the door, horrified at whatever she was seeing. Her eyes were open but I soon discovered she was not awake; she was in the middle of a nightmare. I sat down on the bed next to her and put my hands on her shoulders.

"Shaela, honey, I'm here. What's the matter?"

"Daddy, Daddy, can't you see it?" she said, pointing to the open doorway and screaming at the top of her lungs.

"See what, Shaela? What do you see?"

"The smoke, Daddy—can't you see it? It's coming in all around the door."

"No, Shaela, I can't see the smoke. Where is it?" I said, trying to calm her down with my voice.

"It's coming in all around the door!" she screamed hysterically. "Can't you see it, Daddy?"

"It's all right now, Shaela. The smoke has stopped now. It's not there any more. It's gone. The smoke is not coming back any more," I assured her. She relaxed in a minute or so and lay back down asleep.

CLICK: I was back with Coach again at my place, swinging in one of the hanging chairs.

"You remember?" Coach asked.

"Yes, I remember. Shaela was one of my children during that lifetime. It's part of the reason she's my daughter in this lifetime. I was never able to let go of the two of them after they died in the house fire. The grief and guilt killed me. If I don't heal it, it will follow me from lifetime to lifetime, affecting the lungs of my body. To heal it, I've got to be able to let go of both of them during this lifetime. That is so hard to even think about. It makes me feel very sad."

I sent my healing energy dolphin, Decky, to find and heal that part of myself back in that first Lifeline program. Almost all of the grief has been handled, but I haven't done much about the guilt. That's the source of the pain. The smoke damaged my lungs and I blamed that for my death. I really died because I couldn't stop blaming myself for the death of my children in the fire during that previous lifetime. I never got over the guilt. As my present marriage became more difficult, I wanted so badly to leave but I couldn't. I used to tell myself that the only noble way for a father to leave his children was for him to die. Some of those feelings come from the guilt of that previous lifetime. I realized the effect of thinking that way after the sarcoidosis spread to my right lung. That kind of thinking almost killed me again this time. When I decided my kids would be better off with a live dad who didn't live with them than a dead dad who did, that's when the sarcoidosis in my lung stopped its advance.

"You know what to do at this point?" Coach asked.

"Yeah. I need to go back and recover the guilt and then let it go," I replied.

"I'll be here when you get back."

I relaxed and focused on the pain I could feel in the upper right side of my chest. I found the part of myself still guilt-ridden over the death of my children. I pulled out all his guilt and experienced that guilt to the fullest. It was not an easy thing to do. When I felt I had gathered it all in, I released it in an act of forgiveness, asking for clean spirit to fill in the void left behind. I knew the act of letting go of my children during my present lifetime was still ahead of me. I returned to my place. Coach was still there waiting for me.

"Rebecca taught you well, Bruce. You handled that perfectly," Coach said reassuringly.

"I sure don't feel like I handled it so well. It's such a painful, awful thing to have to go through."

"I think you might want to spin for a while now," Coach suggested.

I felt myself relaxing, lying flat and starting to spin.

"You can do this yourself, you know," Coach said.

"Yeah, I know, just sometimes I forget to do it."

I was still spinning as I brought myself back to C-1. I got up and wrote down everything I could remember. I was feeling a mixture of sadness from the retrieval of that part of myself mixed with my joy at having found Rebecca at last.

The following evening I phoned Rebecca to compare notes about our first meeting I could remember at the flowers. Everything matched to the finest detail! She described our first meeting and mentioned I had been accompanied by someone, a man.

"I just met him just two nights ago. His name is Coach," I told her. I filled her in on the details of my first meeting with Coach.

She confirmed we were having a ball flying together when she got a call and invited me to come along. Rebecca laughed as she recounted our flight to answer the call at the hospital. All her zigzagging had been an intentional, nonphysical game of follow the leader. She related additional details about our trip to the hospital.

When we arrived she had indeed approached Albert first. She had gotten his attention and then asked if there was anything she could do to help him. She'd received a chunk of information, a Rote. From it she confirmed that Albert had felt lost and wanted to be with his mom. Both his parents were still alive and the surrogate aunt I talked about was dead but unavailable. When I had seen the peculiar movements of her hands, she was doing what she referred to as energetic work. The technique she was using was intended to remove Albert's fear. Regarding the shimmering fade-in and fade-out of the scene which had occurred while I was interacting with Albert, Rebecca had some advice.

"Bruce, you appeared to be focusing into yourself too deeply trying to figure out the right thing to do. By focusing into yourself you began to lose the connection with Albert. That's why I pulled in front of you. We almost lost contact with him."

"Yes, I was trying to get information for verification. When I got that the aunt wasn't available I was trying to figure out what to do next."

"In the future," she suggested, "when you find yourself trying to find the right thing to do, turn it over to Coach."

"Turn it over to Coach? What do you mean?"

"In the same way you form your intent to do anything else. Then release it, expecting a reply. Just ask Coach to provide the method and expect that he will."

"Oh, I see. Is that what you did this time?"

"No, every kid loves to fly. When I moved in front of you I needed to reconnect with Albert right away. Flying always works with kids."

She confirmed that she and her mother have been working together for quite a while.

"Mom and I got reacquainted after she died. It's an interesting relationship we have now. We're more on the same level. Mom substitutes sometimes when I need a mom, as in Albert's case. She was the one who met us in Focus 27. You got that correctly."

Rebecca's recollection of all that happened the previous night when we first met at the flowers matched my notes to the last detail. We had spent approximately twenty minutes together from my first contact with her until Coach had interrupted. I had the verification I had been looking for in a way I never expected it to come. I had met Coach and found Rebecca at the flowers. Together with Rebecca we had retrieved Albert, met Rebecca's mother, and I had returned to my place with Coach. Still I could feel resistance within myself to fully accepting the reality of the entire experience.

I discovered that doubts and old beliefs don't dissolve easily as the result of one experience. I could accept that perhaps this experience was more than coincidence. Perhaps we had actually shared and reported the same series of events, in the same order, for a twenty-minute period of time. Perhaps a little boy named Albert had actually been found and retrieved; but still the incident could have been some kind of mutually generated hallucination. It didn't prove decisively that retrievals as a phenomenon were *real*. I'd need more evidence before my doubts in this regard would be gone. What I had gotten was good evidence, I could admit, but I'd have to experience something that was irrefutable.

Energy Work and Retrieval Practice

After that first meeting at the flowers, Rebecca and I continued to meet nonphysically and then compare notes on the phone. Sometimes we arranged ahead of time what we intended to do. Other times, I'd just go looking for her and show up unannounced. One night I went looking for Rebecca, nonphysically, and found her moving her hands in the same way she had been when she had approached Albert.

I was standing behind her and a little to her right. There was a man I didn't know standing calmly in front of her. I could see Rebecca's arms and hands moving through the space around the man's body. Her hands started above his head and she maintained a distance of a foot or so between them and his body. As she moved her hands downward along the length of his body, they looked to be shimmering or vibrating. I couldn't make out exactly what it was that was so peculiar about her hand movements. The space surrounding the man's body appeared to shake and shimmer in response. I observed that a vibration of some sort was building up in the space around him.

I'd watched for perhaps a minute or so when I impulsively decided to join in and try to help Rebecca with whatever it was she was doing. From my position, still behind and to her right, I moved forward beside her and stopped. As soon as I raised my hands and began to mimic her movements, I realized that I was making a mistake. Rebecca didn't say a word to me as she turned and looked into my face, but she made it very clear by the gruff look on her face that I should not be interfering. I stopped immediately and moved back to where I had been standing, feeling a little sheepish and stupid for butting into something about which I knew nothing.

On impulse, I went to my parents' house in Minnesota and found them both sleeping. I tried to engage them in conversation but they were too groggy and tired.

In a moment I found myself visiting with my roommate from my second Lifeline program, somewhere in Canada. I called his name several times with the intent that he hear my voice. He seemed alert and we talked for a while about what we might do to help him remember our meeting. We decided that in my letter back to him I'd put in a key phrase to trigger his memory of our meeting. When he remembered our meeting, after reading the phrase, he was supposed to write me back and let me know he'd remembered. Guess it didn't work since I never got word back from him that he remembered.

After we were finished chatting I decided to go back and see what Rebecca was doing. Just thinking about doing so brought me right back to where I'd been standing before I left. The man was gone and now a woman was standing in front of her. Rebecca was moving her shimmering, vibrating hands in the same peculiar manner in the space surrounding the woman. I knew better than to interfere, so this time I just observed, trying to figure out what was going on. Afterward I came back to my physical house and got up off the sofa to journal my memories of all that had happened.

When we compared notes later on the phone, Rebecca confirmed everything I had seen her doing.

"What was that you were doing with your hands? It looked a lot like what I saw you doing with Albert in the hospital room the other night," I said.

"It's energy work. With both the man and woman you saw I was moving energies within their energy fields."

"Sorry for butting in like that. I acted on impulse again without asking if it was okay."

"I'm continually amazed at how you jump into things, Bruce," she replied. "When you did it this time it caused some disruptions that weren't appropriate to the energies I was moving. I'm glad that when you came back, you just observed."

"Yeah, I figured maybe I could learn by watching, though I didn't understand much about what you were doing or why. Besides, that was quite a look you gave me the first time. It was pretty obvious I had gotten in the way of something."

"I'm sure you'll have opportunities to learn more about moving energy in the future," she said.

The very next time I went looking for her, she was waiting there ready to demonstrate the movement of energy again. Coach had suggested trying a new method of finding her: "Just bring her name into your awareness as you place your intent on being with her."

I followed his instructions and found Rebecca immediately. I could feel her presence but she appeared visually as a very dim image in the surrounding 3-D blackness.

I had the impression of many parallel lines emerging from behind me, perpendicular to the long axis of my body and curved around it from left to right. I started seeing images, pictures and movement swirling through the space between us. Then I lost sight of her.

"Rebecca, are you still there?"

"Yes, Bruce, I haven't moved from where I was before."

She came back into view briefly and then the swirl of pictures and images began in the space between us again and I lost sight of her.

"I seem to be losing contact with you. It feels like you're still standing there and then there's so much going on in the space between us it feels like you're gone," I said.

She faded back in and out like that, with images and pictures swirling in the space between us for the rest of the time we were together. When we compared notes later on the phone, what had been happening became clear.

"I was demonstrating the movement of energy. That's where the parallel lines, images, and pictures were coming from. From what you're telling me of your experience I think you were moving your awareness into that energy and going with it," she explained.

I still didn't feel that I understood much about the energy movement she had demonstrated. I might have understood more if I'd observed instead of joining in.

Many times in these training exercises we wouldn't decide what we were going to do until after we met nonphysically. I still had some doubts somewhere deep in my beliefs about the reality of our nonphysical meetings. By spontaneously deciding on what we would do after we met nonphysically, logical options for disbelief on my part were ruled out.

The next time we nonphysically met, she said, "Someone called me on the phone today and asked me to check on her dad. So I'm going to do that. Would you like to come along?"

"Sure, let's go and I'll just observe without getting in the way this time," I laughed. We didn't play follow the leader this time. Instead I just placed my intent on being wherever Rebecca was going. I materialized next to her in a hospital room and then watched as she approached a man lying on a bed. He was an older man who appeared to be in his eighties. Rebecca stood next to his hospital bed and waited for a moment until the old man noticed her standing there.

She asked, "How can I help you?"

"I know I'm going to die soon," he said, "but I'm afraid. I don't know what to expect when I die and I don't know what to do."

"If you would like we can take a some short trips together. I think it might help with your fear," she suggested.

"Okay," he said. "I'm willing."

All three of us shifted to the Park, part of the Reception Center in Focus 27. We landed in an area that looked like a fine city park, but more beautiful than any I've ever seen. Along the sidewalks that wound their way across the lush green landscape there were wrought iron park benches with wooden plank seats. Brightly colored flowers in lovely little gardens dotted the landscape. A few trees, tall, thick and stately, were scattered around the countryside. A huge oak or maple towered over us as we stood on a sidewalk near one of the park benches. From where we were standing I could see people walking along in twos and threes, enjoying the surroundings. We waited until the old man had had plenty of time to focus into the Park and look around.

"This is the Park," Rebecca explained. "The people you see live here. When you die this is where you'll come. There will be people you know, friends and relatives, waiting here for you when you come."

"Okay," he said matter-of-factly. "When I die I come to this Park and I'll get to meet my friends who have passed on before me. Okay, that makes sense to me. How do I find this place again when the time comes?"

"All you need to do to come here is just picture what the Park looks like in your mind," Rebecca told him. "Just remember what this Park looks like. Remember the trees, the sidewalks or the park benches, anything you can remember at all. When you do, your remembering will automatically bring you here to this very spot. Now I'd like to take us back to your hospital room if that's all right."

"Okay," he said again. The tone of his voice sounded as though he were responding to the guide on a tour bus, as if he had been told it was time to board the bus and head for the next destination on a sightseeing tour. His voice sounded emotionally flat, yet inquisitive, without a hint of fear in the sound of it.

Moments later we were back at the hospital and the old man was once again on his back in his bed. Rebecca repeated the trip back and forth to the Park a couple of more times and I followed them each time.

"Now, I'd like you to practice bringing yourself to the Park," Rebecca told him. "I'll go with you and then we'll come back and practice a few more times. Is that all right with you?"

"Sure, I'm ready to give it try," he said, for the first time I heard a sense of excitement in his voice.

I focused on Rebecca instead of the old man so as not to interfere with his efforts to move himself to the Park. I could feel through her as he brought first the park bench, then the towering tree, and finally the flowers to mind. In just a few seconds we were all standing in the Park next the bench to which Rebecca had first taken him.

"I did it!" he said excitedly. "I did it!" We stayed with him through a few more of his practice runs.

"This time," Rebecca said, "my friend and I will stay here in your room while you go ahead to the Park on your own. After you get there you can use the same method to come back here. We'll be waiting for you here."

The old guy closed his eyes and then dematerialized on his hospital bed. After a half a minute or so, he rematerialized standing on the floor a short distance away.

"You've got the hang of it now," Rebecca said, offering him smiling congratulations. "You can practice on your own now whenever you'd like to. One of us will be back to check on you later."

"Thanks so much for your help," he said with gratitude. "Thank you so very much."

"You're most welcome," Rebecca replied.

With that we left and I returned to write in my journal. Later on the phone Rebecca explained that a friend of hers whose father was dying had called. She was concerned because he seemed to be so afraid. It was more evidence of the reality of retrieval work I had learned to do in Lifeline. I piled it on top of all the other evidence I had gotten so far and still felt I needed more to be convinced. I also learned another facet of what is meant in the Lifeline program by being of service Here and There. The man's daughter would realize he was now approaching his impending death in more comfort. She would see his fear was gone. And her father would now make a smooth, easy transition into the company of friends There, in the Park, when he left his physical body for the last time.

Several days later, I went back to the old man's hospital room by myself to check on his progress. I didn't make my being there known to him. I just observed him from off to the side. As I watched him I could see he was still practicing his trips back and forth to the Park. Rebecca later confirmed on the phone that he was still alive and her checks on him matched with mine. He would have an easy transition when the time came as a result of a phone call to Rebecca by his daughter.

Talking about my activities with friends sometimes led to more opportunities for verification. I had a friend named Jim, with whom I could share some of my experiences. It's not the sort of thing you talk to just anybody about. Most people think you're nuts. There were times I'm sure even Jim wondered about that. To try to lend some reality to discussions about my experience, Jim asked once if I'd try to find him nonphysically sometime. If he could remember our meeting, he felt, it might make it easier for him to accept what I shared with him. I told him I'd attempt to contact him sometime in the next week or two. I waited three or four days to let any excitement either of us felt at the prospect of verification die down. That way, I figured, the excitement wouldn't lead me to think I'd found him when no such thing had actually happen. When I felt calm about, it I decided to pay Jim a visit.

I hadn't told Rebecca beforehand what I was up to: maybe *double blind* describes this kind of testing. I went to find her first, nonphysically, and asked her to accompany me on my visit to Jim. This time I led the way, bringing Jim's name to mind while I placed my intent to be with him. I found him quickly. He was in bed sleeping, and I approached him to get his attention. It took a bit of shaking him awake before the groggy sleepiness left him. He and I gabbed for a while, trying to come up with something together that would make it easier for him to remember our meeting. Then I stepped back and Rebecca stepped forward. She and Jim talked for a short while. When we left, Jim went back to sleep.

The next morning at work Jim found me in my cubicle and told me about a dream he remembered that morning. He remembered seeing me with a little girl that he knew wasn't my daughter, Shaela. Jim didn't remember exactly what we'd said to each other. I told him the little girl he'd seen with me was Rebecca and confirmed that last night was the night that I went looking for him. One more piece of confirming evidence gathered and yet I felt I needed more.

Rebecca and I continued to meet at the flowers. I'd make notes in my journal about everything I could remember of our interaction and phone her later to compare notes. Although our notes continued to match time after time in minute detail, I still felt I had nothing definitive. Meeting Jim was as close as I'd come to any verifiable, physical world evidence. There wasn't any way to check out the details from other experiences since they almost always involved only nonphysical people. I had no way to contact them in the physical world for corroboration.

Black Stuff

On one trip, Rebecca and I each had a person who had requested that we examine her from a nonphysical perspective. A woman named Ellen, who was experiencing a long-term deep depression which resisted medical treatment, had asked Rebecca to examine her remotely, hoping such a nonphysical examination might reveal clues she could use to move out of her depression. Lenora, an acquaintance of mine, had some specific physical health problems which she knew to have a nonphysical, energetic basis, but had been unable to discover the root cause of. This woman, a gifted, well-known psychic, works with a Guide named Shawn, channeling Shawn's answers and advice to her clients. In an effort to improve her physical health, Lenora had recently changed her name to Lydia. She felt that by taking a new name she would be able to build a new identity for herself and eliminate her connection to her previous health problems.

Rebecca and I had decided to do them together as another training exercise. When we met nonphysically, Ellen came into view, standing directly in front of us about eight feet away. Rebecca called my attention to various aspects of Ellen's nonphysical body before us. What stood out most prominently was a black spot about the size of a golf ball, located on one side of where her navel would be. We moved, side by side, closer to Ellen, and I more closely examined the dark spot.

From close up the spot appeared as a black circular area with a squiggly, black tail pointing generally to Ellen's right. The tail looked like a smoke trail, wide where it connected to the black spot and tapering to a very thin stream at its end. It extended about a foot and a half from her body and then either ended or became so thin I could no longer see it. After giving me plenty of time to look this all over closely, Rebecca moved forward and began to do energy work on the spot with her hands. I tried without much success to observe and understand exactly what she was doing. Her shimmering, vibrating hands made passes directly over the spot and the surrounding area. When she stepped back and directed my attention to the area, the spot's appearance had changed. The black, smoke-like squiggly tail was gone and the spot now glowed in a combination of pink and white light that radiated a feeling of complete healing and vitality.

We then moved a short distance away and Rebecca directed my attention back toward Ellen to get a perspective of her whole being. I was immediately struck by the look of fear and anxiety on Ellen's face. I could also see what appeared to be a thick, tarry, black covering surrounding her body. I felt a strong impulse to remove the fear and anxiety this thick black covering represented. Not waiting for Rebecca to demonstrate how, I swooped in and began using my hands, pulling at the black stuff to remove it. At first it felt like very hot, sticky, bubble gum. It stuck to everything with incredible tenacity. Moments after first touching this black stuff it felt like I'd plunged my hands into a bucket full of stinging jellyfish. Intense, burning, stinging pain radiated from my hands and up my arms. I backed away from Ellen and began desperately trying to get the black stuff off my hands.

Pulling at it with my fingers only succeeded in spreading the stinging pain to any place else it touched. This black stuff was such a gooey, sticky, elastic mess that pulling at it only made it stick to my fingers and added to the places from which it needed to be removed. Rubbing my hands together caused it to stick to itself and collect together a little. All the while the burning, stinging pain was intensifying. I finally succeeded in rolling it into a ball, collecting most of the bits and pieces together in one place. I felt the intense pain only where this ball and the few remaining bits contacted my hands. As I thought about throwing this ball of black stuff away, I became concerned that it might hit other people, stick to them, and cause them pain. I heard Coach in the background.

"Don't worry about that; just get rid of it!" he said urgently.

I threw the ball away and then visualized all the rest of this awful, stinging black stuff collecting itself together at my fingertips. As it gathered there I flicked it off into the surrounding blackness. Coach and Rebecca assisted in removing the last bits of this sticky black goo from my hands. Once it was gone, the intense, burning, stinging sensation went away. Then Rebecca directed my attention back to Ellen. For all my frantic, painful efforts I'd made only a small dent in the volume of thick, black goo surrounding Ellen. I was about to dive in and start at it again when Rebecca reached out and stopped me. She made it clear that I was to wait and watch how she dealt energetically with the fear and anxiety surrounding and covering Ellen. I couldn't believe my eyes. One moment Ellen was completely surrounded, the next all the black stuff was gone. It had started to shimmer and vibrate ever so slightly, then it just disappeared all at once. I looked over at Rebecca to get some clue as to what she had done. I couldn't get a clear idea about how she had made the black stuff disappear. She was trying to explain but nothing she said made any sense to me.

We decided to move on to Lenora next and check on her new identity, Lydia. Ellen's image faded into the blackness and I did a slow turning scan to locate Lenora. Almost as soon as I felt the direction she was in, Lenora's image began to form in the blackness in front of me. She had asked that I not interfere with whatever I found. I was to just look and later tell her what I found, without taking any action to change it.

I approached her and stopped about fifteen feet away. My attention was drawn to her neck. I tried to move forward to get a closer look. My progress was stopped because I ran into a twisted mass of tangled black stuff. It resembled a thick briar patch and it completely surrounded her. I couldn't get close enough to clearly see what had attracted my attention to Lenora's neck with all the choking, vine-like black stuff in the way. Not one to learn my lesson quickly from the experience with Ellen, I dove in again.

Every place these black, thorny briars touched my body gave the same burning, stinging sensation I'd experienced with Ellen. I decided I'd have to cut a pathway through them to get close enough to examine her. I had to back out several times to clean the same hot, sticky, stinging black goo off my body. The tangled mess surrounding Lenora extended at least ten feet in every direction around her. It was impossible to approach her without being stung continuously as I came in contact with the thorny web surrounding her.

After a minute or two I had cleared a pathway through this tangle and was able to see Lenora's neck more clearly. A thick, billowing, black smoke-like substance emanated from her neck along its entire length on her right side. It appeared to be moving away from her as it tapered down to a thin stream. I followed this black smoke trail away from her to see where it led. I caught a glimpse of her face as I moved away. It had the look of a terror-stricken animal, trapped by the neck in the jaws of a lion. Like such an animal, she knew that whatever had her by the throat was going to drain the life out of her and kill her. Her fear of dying held her paralyzed in its grip, and the rest of her body hung limply, waiting to die.

When I came to the end of the thin smoke trail I saw her father, brother, and mother (all physically alive), feeding, vampire-style, on the smoke trail leading from her neck. I realized they did not intend to kill her. They only wanted to drain the life out of her to the extent that she'd be immobilized by fear and unable to break away and free herself. They wanted Lenora alive so they could continue to feed on the fear of dying their feeding induced in her. Watching them, I realized that Lenora could break free of their grip by stopping the flow of the fear-of-death energy by sending them love and forgiveness. With their supply of fear gone, they'd have to let go of her and look for some other victim.

At this point in my examination of Lenora I was interrupted by the feeling of a call to stop and carry out a retrieval. Although it seemed to be a random interruption at the time, in retrospect I realized it was a call to retrieve a part of Lenora connected to the fear of death that held her paralyzed. I turned away from the three people feeding on her fear and followed the pull I felt tugging at the top of my head. After a short, quick sensation of movement into Focus 23 through the 3-D blackness, I came upon the scene of a little boy's death. His image was frozen like a still black and white photograph taken a split second before he died. Then I saw the entire sequence of his death as though I were watching a black and white newsreel film of a scene from World War II. As it started I was watching a tank, slinging mud high in the air behind itself, as it sped along a muddy road.

The boy appeared to be about seven years old and had been trying to get across the deeply rutted, muddy road. He had stumbled and fallen, landing on his back. His body was stretched out across one of the ruts. The driver of the tank hadn't seen the boy fall in the road in front of him. The track on the right side of the vehicle had passed over and crushed the boy's body from just below his neck all the way to his knees. He had died in the instants just after the track touched his body. Just before it had crushed him to death, he'd looked up and realized in sheer terror that he was about to die. After the tank had driven past his body I could see the boy's flattened, mangled remains pushed deep into the mud. Then I was looking again at his face in the still photograph I had seen when I first came upon him. I understood that his terror and fear of dying had taken over all his awareness at the instant he realized he was about to die. He'd become trapped in that instant of terror—so trapped that he'd been unaware of his actual death. For his entire existence, since then, he had been locked in his experience of the terror and fear of that instant before his death. That's why he'd become stuck in Focus 23.

I could see the boy had the now-familiar coating of the thick, black, goo of fear surrounding and covering his body. Before I moved closer to the boy to try to assist him, I noticed my daughter and son sitting on their magic flying carpets. They were hovering nearby, watching. They had evidently come to see what it was Dad did when he wasn't out flying with them. They both seemed calm and unafraid as I acknowledged their presence, then I turned my attention back to the boy.

Remembering how painful it had been to come in contact with this black stuff when I encountered it with Ellen and Lenora, I decided to try something different. Instead of grabbing at it and tearing it off, I moved my hands close to the thick black layer and tried to make them shimmer and vibrate the way I'd seen Rebecca do in the past. After five or ten seconds, I felt the terror and fear the black stuff represented loosen its grip on the boy's awareness. He turned his head and looked into my face, confused about what was happening. Once he turned away from the instant before his death, I was able to get his attention. I lifted him up out of the rut in the muddy road and we stepped back and watched that whole scene fade into the blackness.

I removed the rest of the black stuff clinging to him using my hands. I constantly flicked it off my finger tips into the darkness without concern about where it would land. Then I thought about Shaela and Daniel sitting on their magic flying carpet hovering off the ground about ten feet away. I realized they had not just happened along out of curiosity but had come to help me retrieve the boy. He and I walked over to where they were hovering and my kids invited him to hop on for a ride. We started to move forward, slowly at first, and then we picked up speed on our way to the Reception Center at Focus 27. We came in for a landing near a woman who was waiting for us. She was a short, plump woman with jet black hair. From her facial features and coloring she felt Mediterranean. She could have been Italian or Arab; I couldn't tell which. The woman was obviously the boy's mother. As he jumped down off our flying carpet and ran to her, my children and I had the privilege of witnessing their joyous reunion. It was hugs, tears, and kisses all around. I thanked Shaela and Daniel for their help and then I headed back to finish my examination of Lenora.

As I stood just outside the boundary of thick, black briars surrounding Lenora, I wondered what part her Guide, Shawn, played in all of this. I placed my intention on contacting Shawn to examine his relationship to Lenora's problems. In the next moment I felt thrust into a solid mass of stinging, black goo that enveloped my entire body. Intense burning, stinging pain locked me its grip so tightly that I could barely think. It felt like I was being burned and electrocuted at the same time. Instinctively my body doubled over into a fetal position. The pain was so intense I couldn't think of anything else. Then I felt someone grab hold of me. I was pulled out of the boiling goo and I lost my connection with Shawn. As soon as I was clear of Shawn's influence, I could feel Rebecca, Coach, and someone else working frantically to remove all the residue of my encounter with him. For a full minute or so I remained doubled up in pain until the last of it was removed and I could straighten out my body again. There were two things I knew from that encounter: (1) Shawn was connected to the twisted, black mass of fear surrounding Lenora, and (2) I never wanted to come in contact with him again. I thanked Rebecca, Coach, and the other Helper profusely and finally got the message: it might be better to learn another way of dealing with this stinging black stuff. Touching it with any part of my nonphysical body was too painful and ineffective.

I got less of a sense of Lydia's story when I examined Lenora's new identity. As a young woman Lydia had fallen in love with an older man. He'd made promises he had no intention of keeping and then skipped out, leaving her pregnant, humiliated and ashamed. I saw that she had descended into a suicidal depression and taken her own life.

I was then called away again by a request to retrieve someone else. In retrospect this retrieval was a part of my examination of Lenora/Lydia. This retrieval was of a part of Lydia she'd left far behind in her past. I could sense Rebecca following along with me this time and we shifted together into Focus 23.

We arrived at bedside near a young mother grieving over her own death. She was locked in grief and shame at having left her three young children to fend for themselves. She was painfully aware of her own death. She had suicided out of her life and was locked in regret, grief, and guilt over abandoning her children. She was so overcome with these feelings that she was unable to leave the scene of her suicide and break free of them. Rebecca stood back and observed as I moved closer to the young woman. The layer of sticky goo that covered this woman seemed to be a different color and texture then the hot, black bubble gum I'd seen before. Keeping my hands about a foot away, I began to move them up and down along the length of her body where she was lying on the bed. I did so intending to loosen and remove the sticky goo from her body. Shortly after I started, it began to loosen and then it started to disappear. With her grief and guilt dissipated I was able to get her attention and move her to a standing position next to the bed. From there we shifted to Focus 27, where we were met by Helpers who welcomed and comforted the young woman. Rebecca and I left to return to Lydia.

I had a difficult time relocating Lydia and didn't get any more information about her. When I went back to find her I was beginning to lose control of my ability to focus. While I was trying to locate Lydia again I met Coach.

"Bruce," he said sharply to get my attention, "I think you've done enough on this outing. You remember how to spin yourself down, like you learned during Lifeline?"

"Yeah, Coach, I remember."

"Good, relax and let us do that for you now," he said calmly. "Just relax."

Several impressions drifted through my mind as I lay on my back spinning slowly to my right. It felt as though, if I had been wearing a dosimeter badge for the black stuff to which I'd been exposed, it would show I was nearly overloaded. Any more exposure and I'd overdose, resulting in something like radiation burns.

"You've got the picture, Bruce," Coach remarked. "Just relax and let us spin you for clean up and repairs on the way back to C-1."

It probably took more than ten minutes before I felt the spinning stop. A couple of times on the way back to C-1 I started feeling restless and began to move around. Each time Coach stopped me, insisting that I go back to relaxing and spinning until he felt I was ready to stop and get up. After a couple of times I stopped arguing with him and just lay back and relaxed. When the spinning stopped I got up, made a pot of coffee, and then entered all I could remember into my journal.

Seeing It Not There

When I called Rebecca on the phone to compare notes, the first words out of her mouth were, "Bruce, I couldn't believe what I was seeing when you dove in and started pulling at Ellen's fear with your hands. I've never seen anybody ever attempt that before."

"Well, I had the impulse to remove it and went after it like I would anything else, with both hands," I replied, feeling a little sheepish and defensive. "Boy, you know that stuff really has a burning sting to it."

"And then when you started hacking your way through those thick twisted vines of fear surrounding Lenora I couldn't believe anybody would dare do a thing like that. Didn't you learn anything from your encounter with the black stuff around Ellen?"

"After I got if off my hands, I remember, you stopped me from going back to Ellen again. I remember watching you do something I didn't understand, and then all the black stuff around Ellen disappeared. But I couldn't figure out or understand what you had done to make it all go away."

"I used a technique I call *seeing it not there*. I thought you understood when I showed it to you."

"No, I didn't get it."

"That was obvious to me when you went wading into that tangle around Lenora," she responded. "*Seeing it not there* is a technique you can use to remove any clinging emotional energy such as fear. It's not the same as making something go away or disappear. There's a subtle but powerful difference."

"What's the difference between making it disappear and seeing it not there?"

"Trying to make something go away or disappear is an activity that implies resistance. It's implicit that whatever you are trying to force away can resist. The more effort you exert to force it to disappear, the more that effort allows it to resist. See what I mean?"

"Well, I understand that trying to force something to happen does imply that such force is necessary. I don't understand the difference between that and seeing it not there," I replied.

"Okay, let's take the case with Ellen. Seeing it not there implies you are going to see Ellen with the black stuff *not there* around her. You are just going to see Ellen. I know it's a subtle difference, but it implies no resistance from whatever is there. The best way to understand this is by doing. The next time you encounter anything you want to remove without touching it, practice with the intent to see it not there. To remove it energetically, first look at the person and don't get too close. Allow the joy of your own being to build up. Get a buzz of joy on. Then just look at the person and see the black stuff or whatever not there.

Don't interact with it or the person until you can see it all not there. Then interact with the person in whatever way you or Coach feels appropriate. This technique would have worked nicely on the thick field of fear around Lenora. You did pretty well with Lydia."

"Yeah, if I'd known what to do it would have been nice not to have had to hack my way through that stuff. That stuff really hurts when you touch it!"

"And then, after all that, you pushed right into the middle of Shawn's energy. I couldn't believe any one would do such a thing! What did that feel like?"

"Like submerging yourself in a ball of boiling-hot tar while being constantly electrocuted with high voltage electricity," I replied. "You saw me do that too, huh?"

"Saw you!" she replied incredulously. "Saw you! Coach and my Guide had to reach in and pull you out of there."

"Yeah, I was so doubled up with pain I couldn't think straight enough to back out on my own. I thought I felt someone grab me and pull me out."

"Don't interact with that stuff or anyone who's made of it until you can see that it is all gone! That shit was stuck all over your body when they got you out of there. All three of us were working frantically to get it all off of you. I still can't believe anyone would dive into something like that. I just can't believe it."

"Well, I've got to admit, it was a very unpleasant experience."

"In the future, Bruce—"

"Yeah, I get it, see it not there."

"Yes."

It was clear from this interaction with Rebecca that she had indeed met me nonphysically during the experience of examining Ellen, and Lenora/Lydia. After confirming other details of our experience together, she added information from her perspective to round out what I had gotten.

Rebecca had known before we examined Ellen that she'd had an abortion. The black stuff was her leftover feelings of being wounded. Rebecca had seen during her examination that Ellen's specialty was making a plan which someone else must carry out for her. She didn't take responsibility for her own actions and future. The pink and white light I had seen in place of the black spot were to heal her wound and give the opportunity for awareness and insight into her own problem.

Rebecca added more information regarding Lenora. Lenora's father had left the family when she was a child and had returned into her life later. By the time he returned, she saw him as an interloper, who was taking her mother's attention away from her. Lenora became extraordinarily angry and jealous and took on the role of a victim. Like Ellen, Lenora took no responsibility for what happened to her. She would have found great relief by just being able to say to herself, "I am fully and completely responsible for everything that happens to me." She trusted nothing, except that she would always be a victim and that she would always be used. Out of that pain and torture she was able to do the psychic stuff that she did. Her psychic ability was the payoff she got for suffering the pain of her connection to Shawn, with the side effect of ill-health. She couldn't let go of her pain because it would have broken her connection to him. She thought that if that happened she'd lose her psychic ability forever, which was not true. If she had managed to break that connection, and drop her victim style, her ability would have stopped for a while. She then would have been able to rebuild it without the pain and torture of being a victim.

The little boy, retrieved during the examination of Lenora, had, according to Rebecca, the same energetic make up as she. Both were trapped in fear, terror, and pain. The boy was no longer held in that state and was free to develop further.

Rebecca confirmed that the young woman she and I had been called to retrieve had suicided out of her life. She shared the energetic make-up of Lydia. Lydia was an aspect of herself that Lenora had taken on as her identity. It was Rebecca's view that Lenora had changed her identity because the tangle of fear and pain surrounding her had become so strong that she was immobilized and made ill by it. The Lydia personality she had taken on hadn't had as much time to build up such a thick layer of fear and pain. But Lydia had the same basic victim style. Rebecca suggested that Lenora's name change to Lydia would work for a while. If she chose to continue as a victim, Rebecca foresaw Lydia becoming immobilized by the same pain and fear in the future.

Rebecca's opinion of Shawn was that he was not a very nice fellow. His gift, Lenora/Lydia's channeling ability, came at a high price. She had to allow his victim energetic style to express through her body along with his information. By expressing his channeled information, she expressed Shawn's pain and fear as well. As she continued channeling Shawn, she would continue to become less and less able to move and grow. She would have to temporarily give up this *gift* to break free of Shawn's influence. But Lenora/Lydia valued her psychic ability too highly to do so. It wasn't a pretty picture at all.

When I contacted Lenora/Lydia to talk about what I had found, she confirmed the events which Rebecca described in her life as a child. She remembered that when her father had returned to the family she had indeed been very jealous of the attention her mother had given to him. She was very upset at me for having cut through the thick, twisted briars surrounding her. She claimed this did not represent fear or pain or have anything to do with her relationship with her Guide, Shawn. To her it represented, instead, the accumulation of her life experience that she would take with her when she died. I have no idea who gave her that information and I don't agree with her assessment. She totally disagreed with my conclusion that she would have to break her connection with Shawn. The idea of losing her psychic ability and then having to rebuild it based on something other than being a victim was completely unacceptable to her. My examination of Lenora/Lydia didn't result in any change in her condition. Maybe someday she would decide to make a new choice.

As I've mentioned, my mother told me long ago that experience is the best teacher and a hard taskmaster. After my experience encountering and dealing with the black stuff clinging to and surrounding people's nonphysical bodies, I'd have to say she was right. From that point on, in my continuing exploration of the New World of the *Afterlife*, I remembered well the lessons I learned. Experience is a good teacher. Whenever I've come across this black stuff since, I've followed Rebecca's suggestions. I don't interact with it or the person involved until I've succeeded in seeing it not there. It turned out to be easier to do than I thought and I now see the difference between that and trying to make it disappear. I tried the latter on my next few encounters with it and saw how stubbornly it resisted my efforts. In the opening chapter of this book, seeing it not there is the technique I used to retrieve the woman who was convinced she was trapped by fallen debris. Seeing it not there is a simple technique and it works every time.

Ghost Busting

My buddy Walt called me at home one night just as I was finishing dinner. He'd gotten a call from his sister Carol, and her request had quite amazed him. Through Walt, skeptical as he was, she'd heard stories about the kind of nonphysical world exploring I claimed to do, and she figured maybe I could help. In her circle of friends there was no one else to whom she could turn for help.

"I never thought I'd ever hear Carol ask me such a thing," Walt said. "It's about my niece. Carol's oldest girl, Barbara. She claims to have ghosts in her house that are causing problems. Carol called me to ask you if there was anything you could do about it. That's what's so strange."

"Walt, it's not so strange for people to have ghosts in their house, at least not to me. I can accept the possibility. I know you're a bit of a skeptic, but—"

Walt interrupted, "No. I mean what's so strange is that my sister is very religious. She's married to a minister, Bruce, and they don't believe in ghosts."

"What brand is the minister?"

"What do you mean, brand?"

"I'm sorry, force of habit. I didn't mean to be impolite. What religion is your brother-in-law?"

"They're a pretty straight-laced, fundamentalist theology group, Christians," he replied. "It isn't that they don't believe there are such things as ghosts, but they believe ghosts are from the Spirit World. For them that means any dealings with them bears the chance of losing your soul."

"Losing your soul?"

"Yeah, see, for them the Spirit World is inhabited by demons and ruled by Satan. Demons and other minions of Satan are capable of tricking unsuspecting humans into committing acts which could win them over to Satan's side. If that happens, the humans are condemned to eternal damnation in Hell. In their religion, Satan is the Great Deceiver, and he can trick people into giving up their souls. So for people in my sister's religion ghosts might be just a deception of Satan and so any dealings with them are real dangerous."

"What do you think, Walt? Are dealings with ghosts dangerous?"

"Hell, I don't know. I know I don't ever want to see a ghost, too scary for me," he answered. "That's why I think it's so peculiar my sister would call and ask for your help. I guess since it's her daughter who's involved she had to do something. She couldn't talk to any of their friends about it. Imagine how that would sound. The minister's daughter has ghosts in her house! This sort of thing is not supposed to happen to good Christians who believe in the correct theology. It probably wouldn't look too good for the minister's daughter to be involved with ghosts."

"I see what you mean, Walt. I'll have to talk to your niece first."

He gave me her phone number. "Just tell her you're her Uncle Walt's friend. I told her some of your stories while she was here visiting. She's a little more open about this kind of stuff than her mom and dad. Do you think there's anything you can do?"

"I don't know. I'll have to call her and see what's going on," I replied.

"Hey, I'd really appreciate it, and let me know what you find out, okay?"

"If there's anything I can share with you, Walt, I'll let you know," I said.

Later that evening I called Barbara and introduced myself. She had indeed heard some of my stories from her uncle and seemed to at least accept the possibility of ghosts. After answering a few of the usual questions about how I learned and what I thought, we got down to what was going on at her house.

Barbara is a single mom with a three-year-old son named Paul. She and Lisa, another single mom with a little boy about Paul's age, had decided to pool their resources and rent a house together. Not long after Barb and Lisa moved in, neighbors had told them the house was haunted. Two months later, Lisa remarried and her husband, Juan, now lived there too.

"The neighbors said nobody lived in the house more than a month or two before they got too scared and moved out. We thought they were just playing a head trip on us," Barbara said.

"But now you don't think it was a head trip? You think there are really ghosts in your house?"

"I don't just *think* there are ghosts in the house. I've seen them myself! They go dancing through the air, right through the living room. Lisa's seen them. Juan has seen them. Juan's brother, Eduardo, is staying here for a while and even he's seen them. There are definitely ghosts in this house. At first we thought it was no big deal; in fact we joked about them. We called them the *Dancers* because that's what they're doing every time we see them. It's not a joke any more. We're all pretty scared."

"Your uncle Walt said the ghosts were causing problems."

"What really freaks me out is when they touch me at night. I wake up out of a sound sleep because I can feel someone running their hands all over my body. Sometimes they're running their hands through my hair. It gives me the willies just talking about it."

"How often does this happen?"

"At least two or three times a week. It really freaks me out."

"What other problems do they cause?"

"Lights go on and off by themselves. There are noises like doors opening and closing. We hear footsteps when there is no one there. Sometimes we hear voices talking, and it's not any of us doing the talking. Things get moved from one place to another when we're gone."

"Barb, I can understand why you're scared. I'd be scared too if things like that were going on in my house."

"That's not all. Lisa's son and my boy Paul act scared and frightened a lot. It's like they can see something we can't see and whatever it is it really scares them. It's gotten to where they're upset most of the time. They scream and cry sometimes and run over to hang on mommy. It's like they're looking right at something in the air right in front of them that scares them."

"I hear your concern for your son, and it makes sense what you say. I read somewhere once that it's not unusual for little kids to be able to see ghosts. Something about how open they are to things."

"Everybody in this house is pretty upset. Is there anything you can do to stop this stuff from happening?"

"What I can do, to start with, is to check out the situation from my end first and see what I can find out. I'll do that tonight and call you back tomorrow to tell you what I find. That's all I can promise for now."

After I hung up I dialed Rebecca's number in Virginia to tell her what I planned to do. Since retrieving Albert that first time we met at the flowers, Rebecca and I had done three or four other retrievals. It had gotten into a pattern where I'd first meet her at the flowers or somewhere else. Then we would do a retrieval and when I returned I'd write down everything I could remember. We'd compare notes on the phone the next day, and so far we had a string of four or five consecutive experiences in which the notes matched to the finest detail. In the process I had gained a lot of confidence in my ability to perceive in the nonphysical world. On each trip I'd first meet with Coach, who always had some little exercise for me to do. He would accompany me on my trips with Rebecca and I was beginning to rely on his input.

When Rebecca answered the phone I told her a little about my conversations with Walt and Barbara and that I intended to check on it. I didn't want to say I was going to do it that night. If she showed up on her own I thought I might get more *evidence*. After we hung up I puttered around the house until it was bedtime for the kids. When the house was quiet I went into the living room and lay on the sofa in my house in Colorado.

The process of shifting my awareness to Focus 27 was a long, involved procedure using visualizations and non-verbal cues I'd been using for almost a year. This procedure was still something I felt I had to do in order to get to Focus 27. In later years I realized all this formality wasn't necessary, but as I shifted off to find the Dancers I was still a creature of my procedural habit. It took me another three minutes or so to *officially* be in Focus 27. After meeting up with Coach and asking for his assistance, I allowed myself to open up my perception to the people around me.

I thought I recognized Barbara's voice in the scramble of thoughts coming from the house I felt I was in. There was a jumble of *little boy* thoughts there too. After a minute or two, I convinced myself I must be in the right house. Not surprisingly, shortly thereafter Rebecca came into view.

"Rebecca, I only half expected to see you here tonight. Sorry about being vague about when I planned to do this—evidence, you know."

"I suspected as much," she said with a chuckle. "You and your evidence."

"So why'd you come?"

"I just thought this might be a marvelous training exercise and that it might be great fun to see how you do. This one's all yours, though, Bruce. I'm only here to observe."

After our brief exchange I suggested we crouch down and wait to see if we could spot the Dancers. I'm sure

Rebecca felt a little silly crouching down with me, as if we needed to hide from them. It didn't take long for the pair of dancers to show up. They approached from my left and went past us, dancing through the air. It was the most beautiful, graceful, flowing combination of ballroom waltzing and professional figure skating movements I have ever seen. I watched in awe as they gracefully flew past us, looking into each other's eyes as they disappeared a short distance away to my right.

"Rebecca, I think that must be them," I whispered loudly.

"Yeah, they seem to fit the description of the Dancers very well," she replied, jokingly mimicking my loud whisper. She caught my eye with a deadpan expression on her face and we both burst out laughing.

"Come on, let's cut in on their dance," I said in a normal tone, and we took off in the direction we'd last seen them moving. We quickly caught up to them.

To get their attention, we each took up positions behind the Dancers, keeping pace with their moving dance. I floated along behind the man and Rebecca behind the woman. We looked at each other to time it just right and then reached out and tapped them each on the shoulder. I tapped the guy's shoulder with the intention to cut in and dance with his partner. Rebecca did the same to the woman. By the strong, startled sense of shock I felt go through the man as I tapped his shoulder, it was obvious no one had touched him like that in a very long time. As they each turned around to see who was cutting in, Rebecca and I traded places in the blink of an eye. I met the gaze of the startled young woman and we danced off together. Rebecca and the male Dancer did the same. I struck up a small-talk conversation with the woman, as anyone would who was dancing with a stranger. As we waltzed through the air and talked, some of the details I picked up painted a picture of who the Dancers were and why they were in Barbara's house.

They were Southern California party kids in their late twenties or early thirties. They had been on their way to a party at a friend's house when they were both killed in a wreck on the freeway. At first they hadn't realized what had happened to them. They had continued on to the party and were confused about why people there couldn't see or interact with them. Before the party broke up, they decided to go home. Some time later they realized what had happened and remembered the accident in which they had been killed. I made the mistake of asking her how she had died and saw the most grotesque image of her head being crushed flat from the sides like a grape.

She and her man now both knew they were dead and what they wanted most was to get back into physical bodies. They wanted to be able to party again. They didn't really know how to get back into physical bodies. The way they'd been trying to do it wasn't working. I wanted to get more information from her about how they'd been trying to get back into physical bodies, but I fell into my own trap again. I couldn't decide what was the right thing to do next and started searching inwardly for the right questions to ask. This time Rebecca wasn't standing behind me to take over. Instead of remembering to turn it over to Coach, as she had suggested after almost losing contact with Albert, I turned inward. Before I realized what had happened, I'd lost my connection with the young woman and I drifted off to sleep.

I woke up on my sofa, perhaps thirty minutes after I'd started, grabbed my journal, and wrote in as much detail as I could remember what had happened during my intro-duction to the Dancers. During this time in my training I was still very much concerned with gathering evidence to verify my experience in any way I could. Some part of me was still having a very difficult time accepting that all this was real and it demanded more verification. When I phoned Rebecca to compare notes it turned out that this was the sixth consecutive time our notes were identical.

Rebecca told me the story she'd gotten from the male Dancer was pretty much the same as I'd heard from the woman. They really wanted to get back into physical bodies again to enjoy the partying, alcohol, and other drugs they'd been into. They were staying in Barbara's house in hopes of figuring out how to do that. Their attempts so far were the cause of Barb's frightening experiences at night. The Dancers would wait until someone in the house was asleep or passed out from too much alcohol or other drugs. Then they would try to slide into the same space that person's body occupied to *catch a buzz*. They couldn't stay in the person's body or actually inhabit it, but they could vicariously experience the feelings of that person's *high*. This worked only as long as the person was unconscious or only semiconscious. As soon as the person regained consciousness, the Dancers were forced out of the person's space. What Barbara was experiencing as someone running their hands over her body or through her hair was actually the Dancers. As they were trying to move into the space occupied by her body, she experienced their attempt as someone touching her.

As Rebecca and I finished up our phone conversation, she reiterated that this was my training exercise and an excellent opportunity to learn. She would not interfere, so I would be the one to figure out what to do and then do it. I thanked Rebecca again for her assistance and we said our goodbyes.

The following day I phoned Barbara to let her know what I found out. After I filled her in on the details and explained why the Dancers were there, our conversation continued.

"You could tell I'd had too much to drink? I'd appreciate that not getting back to my parents," she said in a voice of concern.

"How you live your life is not my concern and I have no plans to tell anyone your private business," I assured her.

"Can these ghosts take over my body? Could I become possessed?" she asked.

"It's my understanding that can't happen without your permission. They can only try to share your space when you're not conscious enough to push them out."

"You had me scared there for a minute," I heard her say, with a sigh of relief.

"So, do you want these people to leave the house, Barbara?" I asked. "I know it might sound like a silly question, but I've found it's always best to ask permission."

"Of course I want them out of here! Can you do that?" she asked incredulously. "Why would anyone not want ghosts out of their house?"

"Yes, I can remove them from the house. Some people think it's interesting to have a ghost in their house. They want the ghost to stay around so they can investigate it. Sometimes they want to prove to themselves there really are such things as ghosts. I had to ask because it's best that I clearly understand the intentions of the people involved in the situation."

"How soon can you get them out of here?"

"I'll start working on it as soon as I can. It should be in the next day or two but I can't promise exactly when they will actually leave. I'll do my best."

I spent the rest of the day thinking off and on about how to approach the Dancers to get them to leave. Logical thinking and planning is second nature to engineers, which is what I did for a living at the time. My plans for dealing with the Dancers were logical and rational and they turned out to be almost totally useless. My plan centered on contacting the Dancers and offering to take them to where they could get physical bodies as an inducement to leave Barb's house. Moving them to Focus 27 would accomplish that, though not in exactly the manner in which they desired it. That evening I lay on my sofa again, and, after connecting with Coach in Focus 27, I shifted off to Barbara's house. Not surprisingly, Rebecca joined me shortly after my arrival. She took up a position behind me so as to not interfere while she observed. From that vantage point she was also free to chuckle occasionally at my antics, somewhat in private.

I settled myself down and stood there quietly, just looking around. Juan's brother, Eduardo, came into view and while watching him I realized he was bringing illegal, recreational drugs into the house. Some of these felt like Native American drugs used in sacred ritual and ceremony. *Powerful things to be using as toys,* I thought to myself. Easily part of the reason the Dancers were being seen and part of the reason they stayed. I also realized, as I watched him, that Eduardo was gay. Looking around further, I noticed a frightened little boy hiding under a crib. I decided that after the Dancers were gone I would come back for him. Then I stood motionless, waiting for the Dancers to appear. A short time later they moved past me, their smooth flowing waltz through the air a thing of beauty to behold.

"Excuse me, I'd like to talk about helping both of you get back into physical bodies, if you don't mind," I called out in their direction, to get their attention. They stopped their dance in mid-air and looked back toward me in surprise. This was the only part of my plan that went as easily as I expected. I moved toward them while saying, "That is what you want most of all, isn't it?"

"Yes, that's our intention," the young man replied. "We've been trying every way we can think of but we're not having any success as of yet."

By the look and feel of the young man, I could tell I had his interest and attention.

"I know of a place where you can do just that, if it's what you really want."

"What do we have to do?" he asked.

"Just come along with me. I can take you there and then you'll be free to get back into physical bodies," I replied. I tried to make it sound as easy and innocuous as I could. As I watched his reaction I could see that this was a very macho young man. He wasn't used to lowering himself so far as to allow another man to have much to say about what he did or where he went. I could tell this was going to be a problem, one I hadn't anticipated. I probably should have turned it over to Coach right there but I got so involved that the thought of doing so never occurred to me.

I got into a long, rational discussion trying to convince this macho kid to come with me. I laid it out logically.

"You want to get back into bodies, right?"

"Yes we do, like I said before, that's what we've been trying to do."

"Well, I know where to take you to do that. Just come along with me and you can have what you want."

I could feel he didn't trust me and he was definitely not in the habit of going along with the suggestions of a salesman. He was too macho for that and in the habit of having his own way. Nevertheless, I continued to lay it out logically for him, doing the best used-car salesman job I could to convince him to come along.

"OK, man," he finally agreed. "It's what I want for my lady and me so we'll go along with you."

"I'm glad to be able to help you," I said, and I reached out to gently grasp his hand. I could tell immediately this was not a very macho thing to do.

The three of us lifted off and moved slowly, straight up, through the roof of the house. As we gathered speed and gained altitude, I looked down and could clearly see the roof of the house, the yard, and cars parked along the residential streets. Everything went fine until we were about three hundred yards above the house. I felt his hand let go of mine. I looked back and watched as he shot back down through the roof as if he had a bungee cord tied to him. I couldn't believe it was happening; nothing like this ever happened before.

I looked over toward where the young woman was still floating, five or six feet away. She looked over at me and then down at the house, at first confused about what had happened. In her look I could see that he made all the decisions in her life. She was his woman. She might not even have been her own woman, but she was definitely his woman. With a look of resignation on her face, she left and drifted slowly, almost lazily, back down toward the house. I watched until she disappeared as she entered the house through the roof. I'm sure I heard a stifled giggle from Rebecca in the peanut gallery behind me where she was standing.

Nothing like this had ever happened before. Benjie had refused to come along with me at all, but I had had a grip on this guy. He just let go and zipped back down to the house. *Now what I'm I supposed to do?* I hovered there, three hundred yards above the house, trying to figure out what to do next. Best I could come up with was just to go back down to the house and go through the whole spiel all over again. That decided, I headed back down, entered the house via the roof and relocated the Dancers.

Using the same logical, used car salesman approach, I convinced the macho young man to come with me again. He bought my pitch to take them to where they could both get into physical bodies again. It was a tough sell. He still didn't trust me, but he and his lady wanted physical bodies again so he again agreed to come along. I got a firm grip on him and we all lifted off, up through the ceiling again and out the roof. This time as we approached the same altitude above the house I could feel resistance building up just before he let go. Whatever the bungee-cord-like-force was that pulled him back to the house, it snapped him back so fast I almost didn't see it happen. The woman followed him down with her eyes and then looked over at me with an expressionless face. Then she casually floated back down and again disappeared through the roof.

Rats! This isn't working, I thought to myself as I hovered there again, looking down at the house. I tried the same approach two more times with the same results. Rebecca must have been doing a great job of concealing her chuckles because I didn't hear her and I know she had to be laughing! *I'm going to have to come up with some other approach.* So I hovered there, where I'd lost the guy again, three football fields in the air, waiting for something to occur to me.

I was drifting in thought when I realized my mother had just moved up close to me. She's still physically alive and was probably asleep dreaming at the time.

"Bruce, what are you doing here?" she asked, surprised to bump into me.

I filled her in on the Dancers and that I was trying to figure out what to do. While I was explaining it to my mother, Rebecca's mother floated up and listened in. Shee-un, White Bear, Coach, Rebecca, and her Guide were all floating there with me above the house as I pondered what to do. Without any particular plan in mind I decided to go back down to the house and think about it there. Everyone followed me there and stood nearby behind me, adding to the peanut gallery. I found the Dancers and just floated there about fifteen feet away, watching them. They were dancing again. It was a pleasure to watch them. Suddenly I had an idea. I turned around to face the peanut gallery and asked for their help.

"These guys love to dance. Maybe we should start a group dance and invite them to join us. You all game to try that?" I asked. I heard a collective "okay." Both the moms, all the Guides, and Rebecca and I formed a circle around the Dancers. We began to rotate, first one way, then the other in our circle and invited them to join in. They were excited at the prospect of dancing in a group and took their places, side by side in our circle.

I've seen Jewish people dance the way we did with our arms over each other's shoulders in a circle. Laughing and singing, our circle of dancers rotated first in one direction then the other. We'd been dancing half a minute or less when it occurred to me that the Dancers were really enjoying our dancing together. I suddenly realized they were so involved that I could shift us to Focus 27 without them knowing what happened. I knew that neither one of the Dancers knew enough about how things worked to find their way back to the house. Amidst the laughter and joy of our dancing together I began the shift. We kept dancing all the way there. Through dissolving into darkness and approaching Focus 27 we all kept dancing. I had no idea where we would land and I couldn't have planned a better reception myself.

As the scene materialized in front of us, we were still dancing in our circle, laughing and singing with joy. When the new scene fully stabilized, we were at one end of a large living room in a house. The house looked suburban, circa 1970s or '80s, with tables, chairs, and other furniture. There was a fireplace on the wall opposite where we had landed. There was a party going on in the house. I could see at least twenty people, some standing in small groups talking, some with drinks in their hands. Over in a corner of the room, on my right, a man and woman, with drinks in one hand and cigarettes in the other, were obviously putting the moves on each other. On the sofa three woman were laughing as though one had just told a good joke. There were hors d'oeuvres set out on the dining room table near where we had materialized in the room. Although I couldn't see it, there had to be a bar set up somewhere nearby. Our dancing circle stopped and we each let go of each other. It was a few seconds later that the Dancers noticed the party going on in front of them. I could feel their excitement as they slipped away from our circle and moved into the party, eager to join the festivities. I put my finger to my lips and looked at each member of our group.

"Shhhhhh, let's quietly leave them here. If they don't see us leave they won't be able to follow us."

Not that our stealth was necessary at all. The Dancers were mesmerized by the house full of people partying in front of them. We all backed away from the room slowly, until the party scene faded into the blackness. When we had completely withdrawn, I thanked everyone for their help and all of them except Rebecca left, going back to whatever they were doing before joining in to help.

We floated together in the blackness for half a minute and then with Rebecca behind me I headed back down to the house to find the little boy I'd seen earlier under the crib. I found him easily where I'd seen him before. He was afraid and angry and a bit of a brat. He was probably the source of Barb's and Lisa's sons' fear and upset. This was the kind of a mean little boy who would bully and scare other kids out of his own insecurity and fear. While I was looking for him I found another little boy, small and dark-haired. His name was Andrew. When I attempted to move them to Focus 27, neither one of them wanted to go or stay there after they arrived. I didn't understand why either of them felt that way.

I made repeated trips back to Barbara's house, with Rebecca always close by behind me, looking for other ghosts who might be there. Coach broke in after a couple of futile attempts to find anyone else.

"That's enough for now, Bruce. Take a break," Coach said.

Rebecca and I did some recreational flying. High, twisting, vertical barrel rolls, loops and spins and turns. We'd rocket along through the blackness playing follow the leader with quick, snapping turns. Our laughing and giggling made it easier for either of us to follow the other. It was wonderful fun, flying with a friend and playing games. After a while Coach broke in again and suggested I just relax and float for a while.

Like a feather-light cloud in a clear blue sky, I rolled over on my back and basked in the warmth of the sun. While stretched out and relaxed, I could see Rebecca. She was doing something to alter the energy states around me. She was moving her hands, kind of waving and shaking them in the air around me. I began to sense an all-over warmth filling the light, airy cloud that I was. It was warm and relaxing yet had an energizing effect on me.

As usual the next day I phoned Rebecca to compare notes. She again verified every detail I remembered. She laughed out loud when she described the look on my face when the male dancer first snapped back to the house.

"If you could have seen the look on your face!" she giggled. "I could see it coming and I couldn't contain my giggles when you realized he was gone."

"It was quite a shock. Took me completely by surprise the first time," I muttered. "I just couldn't believe it happened and then when it happened again I was really baffled. The second time I could feel increasing resistance just before he snapped back. I just couldn't believe what I was doing wasn't working!"

"Yeah, and you kept it up after that," Rebecca said as she burst out laughing.

"It's funny now," I had to admit, laughing right along with her.

"Do you know why he kept snapping back?" she asked when she stopped laughing.

"Something seemed to be pulling him back to the house, but I didn't understand what it was."

"Well, you were right about Eduardo bringing drugs into the house. Juan likes to pass them around while everybody there is partying. The male Dancer was afraid that leaving the house meant leaving the drugs and the vicarious high he and his woman enjoyed there," she explained. "As he got further and further away from the house his fear grew stronger and stronger. When it built up to sufficient strength, that fear snapped him back to the house. Overall you did quite well, although it took you a while to remember to let Coach handle it when nothing you tried worked.

"I figured that's where the idea to dance with them came from. I didn't hear or feel him give me the idea, but I thought it came from Coach."

We chatted a while longer and I thanked Rebecca for helping me learn the ropes. A week later I called Barbara to see how things were going.

"They've been gone for at least a week," she said when I asked about the Dancers. "The kids have settled down and aren't crying and clingy anymore. None of us have felt or seen them since the last time I talked to you. Thanks. You don't know what a relief it is to have them gone."

"Glad I could help out," I replied, and we made small talk for a few minutes. I suggested everybody take it easy with the drugs and the alcohol, as too much could leave them open to problems. Barb was a little upset I'd found out about that and again asked me not to tell her parents. I assured her it was entirely her business and I would keep her confidence. We said our goodbyes and I thought that would be the last time we talked to each other.

Walt called later in the week, bugging me again. He asked if I'd found out anything about Barbara's ghosts. I told him as much as I could without betraying Barb's confidence. During our conversation, it slipped out that Juan's brother was gay. He called back a week later to gloat.

"The ghosts are back at Barb's house, old buddy. Guess you're not as great a ghost buster as you thought you were," he snickered.

"I'd be very surprised if the same ghosts found their way back to her house," I replied. "I'll check it out."

"Actually, Carol called me and asked if you could do just that."

When I called Barb she told me it didn't feel like the same ghosts. This time they were seeing only one ghost, who appeared to be an old man. I went to her place that night and found the old guy. His name was Wilbur. He was a snoopy old man who enjoyed the sight of young women, lying naked in bed, asleep. He also liked the buzz of booze he felt when he moved in real close to a drunk one. He came along easily with me to Focus 27 and I left him there with Helpers who met us. I went back to the house to see if I could find out if anything other than that the alcohol and drugs had drawn him in. When I got there I was standing in front of Juan. He was doing something unusual but I couldn't understand what it was. I called Barbara the next day.

"Is there anything Juan does that's unusual?" I asked her after a few moments of small talk.

"Well, he does cast spells sometimes," she replied.

"What kind of spells?"

"He's here, if you'd like to like to talk him about," she suggested.

Juan told me he'd learned to cast spells from his mother. She'd brought the ability with her when she came to New York from Puerto Rico. He said he used it only against his enemies, anyone who did something to him he didn't like.

"Nothing real serious," he said to me. "If somebody does something to me that I don't like I just cast a spell to make him lose his job or something like that. Nothing serious."

After talking to him I realized Juan had no idea what consequences spell casting had. He didn't know spell casting and bait casting have a lot in common. His harmful intent is like bait on a hook. He can cast out and hit his *enemy* with it. It can have an effect on that person that matches with his harmful intent. But, like the bait that is cast with a fishing rod, it gets reeled back in before you can cast it again. Like fish bait being pulled through the water, *spirits* who resonate with the harmful intent of the spell follow it back to the person who cast it. What Juan was doing would continue to attract more ghosts into the house. Judging by the intent with which he baited his hook, the ghosts who came in would not be nice people to have visiting.

My suspicions were confirmed when Barb called me again a week later. Someone was running his hands through her hair again and it was freaking her out. She wanted to know what to do.

"I know I can't keep asking you to always be coming back and taking them out of here. I can't stand all the turmoil it causes the kids and it's just to spooky to keep putting it up with. What can I do?"

"As long as Juan continues his spell casting, new ghosts will continue to be drawn into the house. If you don't want to live with that, it appears to me you have two choices. Either Juan has to stop casting spells or you'll have to move out of the house."

Over the next three weeks I made trips to her house once or twice a week and hauled out the riffraff Juan's spell casting lured in. I didn't talk to her on the phone again until she called to say she had decided to move and would be in her new place the following week. She thanked me for all I had done and that was the last time I ever talked to her.

I did get one piece of verifying evidence from an unexpected source. Walt called after Barbara moved to her new place. Evidently he had passed on my comment about Eduardo's being gay to Barb's mother, Carol. Carol told Walt that her husband (who had helped Barb move to her new place and had met Eduardo) was still puzzled. He couldn't understand how someone who had never met Eduardo and lived a thousand miles away could know that Eduardo was gay.

I know it probably doesn't sound like much to anyone else, but something changed in me after I got confirmation that Eduardo was gay. It was the first time I'd ever had something I'd found by myself in the nonphysical world turn out to be verifiably real in the physical world. Rebecca and I had nonphysically met and later compared notes that were identical at least eight consecutive times. That didn't make the same internal change in me. Nothing we did had, to my mind, corroborating evidence in the *real world*. But knowing about Eduardo, and having that confirmed, did something to change my beliefs. It did something to allow me to accept more of my experience as *real*. Not that all my doubts were erased by that single event, but a fair-sized chunk of the skepticism I'd been carrying since my first Lifeline program dissolved and washed away.

Epilogue: Thislife and Afterlife

I'm happy to say I've gotten many answers to the "Three Great Questions" I've carried with me since childhood.

I now know several of the places I came from before I was born here into Thislife. I now know some of the things I'm supposed to be doing while I'm living here. I now know without any doubt where I'll go when I leave.

That complete lack of doubt came about as a result of my continuing voyages beyond the physical world. Each excursion became a process of uncovering more of the truth and building trust in my experience. The story of my journey is not yet finished. There is so much more to tell you about my exploration of the Afterlife, but there just isn't room to put it all in one book. The second book in this series will continue from where we've left off here. There are a couple of things I'd like to say before leaving you for now.

First, I want to make certain I don't leave you with the wrong impression. Not everyone who dies gets isolated or stuck in Focus 23. This happens when fear or beliefs interfere with the natural process of dying. In the natural process of dying, both those entering the Afterlife and those remaining Here know and understand what to expect. They both know that friends, loved ones, or Helpers will be waiting in the Afterlife to meet and care for the dying. They know that those remaining Here can communicate with the newly deceased to assist them through difficult situations should they occur. It is only the interference of our own fears and beliefs that inhibit the natural process of dying.

From my experience I'd say most of the dying are met by friends, relatives, and Helpers when they move into the

New World of the Afterlife. Most people move directly to the Reception Center or the Park or to somewhere else beyond Focus 23. Some move to the Belief System Territories of Focus 24, 25, and 26. They are in the company of only people who believe as they do. In a sense they are stuck too, since their own beliefs bring and hold them there. But they are not isolated and alone, suffering in fear or pain.

The reason these retrieval accounts have concerned people found isolated and stuck in Focus 23 is that the Lifeline program is where I first learned to explore the Afterlife, and Lifeline uses retrievals as a way of teaching one how to explore the Afterlife. Doing retrievals is a port of entry, a way of obtaining access to the Afterlife to learn more about it.

The second book in the *Exploring the Afterlife* series tells about my continuing explorations that built trust in my perception. Verified evidence continued to pile up until something happened—during the retrieval of a friend's father—that washed away the last doubt.

Not all of those in the next book were stuck in Focus 23. Many of these people made transitions into the Afterlife that were quite different. Some made smooth easy transitions and were met by friends or loved ones in joyful reunions as they left their physical bodies for the last time. Some did become stuck in Focus 23, but for entirely different reasons than those I've already discussed. To illustrate these and other aspects of the Afterlife, my next book will include accounts of:

- The time in India when I met the Helpers who were retrieving thousands of people who were killed in an earthquake;
- The grandmother I found sitting on a chair in her kitchen nine months after she died after a long struggle with Alzheimer's disease (information I received during her retrieval was later verified as accurate);
- A friend who was murdered (strange as it might sound, the circumstances of his death were an attempt to

heal wounds from a previous lifetime he and his wife had lived together);

- A man in Hell—but a Hell that was nothing like the descriptions given by most religions and that exactly fit his needs;
- Dr. Ed Wilson, who died on the first day of my third Lifeline program and began communicating with me immediately, continuing for months afterwards;
- A man whose daughter guided him to an immediate reunion with his wife as he died in a hospital;
- A young Israeli killed in terrorist bombing, whose misunderstanding of Atonement held him in Focus 23;
- A man who needed over two months in the Health and Rejuvenation Center in Focus 27 to recover from the effects of the disease that killed him, a story giving insight into how our attitudes and beliefs in the physical world can effect our Afterlife experience; and
- Further contacts with Bob Monroe from the Afterlife.

These are just a few of many voyages I have taken. Hardly a week goes by in which I don't travel there again and come back with more understanding of that realm.

I hope what I've written and will write encourages you to begin exploring beyond the physical world on your own. I hope the second book in this series will give more insight into what the natural dying process is and where it leads. Perhaps it will go some measure toward making it easier for more of us to experience our own death this way when our time comes. Maybe through what you come to understand from your Afterlife exploration you'll be able to assist others when their times come. Most of all I wish that through your own Afterlife exploration you'll come to Know the truth for yourself.

If you desire to begin your own voyage by assisting through service There, I've included some suggested guidelines in Appendix C. From the knowledge I've gained, I know with absolute certainty that you can contact, and if necessary be of assistance to, friends and loved ones who are in or past the dying process. You can communicate your thoughts and feelings to those who now reside in the Afterlife. Some of you may even be able to receive communication from them.

For now I'd like to leave you the way I began.

I'm just an ordinary human being whose curiosity about human existence beyond death led me to extraordinary experience. I've never had a near-death experience. No supernatural happening changed me. I wasn't born with some special psychic gift or talent. If there is any difference between you and me it is *only* that my curiosity has *already* led me to explore and know what lies beyond death in the Afterlife.

Appendix A
The Monroe Institute, Gateway Voyage, and Jargon

Much of the following information regarding The Monroe Institute and its technology and jargon is taken directly from the Monroe Institute's brochures, with their permission.

The Monroe Institute

The Monroe Institute was founded by Robert A. Monroe, a former broadcasting executive who in 1958 began to undergo spontaneous experiences that drastically altered his life. Unpredictably, and without willing it, Monroe found himself leaving his physical body, via a *second body*, to explore locales unbounded by conventional concepts of time and space. He has documented these experiences in his books, *Journeys Out Of The Body*, *Far Journeys*, and *Ultimate Journey*.

FFR and Hemi-Sync

The Monroe Institute is internationally known for its work in the effects of sound wave forms on human behavior. In its early research, the Institute discovered that nonverbal audio patterns had dramatic effects on stages of consciousness.

Certain sound patterns create a *frequency following response* (FFR) in the electrical activity of the brain. These blended and sequenced sound patterns can gently lead the brain into various states, such as deep relaxation or sleep. A generic patent in this field was issued to Robert Monroe in 1975. Drawing upon this discovery and the work of others, Monroe employed a system of "binaural beats" by feeding a separate signal into each ear. When separate sound pulses are sent to each ear with stereo headphones, the two hemispheres of the brain act *in unison* to "hear" a third signal, the difference between the two sound pulses. This third signal is not an actual sound, but an electrical signal that can be created *only by both brain hemispheres acting and working together simultaneously.*

The unique coherent brain state that results is known as hemispheric synchronization, or "Hemi-Sync.®" The audio stimulus which creates this state is not overpowering. It is non-invasive and can easily be disregarded either objectively or subjectively.

While hemispheric synchronization occurs naturally in day-to-day life, it typically exists only for random, brief periods of time. The Hemi-Sync audio technologies developed by The Monroe Institute assist individuals in achieving and sustaining this highly productive, coherent brain state.

Hemi-Sync: My Explanation

If you are a technical type, maybe my own explanation of hemispheric synchronization will be easier to follow.

Using stereo headphones to acoustically isolate each ear, two different-frequency audio tones are supplied, one to the left ear and the other to the right. For example, a 400-cycle-per-second tone might be supplied to one ear and a 402-cycle-per-second tone to the other. If you watched a real-time brain wave frequency pattern analysis of the result, you would see both hemispheres of the brain begin to synchronize to a 2-cycle-per-second brain wave frequency. The brain wave pattern of both hemispheres synchronizes to the difference between the two input frequencies (402-400=2). If this brain wave frequency pattern were the same as, say, REM sleep (which it is not) then the person listening would begin moving into REM sleep. Another pair of audio tones could be simultaneously introduced which match an alert, wide-awake brain wave state. Then the state into which the individual would move would be Mind Awake/Body Asleep—Focus 10 in Monroe Institute jargon.

The most important point seems to be that both hemispheres of the brain come to a balanced, cooperative, information-sharing state which is facilitated by their synthesizing the third tone, two cycles per second in the above example. In this balanced state, both hemispheres of the brain, with their well-documented differences in perception and analysis abilities, cooperate constructively. In that balance comes Knowing.

Focus Levels

Focus 1 (or C1, Full, Physical Waking Consciousness): The level of awareness in which most of us spend our normal, waking lives. The everyday, ordinary reality of the physical world in which we live. The level of consciousness beyond which we learn to move during Gateway programs.

Focus 3 (Basic Hemi-Sync): This level is a participant's first exposure to the concept and technology of Hemi-Sync.

Focus 10 (Mind Awake/Body Asleep): This is the level at which the physical body is asleep but the mind is awake and alert. Consciousness is fully retained without dependence upon signals from the physical body. Conceptual tools are developed that the participant may use to reduce anxiety and tension, for healing, for remote viewing, and for establishing resonance with other individuals. In Focus 10, much like the dream state, we learn to think in images rather than in words.

Focus 12 (Expanded Awareness): This is a state where conscious awareness is expanded beyond the limits of the physical body. Focus 12 has many different facets, including exploring nonphysical realities, decision making, problem solving, and enhanced creative expression.

Focus 15 (No Time): The state of "No Time" is a level of consciousness which opens avenues of the mind that offer vast opportunities for self exploration beyond the constraints of time and place.

Focus 21 (Other Energy Systems): This level offers the opportunity to explore other realities and energy systems beyond what we call time-space-physical-matter.

The Gateway Affirmation

I am more than my physical body. Because I am more than physical matter, I can perceive that which is greater than the Physical World. Therefore, I deeply desire to Expand, to Experience, to Know, to Understand, to Control, to Use such greater energies and energy systems as may be beneficial and constructive to me and to those who follow me. Also, I deeply desire the help and cooperation, the assistance, the understanding of those individuals whose wisdom, development and experience are equal to or greater than my own. I ask their guidance and protection from any influence or any source that might provide me with less than my stated desires.

A Personal Note

I have to say, as an engineer and skeptic, that one of the things that really appealed to me about The Monroe Institute's approach was its technologically based system. The Gateway affirmation was the only bit of ideology I was ever asked to consider. I didn't have to subscribe to any particular set of beliefs, change my diet, give away my fortune or bow to any guru. The technological approach to shifting my awareness repeatedly to specific *altered states* using nonverbal, audio sound patterns greatly appealed to me. I have never liked to have to follow someone else's beliefs to find my own truth. My journey is a quest to find *my* answers to my three great questions. No one else's answers will do.

Appendix B
Lifeline Program Reference Information

The Lifeline program had its genesis in the desire for something Robert Monroe called *death insurance*. His non-physical travels had left clues as to the whereabouts and status of friends who had died. When his wife, Nancy Penn Monroe, was diagnosed with a life-threatening illness, it became important for him to know where she was going to be should she die. He wanted *death insurance*. He claimed the proper name for what he wanted, *life insurance*, had already been taken and its meaning misconstrued. Death insurance meant, to Bob, that what came after this life would become known and he would be assured that he would be able to make contact with Nancy should it become necessary.

He went back through his notes from travels years before, looking for the clues. He revisited the places where he'd found his friends after they had died. You can read about this exploration in all its fascinating detail in his book *Ultimate Journey*. In going back again to find these people and places, he uncovered much about the New World and the Afterlife that I and many hundreds of others continue to explore today. Out of his desire to assure that he would be able to find and communicate with his wife Nancy if she died, the Lifeline program was born.

Focus Levels of Lifeline

In assembling the Lifeline program, Monroe and the Institute staff defined the Focus levels he'd explored and developed Hemi-Sync sound patterns to facilitate exploration by others. These Focus levels, defined below, serve as a starting point to understand the structure and workings of the Afterlife in the New World. These descriptions are taken as quotes from Robert Monroe's book, *Ultimate Journey*.

Focus 22

Where humans still in physical existence have only partial consciousness. In this state would be those suffering from delirium, from chemical dependency or alcoholism, or from dementia. It would also include patients who were anesthetized or comatose. Experiences here might be remembered as dreams or hallucinations. [My personal experience of this arena is that many here appear deranged, lost, or confused. This can make them very difficult to reach and communicate with.]

Focus 23

A level inhabited by those who have recently left physical existence but who either have not been able to recognize and accept that fact or are unable to free themselves from ties of the Earth Life System. It includes those from all periods of time.

[Those who live here are almost always isolated and alone. Often the circumstances of their death have left them confused about where they are; many times they don't realize they've died. Many maintain some form of contact with the physical world and thereby limit their ability to perceive those who come from the Afterlife to assist them.]

Focus 24, 25, 26

These cover the Belief System Territories, occupied by nonphysical humans from all periods and areas who have accepted and subscribed to various premises and concepts. These would include religious and philosophical beliefs that postulate some form of post-physical existence.

[My experience in these realms is limited compared to the rest of the Focus levels I learned to explore during Lifeline. Most of those I have encountered here are not very pleased to have someone appear in their midst talking about things they don't believe. In some ways working with people who have taken up residence in Focus 25 is more difficult than those in any other place. These people typically live within a closed-minded belief system which is fully supported by the fact that only members of that belief system live there. The belief systems represented go way beyond mere religious training. The only place I ever encountered what was like a Hell was in Focus 25.]

Focus 27

Here is the site of what we may call the Reception Center or the Park, which is the hub of it. This is an artificial synthesis created by human minds, a way station designed to ease the trauma and shock of the transition out of physical reality. It takes on the form of various earth environments in order to be acceptable to the enormously wide variety of newcomers.

[This is an incredibly diverse area which seems to contain every conceivable construct to ease newcomers into their existence in the Afterlife. If the person arriving would be most comfortable arriving in a house with a raucous party going on, it's There. If meeting a group of Freemasons at their facility would be best, it's There. A doctor might be met in the surroundings of a doctor's private practice office specifically outfitted with the medical equipment of his era. I am continually amazed at the ability of those who inhabit Focus 27 to direct my arrival to just the right setting for the person I am bringing There. In their literature The Monroe Institute bills Lifeline as a program of learning Service Here and Service There. Service Here means learning to provide assistance to those who live in the physical world. Use of the term Service There means learning to provide assistance to those who live beyond physical world reality or in the Afterlife.]

Lifeline Service Here

Participants learn how they can help others still living in the physical world to know they survive physical death.

Sometimes this takes the form of bringing back communication from departed loved ones. Messages and information which participants would have no other way of knowing many times prove to be valid. In my experience, bringing such information back from a loved one can be very comforting to those left behind.

Another part of Service Here taught during Lifeline is membership in the Dolphin Energy Club or DEC. DEC is a healing system which can be used in several different ways. It can be used for self-healing, for healing of others nearby, and for remote healing of others.

The story of how the Dolphin Energy Club was created is fascinating. The Monroe Institute carries out research into many different states of human consciousness. One of the tools of this research is a twenty-four-channel brain wave analyzer. With this tool, dynamic brain wave patterns can be recorded and displayed for analysis. Development of Hemi-Sync sound patterns for the DEC utilized this sophisticated piece of electronic hardware.

First, healers with demonstrated ability were connected to the brain wave recorder. Their brain wave patterns were then recorded while they carried out their healing methods on patients. After several different healers were recorded in this manner, the resulting brain wave patterns were analyzed for similarities. Once similarities in the patterns were deduced, they were reverse engineered into Hemi-Sync sound patterns which would induce the brain wave patterns of a healer. The resulting Hemi-Sync tapes became the basis for the Dolphin Energy Club. These DEC states of consciousness are taught during Lifeline as part of learning Service Here.

Lifeline Service There

Participants in the Lifeline program become familiar with levels of existence in Focus levels 21 through 27. They learn how to find the newly deceased in Focus 23 and how to contact them. They learn how to offer assistance to those they meet and how to guide them to the Reception Center at Focus 27. They learn how to gather information which might be useable to verify the reality their experience in carrying out these functions.

This process of finding, offering assistance to, and guiding people to the Reception Center is called "retrieval." Some call it "rescue," but that term is too dramatic for me. Doing retrievals is a great vehicle with which to explore and learn about the Afterlife in the New World beyond physical existence.

In doing retrievals, participants come to *know* they will survive physical death. This knowing can come through meetings and communications with their own friends or loved ones who've passed on into this New World before them. This knowing may also come when information received while retrieving a stranger turns out to be undeniably true.

A Place in Focus 27

As part of the Lifeline program, participants also create places for themselves in Focus 27. The form each place takes is entirely up to the participant's imagination and it can be added to or changed at any time. It often becomes a meeting place to communicate with others who inhabit Focus 27 and become friends through repeated contact.

Appendix C
Guidelines for Afterlife Contact

A woman died recently. I never knew her. Seemingly in good health, she'd given all the signs of someone preparing to leave this world. Over the past months she'd satisfied her urge to visit her grandchildren, friends, and relatives who are scattered across the country. Then, quite unexpectedly, she had a stroke. In less than a day's time she entered the Afterlife. Her timing couldn't have been better.

I was attending a seminar at TMI in August 1996 when it happened. My manuscript was finished except that my publisher had asked me to consider writing guidelines for readers who might wish to join in assisting the recently departed. I'd queried other seminar participants, wondering how someone without my formal training and experience could accomplish such a thing. Before breakfast the last day of the seminar I had my answer.

Janet, a fellow seminar participant, had gotten a phone call at midnight from her son telling of her mother-in-law's stroke. The next morning, as I stood alone on the deck outside with my cup of decaf and cigarette, Janet asked me what she could do to help Grandma. I'd been puzzling over this very issue for over a week. As I tried to answer her question, something came through me and out into the air between us as words. We were both hearing them for the first time. I've added more detail to our conversation than actually occurred to clarify the method. In the few minutes of that conversation, the procedure I'd been trying to come up with was born. It's no accident that Janet is a midwife.

"First you need to get Grandma's attention."

"How?"

"Start by relaxing. You're familiar with Focus 10. Lie down, move to Focus 10, and let your mind clear of distractions. Any quiet, meditative state will do. Then bring Grandma to mind; remember a time you and she were together, talking pleasantly. Allow yourself to feel what it was like to be with her."

"Like when she was visiting last spring and we sat out on the patio drinking ice tea?"

"That would do fine. The important thing is to remember what it felt like to be with her. How you felt as you talked to each other, the sound of her voice, your surroundings. Bring it all back to mind, remembering as much detail as you can."

"Surroundings? You mean like the patio table and chairs, the hot sunny day, the shade from the patio umbrella?"

"Exactly. Bring to mind as many details of the time you were together as you need to be able to feel what it was like to be there talking with her. Then begin a pretend conversation with her."

"Pretend?"

"Yes. Pretend you're telling her about the time you were sitting out on the patio, drinking ice tea. Pretend she's listening as you reminisce with her about that time together. You can even pretend that she talks back to you, reminding you of things that happened or things she said."

"Why pretend?"

"It's a way of opening up the power of your imagination. Imagination is a nonphysical means of communication. I use the word *pretend* because it doesn't matter if you believe your conversation is really happening or not. Only that you pretend it is."

"What if I can't actually 'see' Grandma or the patio or 'hear' her voice while I'm pretending?"

"That's completely okay. You are only pretending, after all, just pretending to see and hear her. You don't have to actually see or hear her for you to be able to contact and assist her."

"I don't?"

"No. In fact, it isn't necessary that you have any conscious awareness of Grandma, your surroundings or conversation for you to be able to assist her. The only thing that's necessary is that you pretend to."

"In my pretend conversation with her, could I tell her things I wanted to say before she died? Would she hear me?"

"Yes. From my experience, she'll hear anything you say to her in your imaginary conversation. I know that many times people wish they had told someone something before they died and wish they still could. If there's something you want say to her, I know she'll get your message. You can do this any time."

"Is it possible I might actually 'see' or 'hear' something that is really happening while I'm trying to help her?"

"Yes. That's entirely possible. From my experience, the more willing you are to go along with the pretending the more likely it is such a thing might happen. Something might happen during your pretending that you know you didn't pretend. These are usually small details such as something Grandma might say or do that you had no way of knowing about beforehand. That's a sign of actual conscious contact with Grandma if it happens. But it's not at all necessary that it happen in order to help her."

"Okay, so I'm pretending a conversation with Grandma, feeling what if felt like to be there with her, then what?"

"Next bring to mind another person. This could be someone both you and Grandma know who already lives in the Afterlife."

"That could be Grandpa. He died several years ago."

"Bring Grandpa to mind. Remember how he looked, who he was, and what it felt like to be in his presence at a happy time. Invite him to join you and Grandma. Using your example, you might pretend to invite him to come and sit down on a patio chair at the table. Pretend you are pouring him a glass of ice tea. Pretend you're calling Grandma's attention to the fact that Grandpa is joining the two of you. Pretend a conversation with him in which you tell him you're trying to help Grandma to go to right place for her."

"Like, 'Grandpa, I'm trying to help Grandma go to Heaven'?"

"Sure. I might say 'the Park' or 'the Reception Center,' but you can use Heaven, Paradise, or whatever your own beliefs would allow. Then pretend that Grandpa begins to talk to Grandma. Pretend he tells her he's come to take her to that place. Pretend she sees him and talks to him. Pretend they stand and embrace. Pretend that as she and Grandpa leave together you thank him for coming. You could even pretend he turns and says something to you as they leave."

"That's all there is to it?"

"Yes, it's as simple as that. Afterwards you might want to jot down in your journal any impressions you had during the experience. How it felt, what happened, what was said, things like that."

"After she leaves could I still tell her things I wanted to say before she died, but didn't?"

"Yes, of course. You could use the same patio scene, and invite her to come. Just pretend she comes and in your imaginary conversation tell her whatever it is you'd like her to know. It's a lot like prayer. From my experience, I know your message will get through to her."

"But what if I don't believe any of it really happened?"

"That's perfectly all right. If all you did was pretend you felt any of it happen, I can assure you Grandma heard you and got the assistance she needed. She and Grandpa, or the Helper who came in his place, will be in contact with each other. Once they can communicate, Grandpa or the Helper will be able to do whatever is necessary to assist Grandma from there on."

"The Helper?"

"Sometimes the person you decide to invite may not be available for some reason. I've seen that happen once or twice. In those cases, someone who lives in the Afterlife will come in that person's place. Sometimes it might be someone else Grandma knows. You might even get an impression of who that person is. Sometimes it's a person who volunteers to do these things. I call them Helpers."

"And if I don't believe in any of this?"

"That's okay too, as long as you can pretend it's happening. Besides, what do you have to lose?"

"Well, I personally do believe in an afterlife, but even if I didn't I can't see any harm in trying."

As Janet and I stood talking, a TMI staff member came out to tell her she had a phone call. Moments after she left, the overwhelming sadness I began feeling told me Janet was hearing over the phone that Grandma had died. I also knew that while she and I had stood talking she had been imagining the events as they were described. I knew Grandpa had come to the patio table as we talked about him. I knew Grandma had seen him. And I knew they had left together.

Contact and communication with those in the Afterlife is as easy as thinking about them. As easy as remembering what it felt like to be in their presence when they were living Here. Communication using thoughts, feelings, and impressions is always a component of my explorations in the Afterlife. Even when I believed I was making it all up in my head it still worked. For anyone with a sincere desire to contact and assist a departed loved one, this method of communication will work. It's really not much different than what might be taught in church or Sunday school as silent prayer. Just a quieting of the mind, and then expressing what you want to say in your thoughts.

A week after I returned home from the seminar, I received a letter from Janet. A little while after we had the conversation on TMI's deck, she used the technique to try to assist her mother-in-law. Janet is a powerful woman with a highly developed sensitivity at a nonphysical, energetic level. Her awareness level is more developed than the average person's. She's a skilled meditator and chose to try to assist Grandma during a walking meditation. Janet's description of her experience confirms for me the usefulness of the method. Paraphrasing her letter:

After talking to you, I decided to do a meditation walk and decided to walk the labyrinth. [Note: the labyrinth was a special, circular footpath constructed by two other seminar participants.] As I walked, I thought through the instructions you had given me. I had an immediate awareness of Grandma's presence. Then I called in Grandpa and felt/saw a merging of bright light as the two of them recognized each other and felt their love for each other. As I got to the center of the labyrinth, I felt/saw a blaze of light that seemed to completely surround and interpenetrate me. It was a very ecstatic moment—the three of us connected to the entire universe. I just stood there in glory with them. I felt Grandma's gratitude that this sassy daughter-in-law that she loved like one of her own kids had been there for her. Seems like I also felt some kind of apology from her about some times she had been critical of me. Sort of like she saw me from a different perspective and was being called on to review some of her actions.

Gradually I took my leave and began to walk out of the labyrinth. It was a feeling of great celebration. On a humorous note, I thought I should check in with Grandma about whether or not she was ready to go to the light. She definitely was not! She wanted to stick around with Grandpa for the funeral. Just like her to never miss a family get-together!

Some might question the need for attempting to assist a loved one who now lives in the Afterlife. For the vast majority of them it's most likely true that no such assistance is necessary. In the balance of things, however, it can do them no harm to try and has the potential to do much good. It may provide just what's needed to help your loved ones become aware of their situation. It may provide the means of bringing into their awareness those who've come to meet them. It may bring Afterlife knowledge to you through your own direct experience. All of these things are possible.

Procedure for Assisting a Departed Loved One

To summarize the technique:

1. Lie down in a quiet place where you won't be disturbed or distracted. No ringing telephones, sudden loud noises or interruptions.

2. Close your eyes and allow yourself several minutes to completely relax. If you know how to meditate that's a perfect way to do this step. If you feel you don't know how to relax sufficiently you can contact TMI using the 800 number on the card in this section. They can provide a Hemi-Sync tape especially for this purpose. Use the instructions that come with that tape to learn to relax in a quiet state of mind.

3. Bring to mind the person you wish to assist—say her name is Betty. Pretend to remember a scene in which you and Betty were talking pleasantly while she still lived Here.

4. Bring to mind another person, one both you and Betty know, who previously entered the Afterlife. Let's call him Paul. Invite Paul to join the two of you.

5. Pretend a conversation in which you tell Paul that you would like him to assist in moving Betty to the best place for her. You can use any name for this place that fits with your beliefs.

5. Pretend a conversation in which you introduce Betty to the fact that Paul has joined the two of you.

6. Pretend a conversation between Paul and Betty in which they acknowledge each other's presence.

7. Pretend Paul and Betty leave together.

8. Pretend you thank Paul for coming.

9. Write down in your journal any impressions you had during the experience.

At this writing, The Monroe Institute is considering the possibility of producing a special tape for use with this outlined method. With Hemi-Sync sound support, this tape would provide the relaxation necessary and voiced guidance in the procedure. The card in this section has information for ordering this special tape should it become available.

A Note to Some Readers

While reading this book some of you no doubt have recognized landmarks you've already seen. You may have realized that you've already begun exploring beyond the physical world in your own way. When I've talked to people about my experience, some of them realize they've been doing retrievals. Sometimes they remember meeting a person in a dream and "providing transportation" to an airport, bus, or train station. For some it's to a doctor's office, a hospital, or an introduction to a third person. From my perspective, such dreams are often valid Afterlife experience from which you can begin to explore further. Journaling such dreams and talking about them with others who've had similar experience can be very useful. Just the desire for more experience and information can be the beginning of your own journey. I'd like to encourage you to begin that journey. For me the rewards have been most gratifying.

BOOKS OF RELATED INTEREST

BROTHERS FOREVER
Joseph Gallenberger

When his beloved elder brother Peter committed suicide, the author, a psychotherapist, was forced to deal with his overwhelming grief. Although able to relieve his emotional trauma, Dr. Gallenberger could not answer the ultimate questions that arise from the death of a loved one. Then, using the Hemi-Sync® technology at The Monroe Institute, he was able to walk into dimensions beyond life, where he contacted his brother and came to view Peter's death in light of a greater spiritual perspective. A profound and moving account of love and life that survive death.

5½ x 8½ trade paper, 176 pages, ISBN 1-57174-045-7, $11.95

MY LIFE AFTER DYING
George G. Ritchie, Jr., M.D.,
Introduction by Ian Stevenson, M.D.

"George Ritchie's story of his dying and coming back to life after some magnificent spiritual experiences is worth reading by all those who have any concern in the 'beyond.' As important, though is how he applied what he leraned in his 1942 NDE to the choices he made in the next fifty years of his life. *"To know that he was the inspiration that started Raymond Moody on his series of investigations into the afterlife makes him noteworthy."* — Spiritual Frontier

5½ x 8½ trade paper, 170 pages, ISBN 1-878901-25-7, $9.95

TRAVELING WITH POWER:
The Exploration and Development of Perception
Ken Eagle Feather

Perception is the river that runs through and shapes the landscape of the New Consciousness movement. Here, the author tells of his early travels along the winding paths of perception, beginning with an apprenticeship to the nagual, don Juan Matus, through shamanic practices, lucid dreaming, and OBE's at The Monroe Institute. An original blend of spiritual autobiography and perceptual map-making.

5½ x 8½ trade paper, 280 pages, ISBN 1-878901-28-1, $12.95

OUT OF BODY EXPERIENCES:
How to Have Them and What to Expect
Bob Peterson

Here's an OBE book designed for the hands-on approach. Not only is it a fascinating account of the author's own experiences, but it is simply the best roadmap ever written for anyone who wishes to have an OBE or has had one and wants to know the next step. Most books only give you theory; here you learn not only how to get in and out of the body, but also how to deal with your fear, how to see and navigate, where you can venture, and what you might encounter. It also has more than 170 resources to help with further research. If you actually want to try some traveling yourself, this book is your flight manual.

5 x 8 trade paper, 224 pages, ISBN 1-57174-057-0, $11.95

USING THE WHOLE BRAIN
Ronald Russell, Editor

Tens of thousands of people have used The Monroe Institute's Hemi-Sync technology to gain new control over their lives. *Using the Whole Brain* is the first book to tell what it can do for body, mind, and spirit. Everything from coping with surgery to strengthening concentration to facilitating transcendent events such as out-of-body experiences and remote viewing. Preface by Robert Monroe.

5½ x 8½ trade paper, 264 pages, ISBN 1-878901-86-9, $14.95

HEALING MYSELF
Gari Carter

After a head-on car crash destroyed much of Gari Carter's face, she suffered for months—yet came to realize that she had learned patience, love, and proper priorities. What she learned and then applied from her experiences at the The Monroe Institute, and her use of the Hemi-Sync tapes in place of anaesthesia make a truly inspirational story of physical and spiritual healing. *"Shows how one woman can rise above suffering, pain, disfigurement, dependency and despair to become a symbol of courage."* — The Free Lance-Star

5½ x 8½ trade paper, 208 pages, ISBN 1-878901-75-3, $10.95

Hampton Roads Publishing Company
publishes and distributes books on a variety of subjects,
including metaphysics, health, complementary medicine,
visionary fiction, and other related topics.

To order or receive a copy of our latest catalog, call toll-free,
(800) 766-8009, or send your name and address to:

Hampton Roads Publishing Company, Inc.
134 Burgess Lane
Charlottesville, VA 22902